Memoirs of Jonathan Swift

Volume 1

Sir Walter Scott

Cambridge University Press

CAMBRIDGE UNIVERSITY PRESS

Cambridge, New York, Melbourne, Madrid, Cape Town,
Singapore, São Paolo, Delhi, Tokyo, Mexico City

Published in the United States of America by Cambridge University Press, New York

www.cambridge.org
Information on this title: www.cambridge.org/9781108034180

This edition first published 1826
This digitally printed version 2011

ISBN 978-1-108-03418-0 Paperback

CAMBRIDGE LIBRARY COLLECTION

Books of enduring scholarly value

Literary Studies

This series provides a high-quality selection of early printings of literary works, textual editions, anthologies and literary criticism which are of lasting scholarly interest. Ranging from Old English to Shakespeare to early twentieth-century work from around the world, these books offer a valuable resource for scholars in reception history, textual editing, and literary studies.

Memoirs of Jonathan Swift

Jonathan Swift (1667–1745) was born in Dublin and studied at the city's Trinity College. He gained his B.A. in 1686 before going to England where he took a Master's degree at Oxford in 1692. Subsequently, Swift lived between England and Ireland for a number of years. He moved permanently from England in 1714 after the Tory party he supported lost power. Back in Ireland as Dean of St Patrick's Cathedral in Dublin, he turned his talents to supporting Irish causes. During this period he wrote some of his best work, including *Gulliver's Travels*, the satirical masterpiece which has been continuously in print since its publication in 1726. Written by Sir Walter Scott, this is the first part of a two-volume biography of Swift, first published in 182[illegible]. This volume covers his early life up to his appointment as Dean of St Patrick's and his involvement in Irish politics.

Cambridge University Press has long been a pioneer in the reissuing of out-of-print titles from its own backlist, producing digital reprints of books that are still sought after by scholars and students but could not be reprinted economically using traditional technology. The Cambridge Library Collection extends this activity to a wider range of books which are still of importance to researchers and professionals, either for the source material they contain, or as landmarks in the history of their academic discipline.

Drawing from the world-renowned collections in the Cambridge University Library, and guided by the advice of experts in each subject area, Cambridge University Press is using state-of-the-art scanning machines in its own Printing House to capture the content of each book selected for inclusion. The files are processed to give a consistently clear, crisp image, and the books finished to the high quality standard for which the Press is recognised around the world. The latest print-on-demand technology ensures that the books will remain available indefinitely, and that orders for single or multiple copies can quickly be supplied.

The Cambridge Library Collection will bring back to life books of enduring scholarly value (including out-of-copyright works originally issued by other publishers) across a wide range of disciplines in the humanities and social sciences and in science and technology.

MEMOIRS

OF

JONATHAN SWIFT, D. D.

DEAN OF ST PATRICK'S, DUBLIN.

BY SIR WALTER SCOTT.

IN TWO VOLUMES.

VOL. I.

PARIS:

PUBLISHED BY A. AND W. GALIGNANI,

AT THE ENGLISH, FRENCH, ITALIAN, GERMAN, AND SPANISH LIBRARY,

N° 18, RUE VIVIENNE.

MDCCCXXVI.

NOTICE OF THE PUBLISHER.

The admirers of Sir Walter Scott will be gratified by the separate publication of these Memoirs, which will complete our Edition of his Works. They are now for the first time published distinct from the Works of Swift, with which, at the price of upwards of eight guineas, they can only be purchased in London. Those who possess old Editions of Swift will find these Memoirs a valuable addition to that work.

Paris, Dec. 15, 1825.

ADVERTISEMENT.

NO author in the British language has enjoyed the extensive popularity of the celebrated Dean of St Patrick's. Neither the local and temporary nature of the subjects on which his pen was frequently engaged, nor other objections of a more positive nature, have affected the brilliancy of his reputation. In spite of the antiquated and unpopular nature of his politics, in spite of the misanthropical and indelicate tone of some of his writings, and the trifling character of others,—the vivid and original power of his genius has supported him in the general opinion, to an extent only equalled by his friend Pope, and far sur passing any other of those geniuses who flourished in the Augustan age of Queen Anne.

Although several Memoirs of the life of this celebrated man have been published, yet, from his utter inattention to literary reputation, and the carelessness with which he flung his productions from him, many fugitive pieces, letters and anecdotes, calculated to throw light on his remarkable history, have not been accessible even to the most laborious and accurate of his biographers. The present is an attempt to fill up this blank, and, from the various advantages which have been afforded to the writer, it is trusted that it will supply a distinct and combined account of the life of Swift which has heretofore continued to be a *desideratum*. Among the various original information which has been supplied from authentic sources, are the liberal communications of Theophilus Swift, Esq. of Dublin, son of the learned Deane Swift, the near kinsman and biographer of the celebrated Dean of St Patrick's, a collection of manuscripts of various descriptions concerning Swift and his affairs which remained in the hands of Dr Lyons, the gentleman under whose charge Swift was placed during the last sad period of his existence, together with various letters and original unpublished pieces in Swift's handwriting. In addition to the valuable materials thus furnished, it has been the object of the writer to condense the information afforded by Mr Sheridan, Lord Orrery, Dr Delany, Deane Swift, Dr Johnson, and others, into one succinct and comprehensive narrative.

ABBOTSFORD, 1st June, 1824.

CONTENTS OF VOL. I.

SECTION I.

Swift's parentage and birth—His life at college—His first residence with Sir William Temple—Visits Oxford—He takes orders, and obtains the living of Kilroot—Resigns that living in favour of a friend, and returns to England—His second residence with Sir William Temple—The Battle of the Books, and Tale of a Tub—Verses on the burning of Whitehall—Swift's correspondence with Miss Waryng—He becomes acquainted with Stella—Sir William Temple dies, and bequeaths his works to Swift—Swift's views of promotion at the Court are disappointed. . . . .

SECTION II.

Swift goes to Ireland with Lord Berkeley—His differences with that nobleman—Obtains the living of Laracor—He is displeased with his sister's marriage—His mode of life at Laracor—Mrs Dingley and Stella come to Ireland—Tisdal makes proposals of marriage to Stella—Swift embarks in politics—His opinion of the affairs of church and state—Tale of a Tub. 58

SECTION III.

Swift's Journey to England, in 1710—His quarrel with the Whigs, and union with Harley and the Administration—He writes the Examiner—The character of Lord Wharton—And other political tracts —Obtains the First-Fruits and Twentieth-Parts for the Irish Clergy—His correspondence with Archbishop King—His intimacy with the Ministers—The services which he renders to them—Project for improving the English Language—His protection of Literary Characters—Difficulties attending his church preferment—He is made Dean of St Patrick's—And returns to Ireland. . . 113

SECTION IV.

Swift takes possession of his Deanery—Is recalled to England to reconcile Harley and St John—Increases in favour with Oxford—Engages again in political controversy—Writes the Public Spirit of the Whigs—A reward offered for discovery of the Author — The Dissensions of the ministers increase—Swift retires to the country — Writes Thoughts on the Present State of Affairs—Writes to Lord Oxford on his being displaced—And retires to Ireland on the Queen's Death—His reception—His Society—The interest he displayed in the misfortunes of his Friends. . . . 177

SECTION V.

Swift's first Acquaintance with Miss Vanhomrigh—She follows him to Ireland—Swift's Marriage with Stella—Death of Miss Vanhomrigh—Poem of Cadenus and Vanessa—Swift's Studies during his retirement from 1714 to 1720—His system of Life and Amusements—Engages in Irish Politics—His Proposal for Encouragement of Irish Manufactures —And other Tracts—Drapier's Letters—Swift's subsequent popularity. 226

MEMOIRS

OF

JONATHAN SWIFT, D. D

SECTION I.

Swift's parentage and birth—His life at college—His first residence with Sir William Temple—Visits Oxford—He takes orders, and obtains the living of Kilroot—Resigns that living in favour of a friend, and returns to England—His second residence with Sir William Temple—The Battle of the Books, and Tale of a Tub—Verses on the burning of Whitehall—Swift's correspondence with Miss Waryng—He becomes acquainted with Stella—Sir William Temple dies, and bequeaths his works to Swift—Swift's views of promotion at the Court are disappointed.

THE life of Swift forms an interesting and instructive narrative to all who love to contemplate those alternations of good and evil which chequer the fate of individuals, distinguished by their talents and by their fame. Born under circumstances of the most pressing calamity, educated by the cold and careless charity of relations, denied the usual honours attached to academical study, and spending years of dependence upon the inefficient patronage of Sir William Temple, the earlier part of his history may be considered as a continued tale of depressed genius and disappointed hopes. Yet, under all these disadvantages, Swift arose to be the counsellor of a British administration, the best defender of their measures, and the intimate friend of all who were noble or renowned, learned or witty, in the classic age of Queen Anne. The events of his latter years were not less strongly contrasted. Involved in the fall of his patrons, he became a discontented and persecuted exile from England, and from his friends; yet, almost at once, attained a pitch of popularity which rendered him the idol of Ireland, and the dread of those who ruled that kingdom. Nor was his domestic fate less extraordinary—loving, and beloved by two of the most beautiful and interesting women of the time, he was doomed to form a happy and tranquil union with neither, and saw them sink successively to the grave, under the consciousness that their mortal disease had its source in disappointed hopes, and ill-requited affection. His talents also, the source of his fame and his pride, whose brilliancy had so long dazzled and delighted mankind, became gradually clouded by disease, and perverted by passion, as their possessor approached the goal of life; and, ere he attained it, were levelled far below those of ordinary humanity. From the life of Swift, therefore, may be derived the important lesson, that, as no misfortuness should induce genius to despair, no rank of fame, however elevated, should encourage its possessor to presumption. And those to whom fate has denied such brilliant qualities, or to whom she has refused the necessary opportunities of displaying them, may be taught, while perusing the history of this illustrious man, how little happiness depends upon the possession of transcendent genius, of political influence, or of popular renown.

Jonathan Swift, Doctor of Divinity, and Dean of St Patrick's, Dublin, was descended from the younger branch of the family of Swifts, in Yorkshire, which had been settled in that county for many years. His immediate ancestor was the Reverend Thomas Swift, vicar of Goodrich, in Herefordshire, and proprietor of a small estate in that neighbourhood. At the beginning of the civil wars, this gentleman distinguished himself by his zeal and activity in the cause of Charles I.; and his grandson has recorded, in a separate memoir, his exploits and sufferings during the civil wars. To that memoir, and the notes which accompany it, the reader is referred for farther particulars concerning Swift's family[1] After having been

[1] See No. I. Appendix. Swift put up a plain monument

repeatedly plundered by the parliamentary soldiers, even to the clothes of the infant in the cradle (which, according to family tradition, was Jonathan, father of the Dean), and to the last loaf which was to support his numerous family, Thomas Swift died in the year 1658, leaving ten sons, and three or four daughters, with no other fortune than the small estate to

to his grandfather, and also presented a cup to the church of Goodrich, or Gotheridge. He sent a pencilled elevation of the monument (a simple tablet), to Mrs Howard, who returned it with the following lines, inscribed on the drawing by Pope. The paper is indorsed, in Swift's hand, «Model of a monument for my grandfather, with Mr Pope's roguery.»

JONATHAN SWIFT
Had the gift,
By fatherige, motherige,
And by brotherige,
To come from Gutherige,
But now is spoil'd clean,
And an Irish Dean.
In this church he has put
A stone of two foot;
With a cup and a can, Sir,
In respect to his grandsire;
So, Ireland, change thy tone,
And cry, O hone! O hone!
For England hath its own.

The lines, originally written in pencil by Pope, are traced over in ink by Dr Lyons, as a memorandum bears. It occurred amongst Dr Lyons' manuscripts.

which he was born, and that almost ruined by fines and sequestrations.

The sufferings of this gentleman were of some service to his family after the Restoration; for Godwin Swift, his eldest son, who had studied at Gray's Inn, and had been called to the bar, was appointed Attorney-general of the Palatinate of Tipperary, under the Duke of Ormond. He was a man of talents, and appears to have possessed a considerable revenue, which he greatly embarrassed by embarking in speculative and expensive projects, to which his nephew, Jonathan, ever after entertained an unconquerable aversion. Meantime, how-

One of these projects seems to have been the iron manufactory at Swadlingbar, mentioned sarcastically by the Dean in his Essay on Barbarous Denominations in Ireland. Swift's dislike to projects and projectors, is exhibited in his Essay on English Bubbles, and the subsequent tracts relating to the proposed establishment of a bank in Ireland. The following anecdote is also recorded on the same subject:—

« When Swift was at Holyhead, waiting for a fair wind to sail for Ireland, one Welldon, an old seafaring man, sent him a letter that he had found out the longitude, and would convince him of it; to which the Dean answered, in writing, that if he had found it out, he must apply to the Lords of Admiralty, of whom, perhaps, one might be found who knew something of navigation, of which he was totally ignorant; and that he never knew but two projectors, one of whom (meaning his uncle Godwin) ruined himself and family, and the other hanged ever, the success of Godwin Swift, in his profession, attracted to Ireland three of his brethren, William, Jonathan, and Adam, all of whom settled in that kingdom, and there lived and died.

Jonathan Swift, the father of the celebrated author, was the sixth or seventh son of the Vicar of Goodrich, the number of whose descendants, and the obscurity of their fortunes, does not admit of distinguishing his lineage more accurately. Jonathan, like his brother Godwin, appears to have been bred to the law, though not like him called to the bar He added to the embarrassments of his situation, by marrying Abigaïl Ericke of Leicestershire, a lady whose ancient genealogy was her principal dowry. The Dean has himself informed us, that his father obtained some agencies and employments in Ireland; but his principal promotion seems to have been the office of steward to the society of the King's Inns, Dublin, to which he was nominated in 1665.

This situation he did not long enjoy, for he died in 1667, two years after his appointment, leaving an infant daughter, and his widow,

himself, and desired him to desist, lest one or other might happen to him."—Swiftiana, London, 1804, 12mo., vol. I. p. 177. The other unfortunate projector was probably Joseph Beaumont, often mentioned in Swift's Journal, who committed suicide.

then pregnant, in a very destitute situation, as Mrs Swift was unable, without the assistance

[1] The following original documents, procured by the kindness of Mr Hartstonge, establish the time of his appointment and death, and also the destitute circumstances of the poet's mother. As Mr Swift states himself to have been conversant about the King's Inns for six or seven years before the date of his petition, it is probable that he came to Ireland upon the death of his father, 1658.

«To his Grace the Lord Chancellor, the Right Honourable the Judges, and other the Honourable Benchers of the Honourable Society of the King's Inns, Dublin:

«The humble Petition of Jonathan Swift;

«Humbly sheweth,

«That the stewardship of this Honourable Society is now become void by the death of Thomas Wale, the late steward thereof: That your petitioner, his father, and their whole family, have been always very loyal and faithful to his said Majesty, and his royal father, and have been very great sufferers upon that account: That your petitioner, for these six or seven years last past, hath been much conversant about the said Inns, and is very well acquainted with the duty and employment belonging unto the steward thereof, he having assisted the said Thomas Wale in entering of the orders of your honours, and in the settling and ordering other things belonging to the said employment.

«That your petitioner doubts not but if your honours will be pleased to confer the said employment of steward upon your petitioner, that he shall give your honours all satisfaction imaginable therein.

«He therefore humbly prays that your honours will be pleased to confirm the said stewardship upon him.

And he shall pray.»

of the society, even to defray the expense of her husband's funeral.

[Extracted from the Black-book of the King's Inns, in the library, Henrietta Street, Dublin, p. 242.]

I compared the above extracts with Mr Hartstonge, and can certify its correctness with the original.

B. T. Duhigg,

Presented to a Council held at the King's Inns, Dublin, 14th Nov. 1665.	Librarian to the Honourable Society of King's Inns, Dublin, Dec. 24th, 1810.

"At a Council holden at the King's Inns, Dublin, the 25th day of January, 1665-6,

[Amongst other matters it was]

"Ordered,

"That Jonathan Swift, upon his petition, be admitted steward of this house.

[Signed]

"Michl. Dublin, Can.
J. Temple, [Master of the Rolls.]
W. Aston, [puisne Justice of the King's Bench.]
Jn. Bysse, [Chief Baron.]
Robt. Kennedy, [Baron of the Exchequer.]
Jerome Alexander, [p. Justice of the Common Pleas.]

I also compared the above,

B. T. Duhigg.

The period of the death of the above-mentioned Mr Jonathan Swift is fully ascertained, by the following petition of his widow, Mrs Abigail Swift, to the Honourable Society of King's Inns, presented at a council held the 15th of April, 1667.

"To his Grace the Lord Chancellor, and the Right Honourable the Judges and Benchers of the Honourable Society of King's Inns:

Dryden William Swift, the brother of the deceased, seems to have been active in behalf

« The humble Petition of Abigail Swift, widow;

« Humbly sheweth,

« That it having pleased God to take away your petitioner's husband, the late steward of this Honourable Society, unexpectedly, and your petitioner being left a disconsolate widow, hath this affliction added to her, that there is due to her from the several members of this Honourable Society, for Commons and Cost Commons, about six score pounds sterling, which she is noways able to get in without your honours' assistance: That your petitioner hath desired her late husband's brother, William Swift, to help her in getting in her said money, who hath manifested himself very willing to assist her, but hath been denied by several persons, upon pretence that he had no authority to receive the same.

« Now, for as much as your petitioner hath no friend next your honours, but her said brother, to rely upon, and that he, your petitioner's said brother, cannot befriend her without he be authorized by your honours' orders to the purpose,

« May it therefore please your honours to grant your petitioner an order, wherein the said William Swift may be authorized and appointed to gather in your petitioner's said money.

« And your petitioner shall ever pray. »

[The prayer of which petition was fully granted upon the same day, and her brother-in-law appointed to receive the moneys due.]

[Extracted from the Black-book of the King's Inns, Dublin, page 248.] I also compared the above,

B T. Duhigg.

I have seen another original petition from Mrs Abigail Swift, presented in council to the Society of King's Inns, of his sister-in-law, but Godwin who was sup posed to be wealthy, was her chief support; and, upon the 30th of November, 1667, being St Andrew's day, she was delivered of the celebrated Jonathan Swift. The place of his birth was a small house, now called No. 7, in Hoey's Court, Dublin, which is still pointed out by the inhabitants of that quarter. His infancy was marked by a chance as singular as that of his father, whose cradle had been plundered of the bedding by Kirle's troopers. The nurse to whom he was committed was a na-

in the month of January, less than two months after the birth of her son, which was on the 30th of November, 1667. I am thus irresistibly convinced, and entirely concur in opinion with Mr Duhigg (see his history of the King s Inns, page 248), that the illustrious Jonathan Swift, the Dean of St Patrick's, Dublin, was undoubtedly born in Ireland. This latter petition, here noticed, is in the Black-book of the King's Inns, Dublin, page 276, which states her poverty, and her desire to pay the funeral expenses of her late husband, and praying that the Society do pay her the arrears due, etc.

MATTHEW WELD HARTSTONGE.

I compared the above with Mr Hartstonge,

B. T. DUHIGG.

Entry on the King's Inns Roll.

On the 26th of January, 1665, Jonathan Swift was admitted into this Society."

[Black-book of the King's Inns, p. 197.]

The antiquity of its appearance seems to vindicate the truth of the tradition. In 1809 it was occupied by Mrs Jackson, a dealer in earthen-ware.

tive of Whitehaven, to which town. she was recalled, by the commands of a dying relation, from whom she expected a legacy. She actually stole away her charge, out of mere affection, and carried him to Whitehaven, where he resided three years, for his health was so delicate, that rather than hazard a second voyage, his mother chose to fix his residence for a time with the female who had given such a singular proof of her attachment. The nurse was so careful of the child's education, that when he returned to Dublin he was able to spell, and when five years old he could read any chapter of the Bible.

Swift was now to share the indigence of a mother whom he tenderly loved, and to subsist upon the support afforded by his uncle Godwin. It seems probable, that these irritating and degrading circumstances sunk deep into his haughty temper, even at an early period of life, and that even then commenced that war of his spirit with the world, which only ended when his faculties were utterly subdued by disease. Born a posthumous child, and bred up as an object of charity, he early adopted the custom of observing his birth-day, as a term, not of joy, but of sorrow, and of reading, when it annually recurred, the striking passage of Scripture, in which Job laments and execrates the day upon which it was said in his athfer's house, «that a man-child was born.»

The narrowness of the allowance afforded for his maintenance and education added to his unhappiness, and was naturally imputed by him to the sordid parsimony of his uncle. It is true, that subsequent events shewed that Godwin Swift was under the necessity of regulating this allowance by the real state of his embarrassed circumstances, rather than by the opinion which his nephew, in common with the rest of the world, entertained of his wealth. But although it was afterwards discovered, that his liberality had borne full proportion to the former criterion, Swift appears never to have lost the unfavourable impression which had once been made, and certainly held Godwin Swift's remembrance neither in love nor veneration.

He mentions him with disrespect in the anecdotes of the family, and elsewhere; and I have the following remarkable anecdote from Theophilus Swift, Esq the grandson of Godwin, and grand-nephew of the Dean, to whom it was often related by Mrs Whiteway. The Rev. Dr Whittingham, Archdeacon of Dublin, a bold and ready talker, used to be forward to shew his colloquial courage where few would have chosen to exercise it, by attacking Dean Swift, and that with great rudeness and severity. At a visitation dinner, they chanced to be placed nearly opposite to each other at table, when Dr Whittingham suddenly asked,. «Pray, Mr Dean, was it not your uncle Godwin who educated you?»—Swift affected not to hear this insulting question. At length it was twice repeated, with a loud and bitter accent, when the Dean answered abruptly, «Yes! he gave me the education of a dog.»—

Meanwhile his education proceeded apace. At the age of six years, he was sent to the school of Kilkenny, endowed and maintained by the Ormond family, where his name, cut in school-boy fashion, upon his desk or form, is still shewn to strangers. Here he learned to say, *latino-anglice*, the words *Mi dux et amasti lux*, the first germ of the numerous *jeux d'esprit* of that nature which passed between him and Sheridan, during his declining years.

From Kilkenny, Swift was removed, at the age of 14, and admitted into Trinity College, Dublin, where, as appears from the book of the senior lecturers, he was received as a pensioner under the tuition of St George Ashe, on 24th April, 1682. His cousin, Thomas Swift, was admitted at the same time; and the mention of the two names throughout

« Then, » answered Whittingham, grinning, and clenching his hand, « you have not the gratitude of a dog. » The instant interposition of the Bishop prevented the personal violence which was likely to follow on this colloquy. This story is alluded to by Dr Delany, in his sixteenth letter to Lord Orrery, but the circumstances are concealed and altered. Notwithstanding the violence of this altercation, the Dean and Archdeacon Whittingham were reconciled by the interference of the Bishop, and became afterwards good friends.

Son to his uncle Thomas, who had been bred at Oxford. Swift's college-companion afterwards became Rector of Puttenham in Surrey, and affected to have a share in the original concoction of the Tale of a Tub. Swift used to call him in contempt, his « parson-cousin.

the College records, without the Christian appellative, has thrown uncertainty upon some minute points of the Dean's biography.

When Swift was entered at the university, the usual studies of the period were required of him, and of these, some were very ill suited to his genius. Logic, then deemed a principal object of learning, was in vain presented to his notice; for his disposition altogether rejected the learned sophistry of Smiglecius, Keckermannus, Burgersdicius, and other ponderous worthies now hardly known by name; nor could his tutor ever persuade him to read three pages in one of them, though some acquaintance with the commentators of Aristotle was absolutely necessary at passing examination for his degrees. Neither did he pay regular attention to other studies more congenial to his disposition. He read and studied rather for amusement, and to divert melancholy reflections, than with the zeal of acquiring knowledge. But his reading, however desultory, must have been varied and extensive, since he is said to have already drawn a rough sketch of the Tale of a Tub, which he communicated to his companion Mr Waryng. We must conclude then, that a mere idler of the 17th century might acquire, in his hours of careless and irregular reading,

This fact Mr Waryng often mentioned to Mr Whiteway.

a degree of knowledge which would startle a severe student of the present age. We have few means of judging of the extent of Swift's real learning; it cannot perhaps be termed profound, but it was certainly extensive. His writings evince great general acquaintance with history and poetry, both ancient and modern; nor is he ever at a loss for such classical allusions and quotations as most aptly illustrate the matter of which he treats. Yet although he thought so lightly of his own acquisitions, that he talked of having lost his degree for dulness and insufficiency, and although he used with great vehemence to rebuke those who bestowed the name of scholar on any one whom they could not prove to have spent most of his days in study, the character of a mere plodding student did not stand high in his estimation. Bentley, whom he unjustly ranked in this dull and laborious class, used to be honoured with the epithets of *Jubar Anglicanum, Lux Britanniæ, Sidus Britannicum*, etc. by the foreign literati. This Swift could not bear, and in the predictions of Isaac Bickerstaff, he launches some satirical shafts at the heavy politeness of the High-Dutch *illustrissimi*, and their extravagant compliments to each other.[1]

[1] "If I had leave to have printed the Latin letters transmitted to me from foreign parts, they would fill a volume, and be a full defence against all that Mr Partridge and all

While Swift, however, was pursuing his studies in this vague and desultory manner, they would have been altogether interrupted by the death of his uncle Godwin and the derangement of his affairs, which then first became public, had he not found another patron in his uncle Dryden William Swift. This gentleman gave the necessary support to his orphan nephew, and it would seem with more grace and apparent kindness, though not more liberally in amount than his brother Godwin, for he too was in narrow circumstances. But Swift always cherished his memory, and recorded him as the « best of his relations. » He used also to mention an incident which occurred while he was at college, of which Willoughby Swift, his cousin, the son of Dryden William, was the hero. Sitting one day in his chamber, absolutely pennyless, he saw a seaman in the court below, who seemed inquiring for the apartment of one of the students. It occurred to Swift that this man might bring a message from his cousin

his accomplices of the Portugal Inquisition will be ever able to object; which, by the way, are the only enemies my predictions have ever met with at home or abroad. The most learned Monsieur Leibnitz thus addresses to me his third letter: *Illustrissimo Bickerstaffio astrologiæ instauratori*, etc. Monsieur Le Clerc, quoting my predictions in a treatise he published last year, is pleased to say, *Ita nuperrime Bickerstaffius, magnum illud Angliæ sidus.* »

Willoughby, then settled as a Lisbon merchant, and the thought scarcely had crossed his mind when the door opened, and the stranger approaching him, produced a large leathern purse of silver coin, and poured the contents before him, as a present from his cousin. Swift, in his ecstacy, offered the bearer a part of his treasure, which the honest sailor generously declined. And from that moment, Swift, who had so deeply experienced the miseries of indigence, resolved so to manage his scanty income, as never again to be reduced to extremity. The system by which he regulated his expense was so very rigid, that, from many of his journals still existing, it is clear he could have accounted for every penny of his expenditure, during any year of his life, from the time of his being at college, until the total decline of his faculties.

Pleasure, as well as necessity, interfered with Swift's studies. Poverty, and the sense of the contempt which accompanies it, often gives to a lofty temper a cast of recklessness and desperation, and Swift's mind was by one of his friends well likened to an evoked spirit, that would do mischief if not supplied with constant employment. Johnson, who studied at college under similar disadvantages, has expressed such feelings in his own nervous language. Hearing from Mr Boswell that he had been considered as a gay and frolicsome fellow, while at Pembroke, he answered, « Ah! Sir, I was mad and violent. It was bitterness that they mistook for frolic. I was miserably poor, and I thought to fight my way by my literature and my wit; so I disregarded all power, and all authority. » Even such a rebel against college discipline Swift appears to have been, under similar circumstances; and it is remarkable, that, though far inferior in humour, in purity of style, and in comprehensive genius, Johnson bore a strong resemblance, in his morbid temperament, political opinions, and habits of domination in private society, to the Dean of St Patrick's. Swift, therefore, while under the dominion of this untamed spirit, was guilty of many irregularities, some which occasioned reproof, and some which led to yet more severe consequences. He repeatedly neglected, and affected to contemn the discipline of the college, and frequented taverns and coffee-houses. In the wantonness of his wit he assailed the fellows of the University with satirical effusions, to which the speeches occasionally delivered by the *Terræ Filius*, gave sufficient scope. But though this species of saturnalia had a prescriptive licence, experience might have taught Swift that it was not to be relied on, and that the individual ridiculed watched his time and opportunity to retort upon the satirist the pain which he had inflicted. The earlier part of Swift's academical course was more slightly marked with these irregularities, for no record of penal infliction occurs, until a *special grace* for the degree of Bachelor of Arts was conferred upon him, on 13th February, 1685 6. We are not therefore to look for the cause of the degrading manner in which this degree was bestowed (as flowing, not from the merit of the student, but the unearned favour of the University,) in Swift's irregularities, but in the neglect of those studies which were then held essential parts of education. In going through the preliminary dissertation, he was ignorant even of the necessary syllogistic forms. He answered the arguments of the impugners in common language, and the proctor reduced his replies into syllogism, the candidate thus displaying a degree of ignorance of what was then miscalled the art of reasoning, which must of itself have called for the mark of incapacity which was attached to his degree. Yet such was the strength of Swift's memory, that, after thirty or forty years, he could repeat to Sheridan the propositions, as they were attacked and defended, in their proper scholastic technicality.

The disgraceful note with which his degree had been granted, probably added to Swift's negligence, and gave edge to his satirical propensities. Between the periods of 14th November, 1685, and 8th October, 1687, he incurred no less than seventy penalties for non-attendance at chapel, for neglecting lectures, for being absent from the evening roll-call, and for town-haunting, which is the academical phrase for absence from college without licence. At length these irregularities called forth a more solemn censure, for, on 18th March, 1686-7, with his cousin, Thomas Swift, his chum, Mr Warren, and four others, he incurred the disgrace of a public admonition for notorious neglect of duties. His second public punishment was of a nature yet more degrading. On 20th November, 1688, Swift, the future oracle of Ireland, was, by a sentence of the vice-provost, and senior fellows of the University, convicted of insolent conduct towards the junior dean (Owen Lloyd), and of exciting dissension within the walls of the college. He shared with two companions the suspension of his academical degree, and two of the delinquents, Swift being one, further were sentenced to crave public pardon of the junior dean.[1] The bitterness of spirit with

Such is the account of this matter inferred by the late Dr Barrett from the college records; and his acquaintance with the mode of keeping them, and the purposes for which they are made up, entitle his judgment to the greatest weight. His opinion is also confirmed by that of Mr Theophilus Swift, who expresses his conviction that, in consequence of his share in the academical satires upon the Fellows of Trinity College, Swift was in danger which Swift submitted to this despotic infliction, if indeed he obeyed it, for of this there

of losing the testimonium of his degree, without which he could not have been admitted *ad eundem* at Oxford. And he supposes that, mortified at the recollection of the humiliating conditions imposed as his terms of pardon, his great kinsman was not unwilling that the particulars of the case should be sunk in a general report, that he had been refused his degree for insufficiency,—a mode of stating the fact, which was likely to throw more discredit on the discernment of the heads of the university, than on his own acknowledged talents. Yet an ingenious correspondent has alleged the following reasons, to prove that this degrading ceremony never was submitted to.

«From Dr Barrett's Life of Swift, it appears that he graduated above a year *before* the usual time, which in Trinity College, Dublin, is four years and a half, therefore *speciali gratia* must mean that he got it by interest or merit; or, if it was suspended after, as Dr B. suggests, it might have been restored to him on intercession of friends. But there appears little to countenance the supposition, that he was ordered to beg pardon on his knees, and nothing to warrant the assertion that he *submitted* to such an indignity, as there is no trace of his remaining in college after the revolution, which is the date Dr B. assigns for that censure. The dates are very confused and contradictory as to the two Swifts; and, while he allows Thomas Swift to have had a scholarship, and suspects that Jonathan had not, he forgets that very few ever remain in Trinity College, Dublin, after graduating, unless they enjoy scholarships; and that Jonathan Swift had one, appears farther from his remaining in Commons, and being, according to Dr B., suspended from Commons, by way of punishment, after graduating, which could be no punishment at all to him, if his Commons were not at the charge of the University.»

is no absolute proof, may be more easily conceived than described. The sense of his resentment shews itself in the dislike which he exhibits to his Alma Mater, the Trinity College of Dublin, and the satirical severity with which he persecutes Dr Owen Lloyd, the junior Dean, before whom he had been ordained to make this unworthy prostration. [1]

This unpleasant circumstance of the Dean's academical life has become gradually confounded with the yet more severe penalty of expulsion, inflicted upon John Jones, one of his companions. Mr Richardson has recorded a tradition, that Swift was expelled from college for writing a Tripos, as it is called, or satirical oration, uttered by him as Terræ-Filius. [2] The research of the learned Dr Bar-

[1] Dr Lloyd is said to have been bribed by a deanery to take a cast-mistress off the hands of Lord Wharton.

[2] Richardson to Lady Bradshaigh, April 22, 1752.—"I am told my Lord (Orrery) is mistaken in some of his facts; for instance, in that wherein he asserts, that Swift's learning was a late acquirement. I am very well warranted by the son of an eminent divine, a prelate, who was for three years what is called his chum, in the following account of that fact. Dr Swift made as great a progress in his learning at the University of Dublin in his youth, as any of his contemporaries; but was so very ill-natured and troublesome, that he was made Terræ-Filius, on purpose to have a pretence to expel him. He raked up all the scandal against the heads of that university, that a severe inquirer, and a still severer temper, could get together into his harangue. He was expelled in

rett has ascertained, that such a tripos was actually delivered, 11th July, 1688. He had published its contents, which are preserved in the Lanesborough MS., and he has proved, from the college records, that Jones, the Terræ-Filius of the period, was actually deprived of his degree, for the false and scandalous reflections contained in that satire, though the sentence was afterwards mitigated into a temporary suspension of his degree and academical rights. But Jones, not Swift, was the Terræ-Filius so degraded. The inaccuracy of Richardson's informer may be easily pardoned: he was recollecting the events of a remote period, when Swift and Jones, friends and associates, both experienced punishment for petulant satire and insubordination. It is not, therefore, wonderful, that he confounded the circumstances attending their delinquencies, and attributed the more weighty offence, an offence, too, of which Swift was likely to have been guilty, and the more severe punishment, to him who afterwards became the object of general attention. It is probable, likewise, that the tripos may have been heightened by the satirical strokes of Swift; though I cannot think it likely that he was the principal author of the work, for which Jones sustained the

consequence of his abuse; and having his *discessit*, afterwards got admitted at Oxford to his degree.

sentence of expulsion, since, with all his grossness, it exhibits little of his humour.

In 1688, the war broke out in Ireland; and Swift, then in his twenty-first year, without money, and if not without learning, at least without the reputation of possessing it, with the stains of turbulence and insubordination attached to his character, and without a single friend to protect, receive, or maintain him, left the College of Dublin. Guided, it may be supposed, more by affection than hope, he bent his course to England, and travelled on foot to his mother's residence, who was then in Leicestershire. Herself in a dependent and precarious situation, Mrs Swift could only recommend to her son to solicit the patronage of Sir William Temple, whose lady was her relation, and had been well acquainted with the family of the Swifts, and in whose house Thomas Swift, the cousin of our author, had already resided as a chaplain.

The application was made, and succeeded; but for some time Sir William Temple's patronage seemed to be unattended either by confidence or affection. The accomplished statesman, and polite scholar, was probably, for a time, unreconciled to the irritable habits, and imperfect learning of his new inmate.[1]

[1] In the letter to Lady Bradshaigh, already quoted, Richardson says, «Mr Temple, nephew to Sir William Temple, and brother to Lord Palmerston, who lately died

But Sir William's prejudices became gradually weaker, as Swift's exquisite power of observation increased his faculties of pleasing, while his knowledge was expanded by a course of study so hard, that it engaged eight hours of every day. Such a space of time, well employed, soon rendered a man of Swift's powers an invaluable treasure to a patron like Temple, with whom he remained about two years. His studies were partially interrupted by bad

at Bath, declared to a friend of mine, that Sir William hired Swift, at his first entrance into the world, to read to him, and sometimes to be his amanuensis, at the rate of L.20 a-year and his board, which was then high preferment to him; but that Sir William never favoured him with his conversation because of his ill qualities, nor allowed him to sit down at table with him. Swift, your ladyship will easily see, by his writings, had bitterness, satire, moroseness, that must make him unsufferable to his equals and inferiors, and unsafe for his superiors to countenance. Sir William Temple was a wise and discerning man. He could easily see through a young fellow, taken into a low office, and inclined to forget himself. Probably too, the Dean was always unpolite, and never could be a man of breeding. Sir William Temple was one of the politest men of his time."—*Richardson's Correspondence.* The outlines of this unfavourable statement are probably true, if restricted to the earlier part of Swift's residence at Moorpark. But we must not forget, that the enmity which subsisted between him and all the descendants of Sir William Temple, may account for Mr Temple's placing his conduct in a disreputable light.

health. He had contracted, from a surfeit of stone-fruit, a giddiness and coldness of stomach, which almost brought him to his grave, and the effects of which he felt during his whole life-time.[1] At one time he was so

[1] It here becomes the indispensable duty of an editor, briefly to notice the opinion expressed by the learned Dr Beddoes, who, in the ninth essay of his work, entitled Hygeia, has directly ascribed the vertigo of Swift, with all its distressing consequences, to habits of early and profligate indulgence. And he has argued upon our author's conduct towards Stella and Vanessa, as indicating the inflamed imagination, and the exhausted frame of a premature voluptuary, who still courted pleasures he was unable to enjoy. The same conclusion, Dr Beddoes is disposed to derive, from the tone of gross indelicacy, of which Swift's writings afford too many proofs. To the hypothesis of this ingenious writer, we may oppose, first, the express declaration of Swift himself, that this distressing malady originated in the surfeit mentioned in the text, a cause which medical professors have esteemed in every respect adequate to produce such consequences. Secondly, His whole intercourse with Stella and Vanessa indicates the very reverse of an ardent or licentious imagination; and proves his coldness to have been constitutionally inherent, both in mind and person, and utterly distinct from that of one who retains wishes which he has lost the power to gratify. Those who choose to investigate this matter further, may compare Swift's Journal to Stella, with Pope's Letters to the Miss Blounts, in which there really exists evidence of that mixture of friendship, passion, and licentious gallantry, which the learned author of Hygeia has less justly ascribed to the correspondence between Swift and Stella.

ill that he visited Ireland, in hopes of experiencing benefit from his native air; but finding no advantage from the change, he again returned to Moorpark, and employed in his studies the intervals which his disorder afforded.

Lastly, Without raking deeper into such a subject, it may be briefly noticed, that the coarse images and descriptions with which Swift has dishonoured his pages, are of a nature directly opposite to the loose impurities by which the exhausted voluptuary feeds his imagination. The latter courts the seductive images of licentious pleasure; but Swift has indulged in pictures of a very different class, and has dwelt on physical impurities, calculated to disgust, and not to excite the fancy. We may, therefore, safely take Swift's word for the origin of his malady, as well as for his constitutional temperance. And, until medical authors can clearly account for, and radically cure the diseases of their contemporary patients, they may readily be excused from assigning dishonourable causes for the disorders of the illustrious dead.

The following receipt for his malady, by the celebrated Dr Ratcliffe, was found among Mr Smith's papers, indorsed in the Dean's hand:—

« R. *Nov. 3d,* 1733. *Dr Ratcliff's Rec^t. for Deafness, sent by my Lady Moncastell.*

« Docter Ratcliff's prescription for a noisse in the head and deffness, proseeding from a cold moyst humor in the head.

« Take a pint of sack whay, make very clear, halfe sack and halfe water, boyle in it sum plain reael sage, and a sprige of Rossmery; take it gowing to rest, with thirty or forty drops of spirit of hartshorn, continue it as long as you find benifet by it, expectly the wintor

It was now that he experienced marks of confidence from Temple, who permitted him to be present at his confidential interviews with King William, when that monarch honoured Moorpark with his visits, a distinction which Temple owed to their former intimacy in Holland, and which he received with respectful ease, and repaid by sound and constitutional advice. Nay, when Sir William's gout confined him to his chamber, the duty of attending the king devolved upon Swift; and it is recorded by all the poet's biographers, that William offered him a troop of horse, and shewed him how to cut asparagus the Dutch way. It would be unjust to suppress the additional advantage he acquired in learning, by the royal example, to eat the same vegetable with Dutch economy, on which subject the reader will find a lively anecdote at the bottom of the page.[1] Other advantages of a more solid na-

seson; he may swetn or not with sirop of Cowslep. He orderd allsoe a spice capp : to be made of clowes, masse, and *pepper mingled finely*, pownded and put betwen too silke, and quelted to wear next the head, and for a man to be sowdd within side his wigg."

[1] This characteristic story is given on the authority of the father of my friend, Mr M. Weld Hartstonge. Alderman George Faulkner of Dublin, the well-known bookseller, happening one day to dine in company with Dr Leland the historian, the conversation adverted to the

ture were, however, held out to his ambition; and he was led to hope that he would be provided for in the church, to which profession he was destined, as well by inclination as by so fair a prospect of preferment:[1] The high trust reposed in him warranted these hopes. For he was employed by Sir William Temple to lay before King William the reasons why his majesty ought to assent to the bill for triennial parliaments; and he strengthened Temple's opinion by several arguments drawn from English history. But the king persevered in his opposition, and the bill was thrown out by

illustrious Dean of St Patrick's. Faulkner, who was the Dean's printer and publisher on many occasions, mentioned, that one day being detained late at the Deanery-house, in correcting some proof-sheets for the press, Swift made the worthy alderman stay to dinner. Amongst other vegetables, asparagus formed one of the dishes. The Dean helped his guest, who shortly again called upon his host to be helped a second time; when the Dean, pointing to the alderman's plate, « Sir, first finish what you have upon your plate. »—« What, Sir, eat my stalks? »—« Ay, Sir! King William always eat the stalks! » —« And George, » rejoined the historian, (who was himself remarkably proud, and very pompous), « what, were you blockhead enough to obey him? »—« Yes, doctor, and if you had dined with Dean Swift, *tête-à-tête*, faith, you would have been obliged to eat your stalks too! »

[1] He writes to his uncle, William Swift, 29th November, 1692, « I am not to take orders till the king gives me a prebend. »

the influence of the Crown, in the House of Commons. This was the first intercourse that Swift had with courts; and he was wont to tell his friends that it helped to cure him of vanity: having probably anticipated success in his negotiation, and being mortified in proportion by its unexpected failure.

In 1692, Swift went to Oxford for the purpose of taking his master's degree, to which he was admitted on the 5th July in that year. He seems to have been pleased with the civilities he met at Oxford, and observes, that he was ashamed to have been more obliged, in a few weeks, to strangers, than ever he was, in seven years, to Dublin college.[1] The favour of Oxford necessarily implies learning and genius. In the former Swift was now eminent, and in the latter shewed the fair promise of an active and enterprizing mind. Even in 1691, he informs his friend, Mr Kendal, that he had « written, and burned, and written again upon all manner of subjects, more than perhaps any man in England. » Amidst these miscellane-

[1] The passage reminds us of a similar expression in Dryden's prologue to the University of Oxford.

> Oxford to him a dearer name shall be
> Than his own mother university;
> Thebes did his green unknowing youth engage,
> He chooses Athens in his riper age.

Both poets had received some censure from their Alma Mater.

ous efforts, poetry was not neglected. The Muses met him on their own sacred ground, and it is at Oxford that Swift produced his first verses (reserving only his claim to any of those contained in the Tripos of Jones). It is a version of Horace, Book II. Ode 18,[1] which will be found in its place:

'Tis true, my cottage, mean and low,
  Not built for grandeur, but for ease,
No ivory cornices can show,
  Nor ceilings rough with gold displays.

No cedar beams for pomp and state.
  (To nature names confest unknown,)
Repose their great and precious weight
  On pillars of the Parian stone.

Not dropt an accidental heir
  To some old kinless miser's m ans;
No wealthy vassal's gifts I wear,
  Rich purple vests, and sweeping trains;

But virtue and a little sense
  Have so endear'd me to the great,
That, thanks to bounteous Providence,
  Nor have, nor want I, an estate.

Blest in my little Sabine field,
  I 'll neither gods above implore,
Nor, since in sneaking arts unskill'd,
  Hang on my wealthy friends for more.

These verses were copied by Dr Hill of Dublin, from the original in the possession of Mr Worrall, who was one of the Dean's curates, and lived in great habits of friendship with him.

From day to day, with equal pace,
  Our sliding moments steal away,
Nor is the fleeting moon's increase
  Aught but her progress to decay.

Yet you, amused with airy dreams,
  Forgetful that the grave is near,
Are busied with your endless schemes
  Of pleasant seats and houses here.

The bounds of nature for your mind
  Too little seem, and you are poor,
Unless the ocean be confined
  T'enlarge your borders on the shore.

Nay, more, profanely you leap o'er
  Your peaceful neighbour's ancient bounds,
Invade the weak, unfriended poor,
  And seize his patrimonial grounds.

Expell'd by you from their abodes,
  The tender wife and husband fly;
In vain they invocate their gods,
  In vain their helpless infants cry.

And yet this dearly bought estate
  How quickly must its owner leave!
The wealthy miser's last retreat,
  And surest portion, is the grave.

What would you more? impartial earth
  Wraps in her lap with equal care
The high and low, nor royal birth
  Preserves its poor distinctions there.

Not all Prometheus' boasted art
  Could ever surly Charon sway,
Nor gold itself work on his heart
  To wake him back into the day.

Proud Tantalus, and all his race,
He holds in chains; the royal kin
In vain implores the smallest grace,
No patient empire his for sin.

Yet, call'd or not, the poor he hears,
And in his last and painful strife,
To his assistance straight repairs,
And carries off his load of life.

Besides these verses. we find Swift attempting another style of poetical composition less favourable to his fame. This produced his Pindaric Odes, the only kind of writing which he seriously attempted without attaining excellence, and which must therefore be accounted among the injudicious efforts of a genius which had not yet become acquainted with its own powers. The undertaking is said to have been pressed upon him by Sir William and Lady Temple, who were admirers of Cowley. But it is reasonable enough to suppose that Swift should have turned voluntarily towards that kind of metaphysical poetry, in which wit (if wit consists in presenting unexpected and ingenious combinations) is the leading and distinguishing feature; and, after all the vituperation which has been heaped upon these odes, they are not, generally speaking, worse than the pindarics of Donne and Cowley, which, in the earlier part of the century, gained these authors unbounded applause. It is said that Swift communicated these poetical exercises to Dryden, whose concise reply,—« Cousin Swift, you will never be a poet,»—he neither forgot nor pardoned One of the Odes is inscribed to the Athenian Society, in strains of eulogy of which Swift must have been afterwards ashamed, when he recollected that the Apollo of this English Athens was no other than John Dunton the bookseller. With the exception of these abortive attempts at a species of poetry of which the fashion had passed away, it does not appear that Swift made any efforts towards literary distinction; for the verses addressed to Congreve, November 1693, and those to Sir William Temple, in December following, seem to have been the effusions of private friendship. From the first we learn, that Swift's talents had raised him above the obscurity which attended his first years at Moorpark, and that he was now on friendly terms with Congreve, a man of the brightest comic genius that Britain has produced. The same verses teach us, that he already felt confidence in his powers of satire, and could predict the effects of that « hate to fools,» which he afterwards assumed as his principal characteristic.

« My hate—whose lash just Heaven had long decreed,
Shall on a day make sin and folly bleed.»

The verses on Sir William Temple's illness

and recovery, are of a different mood, and express strongly and pathetically the miseries of the precarious situation under which his proud and independent spirit was then struggling. He thus addresses his Muse, which, since Cowley's time, was the established mode in which a poet expressed his complaints:—

« Wert thou right woman, thou shouldst scorn to look
On an abandon'd wretch, by hopes forsook;
Forsook by hopes, ill fortune's last relief,
Assign'd for life to unremitting grief;
For let Heaven's wrath enlarge these weary days,
If hope e'er dawn the smallest of its rays,
Time o'er the happy takes so swift a flight,
And treads so soft, so easy, and so light,
That we the wretched, creeping far behind,
Can scarce th' impression of his footsteps find.——

— — — — —

To thee I owe that fatal bent of mind,
Still to unhappy restless thoughts inclined
To thee, what oft I vainly strive to hide,
That scorn of fools, by fools mistook for pride;
From thee whatever virtue takes its rise,
Grows a misfortune, or becomes a vice;
Such were thy rules to be poetically great:—
'Stoop not to interest, flattery, or deceit;
Nor with hired thoughts be thy devotion paid
Learn to disdain their mercenary aid;
Be this thy sure defence, thy brazen wall,
Know no base action, at no guilt look pale,
And since unhappy distance thus denies
T' expose thy soul, clad in this poor disguise;
Since thy few ill-presented graces seem
To breed contempt where thou hast hoped esteem.'»

These last lines probably allude to the coldness of Sir William Temple, and to a disagreement which began to take place between them. Swift sighed after independence, and seems to have thought that Temple delayed providing for him, from the selfish view of retaining his assistance, now become necessary to him Temple, on the other hand, regarded his dependent's impatience as if tinctured with ingratitude. He offered him, but with coldness, an employment worth 100*l.* a-year, in the office of the rolls in Ireland, of which he was then master. To this Swift answered, that since this offer relieved him from the charge of being driven into the church for a maintenance, he was resolved to go to Ireland to take holy orders. And thus they parted in mutual displeasure: Temple positively refusing to pledge himself by any promise of provision, in the event of his consenting to remain with him; and Swift determined to exert and maintain his independence.

When Swift arrived in Ireland, he found that the bishops, to whom he applied for orders, required some certificate of his conduct during the time he had resided with Sir William Temple. This must have been a grating task; for to obtain such a testimonial, required both submission and entreaty; and, accordingly, Swift appears to have paused nearly five months before endeavouring to procure it. The submission, however, was at length made, the entreaty listened to, and « Swift's penitentiary letter» formed, probably, the ground-work of reconciliation with his patron. Within less than twelve days after the date of that letter, he must have received the testimonial he desired, for his letters for deacon's orders are dated 18th October, 1694, and those for priest's orders on the 13th January following[2] It seems probable that Sir William Temple added to the certificate desired, some recommendation to Lord Capel, then Lord-deputy of Ireland; for, almost immediately upon taking orders, Swift obtained the prebend of Kilroot, in the diocese of Connor, worth about one hundred pounds a-year. To this small living he retired, and assumed the character of a country clergyman.

Swift's life at Kilroot, however, so different from that which he had led with Sir William Temple, where he shared the society of all that were ennobled, either by genius or birth, soon became insipid. In the meanwhile,

Swift's letter to his cousin, Deane Swift, is dated at Moorpark, 3d June, 1694, and he then says he left Sir William Temple a month before. The penitentiary letter is dated 6th October following.

[2] Mr Sheridan believed him to be ordained in the preceding September, but that he was mistaken is obvious from the letter to Sir William Temple, and from the dates of the official certificates of ordination, which are now before the editor.

Temple, who had learned, by the loss of Swift, his real value, became solicitous that he should return to Moorpark. While Swift hesitated between relinquishing the mode of life which he had chosen, and returning to that which he had relinquished, his resolution appears to have been determined by a circumstance highly characteristic of his exalted benevolence. In an excursion from his habitation, he met a clergyman, with whom he formed an acquaintance, which proved him to be learned, modest, well-principled, the father of eight children, and a curate at the rate of forty pounds a-year. Without explaining his purpose, Swift borrowed this gentleman's black mare, having no horse of his own,—rode to Dublin, resigned the prebendary of Kilroot, and obtained a grant of it for this new friend. When he gave the presentation to the poor clergyman, he kept his eyes steadily fixed on the old man's face, which, at first, only expressed pleasure at finding himself preferred to a living; but when he found that it was that of his benefactor, who had resigned in his favour, his joy assumed so touching an expression of surprise and gratitude, that Swift, himself deeply affected, declared he had never experienced so much pleasure as at that moment. The poor clergyman, at Swift s departure, pressed upon him the black mare, which he did not choose to hurt him by refusing; and thus mounted, for the first time, on a horse of his own, with fourscore pounds in his purse, Swift again embarked for England, and resumed his situation at Moorpark, as Sir William Temple's confidential secretary.

These are the outlines of a transaction, upon which, long after Swift's death, malice or madness endeavoured to fix a construction fatal to his reputation. This scandalous falsehood is only mentioned here, that it may never be repeated on any future occasion.

In an edition of the Tatler in six volumes, 1786, executed with uncommon accuracy and care, there occurs a note upon No. 188, which, among other strictures on Swift's history, mentions the following alleged fact:— «Lord Wharton's remarkable words allude, not only to the odium Swift had contracted as the known or supposed author of the Tale of a Tub, etc but they seem to point more particularly to a flagrant part of his criminality at Kilroot, not so generally known. A general account of this offence is all that is requisite here, and all that decency permits. In consequence of an attempt to ravish one of his parishioners, a farmer's daughter, Swift was carried before a magistrate of the name of Dobbs (in whose family the examinations taken on the occasion are said to be still extant to this day), and, to avoid the very serious consequences of this rash action, immediately resigned the prebend, and quitted the kingdom. This intelligence was communicated, and vouched as a fact well known in the parish even now, by one of Swift's successors in the living, and is rested on the authority of the present prebendary of Kilroot, February 6, 1785.»

It was not to be supposed, that a charge so inconsistent with Swift's general character for virtue, religion,

Swift returned to the house of Sir William Temple rather as a confidential friend, than as a dependent companion. The mark of kind-

and temperance, should remain unanswered. Accordingly, a reply was addressed to the Editor of the Gentleman's Magazine, by Theophilus Swift, Esq., who was justly zealous for the honour of his great relative, but it was refused admission on account of its length. An answer is also to be found in Mr Monck Berkeley's Reliques; and, in both cases, the advocates of Swift, or rather his vindicators, urge the utter improbability of the charge, considering the circumstances of the case. It was shewn by Mr Berkeley, that had such a criminal stigma ever stained the character of Swift, some allusions to it must have been found amid the profusion of personal slander with which, at one time, he was assailed, both in Britain and Ireland. It was farther remarked, that had Swift been conscious of meriting such an imputation, his satire upon Dean Sawbridge, for a similar crime, argues little less than insanity in the author. To which it might have been added, that the same reproach is thrown by Swift on Sir John Browne, in one of the Drapiers. Above all, the proofs of this strange allegation were loudly demanded at the hand of those who had made public a calumny unknown to the eagle-eyed slander of the age in which Swift lived. To these defiances, no formal answer was returned, but the story was suffered to remain upon record. That this most atrocious charge may no longer continue without an explicit contradiction, I here insert the origin of the calumny, upon the authority of the Rev. Dr Hutcheson, of Donaghadee.

The Rev. Mr P——r, a successor of Dean Swift in the prebend of Kilroot, was the first circulator of this extraordinary story. He told the tale, among other public occasions, at the late excellent Bishop of Dromore's, who ness and confidence which he had exhibited in relinquishing that independence after which he had longed so earnestly, marked at once

committed it to writing. His authority he alleged to be a Dean Dobbs, who, he stated, had informed him that informations were actually lodged before magistrates in the diocese of Down and Connor, for the alleged attempt at violation. But when the late ingenious Mr Malone, and many other literary gentlemen, began to press a closer examination of the alleged fact, the unfortunate narrator denied obstinately his having ever promulgated such a charge. And whether the whole story was the creation of incipient insanity, or whether he had felt the discredit attached to his tergiversation so acutely as to derange his understanding, it is certain the unfortunate Mr P——r died raving mad, a patient in that very hospital for lunatics, established by Swift, against whom he had propagated this cruel calumny. Yet, although P——r thus fell a victim to his own rash assertions, or credulity, it has been supposed that this inexplicable figment did really originate with Dean Dobbs, and that he had been led into a mistake, by the initial letters, J. S. upon the alleged papers, which might apply to Jonathan Smedley (to whom, indeed, the tale has been supposed properly to belong), or to John Smith, as well as to Jonathan Swift. It is sufficient for Swift's vindication to observe, that he returned to Kilroot, after his resignation, and inducted his successor in face of the church and of the public; that he returned to Sir William Temple with as fair a character as when he had left him; that during all his public life, in England and Ireland, where he was the butt of a whole faction, this charge was never heard of; that when adduced so many years after his death, it was unsupported by aught but sturdy and general averment; and that the chief propagator of the calumny first retracted his assertions, and finally died insane.

2.

the generosity and the kindness of his disposition, and Sir William was insensible to neither. He resided with that great man from his return to England in 1695, till Temple's death in 1699, scarce a cloud intervening to disturb the harmony of their friendship. A cold look from his patron, such was the veneration with which Swift regarded Temple, made him unhappy for days;[1] his faculties were devoted to his service, and, during his last decline, Swift registered, with pious fidelity, every change in his disorder; and concluded the Journal, « He died at one o'clock this morning (27th January, 1698-9), and with him all that was good and amiable among men.» From another memorandum, copied by Thomas Steele, Esq. junior, we have this farther character by our author of his early patron: « He was a person of the greatest wisdom, justice, liberality, politeness, eloquence, of his age and nation; the truest lover of his country, and one that deserved more from it by his eminent public services, than any man before or since: besides his great deserving of the commonwealth of learning; having been

[1] In the Journal to Stella, he says, « Dont you remember how I used to be in pain, when Sir William Temple would look cold and out of humour for three or four days, and I used to suspect a hundred reasons? I have plucked up my spirit since then, faith; he spoiled a fine gentleman.»—S.

universally esteemed the most accomplished writer of his time.»

Among the most acceptable services which Swift could render Temple during this period, was his powerful assistance in the dispute concerning the superiority of ancient or modern learning, in which his patron had taken an anxious share, and had experienced some rough treatment from Wotton. This controversy, with other foolish fashions, had passed to England from France, where Fontenelle and Perrault had first ventured to assert the cause of the moderns. Upon its merits it may be sufficient to observe, that the field of comparison is infinitely too wide to admit of precise parallels, or of accurate reasoning. In works of poetry and imagination, the precedence may be decidedly allotted to the ancients, owing to the superior beauties of their language, and because they were the first to employ these general and obvious funds of illustration, which can appear original in those only by whom they were first used. On the other hand, in physical science, which necessarily is gradually enlarging its bounds, both by painful research and casual discovery, and in ethics, where the moderns enjoy the advantages of a pure religion and more free polity, it seems that they have far outshone their predecessors. But there is an ardour in literary controversy which does not rest contented with a drawn-battle. The arguments in favour of the moderns were adopted in England by Mr Wotton, in his Reflections on Ancient and Modern Learning, and indignantly combated by Sir William Temple, in his treatise on the same subject. Among other works of the ancients on which he founded the plea of their pre-eminence, Temple unhappily referred to the Epistles of Phalaris, now generally regarded as spurious, but which he pronounced to exhibit « such diversity of passion, such freedom of thought, such knowledge of life and contempt of death, as breathed in every line the tyrant and the commander. » Wotton replied to this treatise, and was seconded by the learned Bentley, who had the double motive of detecting the spurious Phalaris, and of vindicating himself from the charge of incivility, respecting the loan of a manuscript from the King's library to the Honourable Mr Boyle, then engaged in an edition of the Epistles. This gave occasion to the treatise called Boyle against Bentley, and to the reply of that profound scholar, known by the name of Bentley against Boyle. Swift felt doubly interested in this dispute, first, on account of the share his patron had in the controversy, and secondly, because the literati of Oxford, with whose conduct towards him he had been so highly satisfied, were united against Bentley, and in the cause of his antagonist. The battle of the Books was the consequence of Swift's interest in behalf of Sir William Temple, and it was probably shewn and handed about in manuscript during his lifetime, although it was not printed until some years afterwards. The idea is taken from Coutray's « Histoire Poétique de la Guerre nouvellement declarée entre les anciens et les modernes,» a spirited poem, divided into eleven books, inferior to Swift's work in personal satire and raciness of humour, but strongly resembling the Battle of the Books in the plan and management of the literary warfare. About the same time, Swift appears to have revised and completed his Tale of a Tub, one of his most remarkable productions. The preliminary advertisements of the bookseller in 1704, mention, that both these treatises appear to have been arranged for publication in 1697, the last year of Sir William Temple's life; there is, therefore, reason to believe that his death prevented their being then given to the world.

During this period, Swift's muse did not remain entirely idle. The following nervous verses on the burning of Whitehall, occur in his hand-writing, and with his corrections, among the papers of Mr Lyons. It is remarkable, that while the first couplet breathes that zeal for the property of the church, which afterwards dictated so many of Swift's publications, the tenor of the whole is completely in unison with revolution principles, and perhaps they are more violently expressed respecting the execution of Charles the First, than would have received the applause of many determined Whigs. The rough satirical force of the lines somewhat resembles the poetry of Churchill.

ON THE BURNING OF WHITEHALL, IN 1697.[1]

This pile was raised by Wolsey's impious hands,
Built with the church's patrimonial lands.
Here bloody Henry kept his cruel court,
Hence sprung the martyrdoms of every sort.
Weak Edward here, and Mary the bigot,
Did both their holy innovations plot.
A fiercer Tudor fill'd the churchman s seat,
In all her father's attributes complete.
Dudley's lewd life doth the white mansion stain,
And a slain guest obscures a glorious reign.[2]
Then Northern James dishonour'd every room
With filth and palliardisme brought from home.[3]
Next the French consort dignified the stews,
Employing males to their first proper use.
A bold usurper next did domineer,
Whirl'd hence by the angry demons of the air.

[1] Such is the date upon the manuscript. But Whitehall was burned in April 1690-1; the date therefore must be that of the year in which the verses were composed, not that in which the accident took place.

[2] Beheading of Queen Mary.

[3] After this a line scratched out,

And here did under the black plaster groan.

When saunt'ring Charles returned, a fulsome crew
Of parasites, buffoons, he with him drew—
Nay, worse than these fill the polluted hall,
Bawds, pimps, and panders, the detested squawl
Of riots, fancied rapes, the devil and all.
This pious prince here too did breathe his last,
His certain death on different persons cast.
His wise successor brought a motley throng,
Despising right, strongly protecting wrong
To these assistant herds of preaching cowls,
And troops of noisy, senseless, fighting fools.
Guerdon for this: he heard the dread command,
"Embark, and leave your crown and native land."
He gone, the rank infection still remains,
Which to repel requires eternal pains.
No force to cleanse it can a river draw,
Nor Hercules could do t, not great Nassau.
Most greedy financiers, and lavish too,
Swarm in, in spite of all that prince could do;
Projectors, peculats, the palace hold,
Patriots exchanging liberty for gold,
Monsters unknown to this blest land of old.
Heaven takes the cure in hand, celestial ire
Applies the oft-tried remedy of fire;
The purging flames were better far employ'd,
Than when old Sodom was, or Troynovant, destroy'd.
The nest obscene of every pamper'd vice,
Sinks down of this infernal paradise,
Down come the lofty roofs, the cedar burns,
The blended metal to a torrent turns.
The carvings crackle and the marbles rive,
The paintings shrink, vainly the Henries strive,
Propt by great Holbein's pencil, down they fall,
The fiery deluge sweeps and swallows all.

Originally thus

Of spurious brats, abhorr'd by all.

But mark how Providence with watchful care,[1]
Did Inigo's famed building spare,
That theatre produced an action truly great,
On which eternal acclamations wait;
Of kings deposed, most faithful annals tell,
And slaughter'd monarchs would a volume swell.
Our happy chronicle can shew alone
——————tyrants executed *one.*[2]

Another copy of verses, written about the same period «in a lady's ivory table-book,» are curious, as the first specimen of that peculiar talent which Swift possessed, of ridiculing the vain, frivolous, and common-place topics of general society.

Meantime, amid the ease of a literary life, and with the prospect which Temple's confirmed friendship appeared to open to him, Swift was imperceptibly laying the foundation for a train of misery which was to embitter his future years; for it was during his second residence at Moorpark, that he formed his acquaintance with Esther Johnson, better known by the poetical name of Stella. And before entering upon this ominous part of his history,

[1] The banqueting-house, built upon a plan by the celebrated Inigo Jones, alone escaped the conflagration. It is unnecessary to add, that in front of this structure Charles I. was beheaded.

[2] The last line originally ran

On this day tyrants executed one;

But the first three words are blotted out, and the word «memorandum» written below them.

it is necessary to notice some previous circumstances, which have been reserved to this place.

While Swift pursued his studies at Trinity College as a secluded and indigent scholar, his intercourse with female society was probably much limited. On his return to Leicestershire, his mother appears to have had some apprehensions of his forming an imprudent attachment to a young woman of their neighbourhood,[1] fears which Swift himself treats as visionary, in a letter to a friend.[2] As that letter forms a sort of index to the views with which he frequented female society, and to his plans of settling in life, the reader will excuse an extract. He alludes to his «cold temper, and unconfined humour,» as sufficient hinderances to any imprudent attachment. He mentions his resolutions not to think of marriage until his fortune was settled in the world,

[1] See a Letter to Dr Worrall, 16th January, 1728-9.—«When I went a lad to my mother, after the Revolution, she brought me acquainted with a family, where there was a daughter, with whom I was acquainted. My prudent mother was afraid I should be in love with her: but when I went to London she married an innkeeper in Loughborough, in that county, by whom she had several children.» The name of this fair seducer was Betty Jones, who, by her marriage above mentioned, became Mrs Perkins, of the George Inn. Her daughter afterwards claimed Swift's protection, and was befriended by him.

[2] Letter to the Reverend John Kendall, dated 11th February, 1691-2.

and hints, that, even then, he would be so hard to please, he might probably put it off till doomsday.[1] But he charges these appearances of attachment, which his friend had deemed symptoms of passion, to an active and restless temper, incapable of enduring

[1] A singular anecdote is told, which seems to shew that, at a late period of life, he retained his sentiments concerning early marriages. « A young clergyman, the son of a bishop in Ireland, having married without the knowledge of his friends, it gave umbrage to his family, and his father refused to see him. The Dean being in company with him some time after, said he would tell him a story: 'When I was a schoolboy at Kilkenny, and in the lower form, I longed very much to have a horse of my own to ride on. One day I saw a poor man leading a very mangy lean horse out of the town to kill him for the skin. I asked the man if he would sell him, which he readily consented to, upon my offering him somewhat more than the price of the hide, which was all the money I had in the world. I immediately got on him, to the great envy of some of my schoolfellows, and to the ridicule of others, and rode him about the town. The horse soon tired and laid down. As I had no stable to put him into, nor any money to pay for his sustenance, I began to find out what a foolish bargain I had made, and cried heartily for the loss of my cash; but the horse dying soon after upon the spot, gave me some relief.' To this the young clergyman answered, 'Sir, your story is very good, and applicable to my case; I own I deserve such a rebuke;' and then burst into a flood of tears. The Dean made no reply, but went the next day to the lord-lieutenant, and prevailed on him to give the young gentleman a small living, then vacant, for his immediate support: and not long after brought about a reconciliation between his father and him.»

idleness, and, therefore, catching at such opportunities of amusement as most readily occurred, and frequently seeking and finding it in the sort of insignificant gallantry which he had used towards the girl in question; a habit, he adds, to be laid aside, whenever he began to take sober resolutions, and which, should he enter the church, he would not find it hard to lay down in the porch. Swift proved unable to keep the promise which, doubtless, he had made to himself, as well as to his friend; and it is probably to a habit, at first indulged merely from vanity, or for the sake of amusement, that we are to trace the well-known circumstances which embittered his life, and impaired his reputation.

His next attachment assumed a more serious complexion. It was contracted in Ireland, and the object was Jane Waryng, the sister of his ancient college companion, whom by a cold poetical conceit he has termed Varina. From the letter which he wrote to that lady, 29th April, 1696, his passion appears to have been deep and serious, with too much of the tragic mood to accord exactly with his account of those petty intrigues, in which

> Cadenus, common forms apart,
> In every scene had kept his heart;
> Had sigh'd and languish'd, vow'd and writ,
> For pastime, or to shew his wit.

On the contrary, the letter to Varina proposes, in the most pressing terms, matrimony as a « just and honourable action, which would furnish health to her, and unspeakable happiness to both.» It is a pleading of vehemence and exclamation, containing a solemn offer to forego every prospect of interest for the sake of Varina; and a pathetic complaint, that her love was more fatal than her cruelty. Another letter, which we find addressed to the same lady, is addressed to Miss Jane Waryng (no longer Varina) and is written in a very different tone from the first. Four years had now elapsed, an interval in which much may have happened to abate the original warmth of Swift's passion; nor is it perhaps very fair, ignorant as we are of what had occurred in the interim, to pass a severe sentence upon his conduct, when, after being mortified by Varina's cruelty during so long a period, he seems to have been a little startled by her sudden offer of capitulation. It is, however, certain, that, just when the lover, worn out by neglect, or disgusted by uncertainty, began to grow cool in his suit, the lady, a case not altogether without example, became pressing and categorical in her inquiries what had altered the style of her admirer's letters. In reply, Swift charges Varina with want of affection, and indifference, states his own income in a most dismal point of view, yet intimates he might well pretend to a better fortune than she was possessed of. He is so far from retaining his former opinion as to the effects of a happy union, that he inquires whether the physicians had got over some scruples they appeared to entertain on the subject of her health. Lastly, he demands peremptorily to know whether she could undertake to manage their domestic affairs, with an income of rather less than three hundred pounds a-year; whether she would engage to follow the methods he should point out for the improvement of her mind; whether she could bend all her affections to the same direction which he should give his own, and so govern her passions, however justly provoked, as at all times to resume her good humour at his approach; and, finally, whether she could account the place where he resided more welcome than courts and cities without him? These premises agreed (as indispensable to please those, who, like himself, were « deeply read in the world »), he intimates his willingness to wed her, though *without* personal beauty or large fortune. It must remain uncertain whether the positive requisites, or the proffered abatements, were least acceptable to the lady; but, under all circumstances, she must have been totally divested of pride and delicacy, if she could, upon such terms, have exacted from her reluctant lover, the faith which he seemed so unwilling to plight. Thus separated Swift and Varina.

Much, as we have already noticed, may no doubt have happened, in the course of their correspondence, to alter his opinion of that lady, or lead him to imagine that, in delaying a positive answer to his proposals, she was trifling with his passion. But ere she was dismissed from the scene, he had learned to know one with whom much of the good and evil of his future life was to be inseparably blended.

Esther Johnson, who purchased, by a life of prolonged hopes and disappointed affection, a poetical immortality under the name of Stella, became first known to Swift during his second residence with Sir William Temple. The birth of Stella has been carefully investigated, with the hopes of discovering something that might render a mysterious and romantic history yet more romantic. But there are no sound reasons for supposing that she had other parents than her reputed father and mother, the former the younger brother of a good family in Nottinghamshire, and by profession a merchant in London,—the latter a woman of acute and penetrating talents, the friend and companion of Lady Gifford, Temple's favourite sister, and cherished by her with particular respect and regard until the end of her life. Johnson, the father, died soon after Stella's birth, but Mrs Johnson and her two daughters were inmates of Moorpark for several years.

General interest was taken by all the inhabitants of this mansion, in the progress which little Hetty made in her education, and much of the task of instruction devolved upon Swift, now a man of thirty, who seems to have, for some time, regarded his lovely pupil with the friendship of an elder brother. But the constant and habitual intercourse of affectionate confidence between the master and the pupil, by degress assumed a more tender complexion; and it will be presently seen,

He taught her even the most ordinary parts of education, and, in particular, instructed her in the art of writing. Their hands resemble each other in some peculiarities. But though he instructed her in the necessary branches of education, there is evidence he went no farther, and that Stella, far from being a learned lady, was really deficient in many of the most ordinary points of information. The editor is possessed of an exact transcript of marginal notes, written by Swift for elucidation of an edition of Milton, 1669, which is inscribed, « The gift of Dr Jonathan Swift to Mrs Dingley and Mrs Johnson, May 1703. » The notes are numerous, but the information which they convey is such as could only be useful to persons of a very indifferent education. Thus, Palestine is explained to be the Holy-land, Rhene and Danau, two German rivers, Pilasters are rendered pillars, Alcides, Hercules; Columbus is designated as he « who discovered America, » and Xerxes as having « made a bridge with ships over the Hellespont. » It does not seem likely that Swift would have taken all this trouble merely for the illumination of Mrs Dingley, and the inference plainly must be, that Stella was neither well informed nor well educated.

that when fortune appeared disposed to separate them, they were both unwilling to submit to her dictates. There is little doubt, that the feelings which attended this new connexion, must have had weight in disposing Swift to break off the lingering and cold courtship which he had maintained with Mrs Jane Waryng. And from this period, the fates of Swift and Stella were so implicated together, as to produce the most remarkable incidents of both their lives.

Four years of quiet and happy residence at Moorpark were terminated by the death of Sir William Temple, in 1698 9. He was not unmindful of Swift's generous and disinterested friendship, which he rewarded by a pecuniary legacy, and with what he, doubtless, regarded as of much greater consequence, the bequest of his literary remains. These, considering the author's high reputation and numerous friends, held forth to his literary executor an opportunity of coming before the public, in a manner that should excite at once interest and respect. And when it is considered, that all Swift s plans revolved upon making himself eminent as an author, the value of such an occasion to distinguish himself could scarcely be too highly estimated.

The experiment, however, appeared at first to have in a great measure disappointed these reasonable expectations. The works of Temple were carefully edited, with a dedication to King William; and at the same time a petition was presented for Swift, reminding his Majesty of a promise made to Sir William Temple, to bestow on him a prebend of Canterbury or Westminster. Swift has expressed his belief, that the Earl of Romney, who promised to second this petition, did in reality suppress it; and William, when he ceased to reap the benefit of Temple's political experience, was not likely to interest himself deeply in his posthumous literary labours. After long attendance upon court, therefore, Swift's hopes of promotion disappeared, and the revolution principles, which he certainly strongly professed, did not prevent his regarding King William, and his memory, with very little complacence.

SECTION II.

Swift goes to Ireland with Lord Berkeley—His differences with that nobleman—Obtains the living of Laracor—He is displeased with his sister's marriage—His mode of life at Laracor—Mrs Dingley and Stella come to Ireland—Tisdal makes proposals of marriage to Stella—Swift embarks in politics—His opinion of the affairs of church and state—Tale of a Tub.

SWIFT, now in the prime of life, and well known both to the great and learned, could not long want an honourable provision, and accordingly received and accepted an invitation to attend the Earl of Berkeley, one of the Lords Justices of Ireland, to that country, in the capacity of chaplain and private secretary. But these plurality of offices gave umbrage to a Mr Bushe, who had pitched upon the latter situation for himself, and who contrived, under pretence of its incompatibility with the character of a clergyman, to have Swift superseded in his own favour. Lord Berkeley, « with a poor apology,» promised to make his chaplain amends, by giving him the first good church living that should become vacant. But neither in this did he keep his word; for, when the rich deanery of Derry was in his gift, Bushe entered into a negotiation to sell it for a bribe of a thousand pounds, and would only consent to give Swift the preference, upon his paying a like sum. Incensed alike at the secretary and his principal, whom he supposed to be accessary to this unworthy conduct, Swift returned the succinct answer, « God confound you both for a couple of scoundrels,» and instantly left Lord Berkeley's lodgings in the castle. He had already given

Lord Orrery intimates, that, notwithstanding what is above stated, Swift would actually have obtained this preferment, but for the interference of the learned Dr King. « The rich deanery of Derry became vacant at this time, and was intended for him by Lord Berkeley, if Dr King, then Bishop of Derry, afterwards Archbishop of Dublin, had not interposed; entreating that the deanery might be given to some grave and elderly divine, rather than to so young a man; because, added the bishop, the situation of Derry is in the midst of Presbyterians, and I should be glad of a clergyman who could be of assistance to me. I have no objection to Mr Swift. I know him to be a sprightly, ingenious young man; but, instead of residing, I dare say he will be eternally flying backwards and forwards to London; and therefore I vent to his resentment in one or two keen personal satires; and his patron, alarmed for the consequences of an absolute breach with a man of his temper and talents, was glad to reconcile, or at least to pacify him, by presenting him with the rectory of Agher, and the vicarages of Laracor and Rathbeggan. These livings united, though far inferior in value to the deanery of Derry, formed yet a certain and competent fund of subsistence, amounting to about L.230 yearly. The Prebend of Dunlavin being added in the year 1700, raised Swift's income to betwixt L.350 and L.400, which was its amount until he was preferred to the deanery of St Patrick's. These facts are ascertained from his account-books for the years 1701 and 1792, which evince, on the one hand, the remarkable economy with which Swift managed this moderate income, and on the other, that, of the expenses which he permitted himself, more than one-

entreat that he may be provided for in some other place.» *Lord Orrery's Life of Swift*, London, 1752, p. 22. Archbishop King was afterwards himself disappointed of preferment on account of his age. When Dr Boulter was preferred to be Primate of Ireland, in spite of his claims, as Archbishop of Dublin, King received him seated in his chair, with the sarcastic apology, «My lord, I am certain your grace will forgive me, because you know I am *too old* to rise.»

tenth part was incurred in acts of liberality and benevolence.[1]

Swift's quarrel with Lord Berkeley did not disturb his intercourse with the rest of the family, in which he retained his situation of chaplain. Lady Berkeley stood high in his opinion as an amiable and virtuous woman, in whom the most easy and polite conversation, joined with the truest piety, might be observed united to as much advantage as ever they were seen apart in any other persons.[2] The company also of two amiable and lively

[1] Account of expenses from November 1, 1700, to November 1, 1701.

Articles per Account,	*L.*	*s.*	*d.*
Shoes and books,	3	0	0
A servant's wages, etc.	7	0	0
Washing, etc.	4	0	0
Linen,	5	0	0
Clothes,	13	0	0
Journeys,	10	0	0
J. B.	5	0	0
Accidents,	5	0	0
Horse,	12	0	0
Letters,	1	10	0
Play,	5	0	0
Gifts and charity extraordinary,	10	0	0
Charity common,	2	10	0
Expenses common,	17	0	0
	L.100	0	0

[2] This excellent lady was daughter of Baptist Noel, Viscount Campden, and sister to Edward, first Earl of Gainsborough. She died 30th July, 1719.

young ladies of fashion, daughters of the earl, must have rendered the society still more fascinating; and, accordingly, it is during his residence with Lord Berkeley, that Swift appears first to have given way to the playfulness of his disposition in numerous poetical *jeux d'esprit,* which no poet ever composed with the same felicity and spirit. Of this class are the inimitable petition of Mrs Frances Harris, the verses on Miss Floyd, a young lady of beauty and spirit, who was also an inmate of the family, and some other pieces, written during this period. But the most solemn waggery was the Meditation on a Broomstick, composed and read with infinite gravity, as an existing portion of the Honourable Mr Boyle's Meditations, which, it seems, Lady Berkeley used to request Swift to read aloud more frequently than was agreeable to him. In such company, and with such amusements, his time glided happily away, and he retained a high regard for the ladies of the family during the rest of his life. Lady Betty Berkeley, in particular, afterwards Lady Betty Germaine, was, to the end of his career, one of his most valuable and most valued correspondents.

[1] Ladies Mary and Elizabeth Berkeley. The former married Thomas Chambers, of Hanworth, in the county of Middlesex; the latter Sir John Germaine, of Drayton, in the county of Northampton. A third daughter of the Earl, Lady Penelope, died during his residence at Dublin.

During this period of Swift's life, his sister contracted an imprudent marriage with a person called Fenton, to his very high and avowed displeasure, which, Lord Orrery has informed us, was solely owing to his ambition being outraged at her matching with a tradesman. This, however, was by no means the case. Fenton was a worthless character, and upon the eve of bankruptcy, when Swift's sister, against his warm remonstrances, chose to unite her fate to his. And although he retained his resentment against her imprudence, Lord Orrery ought not to have omitted, that, out of his own moderate income, Swift allowed Mrs Fenton what was adequate to her comfortable support, amid the ruin in which that imprudence had involved her.[1]

Having now taken leave of Lord Berkeley's family, at least as resident chaplain, Swift, in the year 1700, took possession of his living at Laracor, and resumed the habits of a country clergyman. He is said to have walked down, *incognito*, to the place of his future residence; and tradition has recorded various anecdotes[2]

[1] These particulars concerning Fenton are on the authority of Mr Theophilus Swift.

[2] Among these may be reckoned the doggrel lines, in which he is said to have commemorated various towns and villages through which he passed in his way to Laracor.

Dublin for a city, Dunshaughlin for a plow,
Navan for a market, Ardbracken for a cow;

of his journey. He walked straight to the curate's house, demanded his name, and an-

> Kells for an old town, Virginia poor,
> Cavan for dirt, and Belturbet for a whore.
>
> SWIFTIANA.

Swift was very much addicted to this sort of proverb-making, as it may be called. In the following couplet on Carlow, I understand the first line is highly descriptive; but that the town and inhabitants do not now merit the reproach contained in the second:

> High church and low steeple,
> Dirty town and proud people.

Many instances of this humour may be observed in the Journal to Stella.

Another anecdote of this journey is preserved by Mr Wilson: "There were three inns in Navan, each of which claim, to this day, the honour of having entertained Dr Swift. It is probable that he dined at one of them, for it is certain that he slept at Kells, in the house of Jonathan Belcher, a Leicestershire man, who had built the inn of that town on the English model, which still exists; and, in point of capaciousness and convenience, would not disgrace the first road in England. The host, whether struck by the commanding sternness of Swift's appearance, or from natural civility, showed him into the best room, and waited himself at table. The attention of Belcher seems so far to have won upon Swift as to have produced some conversation. 'You're an Englishman, sir?' said Swift. 'Yes, sir.' 'What is your name?' 'Jonathan Belcher, sir.' 'An Englishman, and *Jonathan* too, in the town of Kells—Who would have thought it! What brought you to this country?' 'I came with Sir Thomas Taylor, sir; and I believe I could reckon *fifty Jonathans* in my family.' 'Then you are a man of family?' 'Yes, sir; and I have nounced himself bluntly « as his master. » All was bustle to receive a person of such consequence, and who, apparently, was determined to make his importance felt[1]. The curate's

four sons and three daughters by one mother, a good woman of true Irish mould.' 'Have you long been out of your native country?' 'Thirty years, sir.' 'Do you ever expect to visit it again?' 'Never.' 'Can you say that without a sigh?' 'I can, sir; my family is my country.' 'Why, sir, you are a better philosopher than those who have written volumes on the subject: Then you are reconciled to your fate?' 'I ought to be so; I am very happy; I like the people, and though I was not born in Ireland, I'll die in it, and that's the same thing.' Swift paused in deep thought for a minute, and then, with much energy, repeated the first line of the preamble of the noted Irish statute—*Ipsis Hibernis Hiberniores!* ('The English settlers are more Irish than the Irish themselves.')»—*Swiftiana,* London, 1804, Vol. I. 58.

[1] His mode of introducing himself was often whimsical and alarming. The widow of Mr Watson, a miniature-painter in Dublin, who, herself, followed the same profession, used to mention, that, while a girl in her father's house (a Mr Hoy, of the county of Wicklow), a gentleman rode up to the door, was admitted to the parlour where the family were sitting, and held some conversation with Mr Hoy, probably upon a literary topic, as her father left the room to seek a book referred to. During his absence, the stranger, stealing softly behind her, gave her a smart and unexpected slap on the cheek, saying, at the same time, to the astonished girl, « You will now remember Dean Swift as long as you live; » in which he prophesied very truly. Even in hiring servants, it was his custom to begin by asking them their qualifications for discharging the lowest and most mortifying offices.

3.

wife was ordered to lay aside the doctor's only clean shirt and stockings, which he carried in his pocket; nor did Swift relax his airs of domination until he had excited much alarm, which his subsequent kind and friendly conduct to the worthy couple, turned into respectful attachment. This was the ruling trait of Swift's conduct to others; his praise assumed the appearance and language of complaint; his benefits were often prefaced by a prologue of a threatening nature; his most grave themes were blended with ironical pleasantry, and, in those of a lighter nature, deep and bitter satire is often couched under the most trifling levity.

Swift's life at Laracor was regular and clerical. He read prayers twice a-week, and regularly preached upon the Sunday. Upon the former occasions the church was thinly attended; and it is said, that the ludicrous and irreverent anecdote of his addressing the church service to his parish clerk, occurred when he found the rest of the congregation absent upon such an occasion. The truth of the story has been, however, disputed, although the friends of Swift allow that it had much of the peculiarity of his vein of humour. The

If they answered saucily, or expressed themselves affronted, the treaty was ended; if not, he set their submissive replies to the account of their good sense, and usually engaged them.

reader will find beneath, the reasoning of Mr Theophilus Swift upon this curious anecdote, to which there can be but one objection, namely, that Swift was more likely to do such a thing, than Orrery to invent it; and that to Swift, notwithstanding his sincere piety, a jest was irresistibly seductive.[1] On Sundays the church at Laracor was well attended by the neighbouring families; and Swift, far from having reason to complain of want of an audience, attained that reputation which he pronounced to be the height of his ambition, since inquiries were frequently made of his faithful clerk, Roger Coxe,[2] whether the Doctor was to preach that Sunday.

[1] « I perfectly recollect, that neither my father or Mrs Whiteway had ever heard the story of 'Dearly beloved Roger,' till Orrery's book made its appearance. I have frequently heard them say so. They allowed it was possible, and not unlike the Dean; but they believed it an invention of Orrery's, to discredit the Dean's respect for religion. They thought it very singular that such a circumstance, had it been true, should not have been known to them; especially as my father had a considerable estate near Laracor, and resided very much upon it. For myself, I give no credit to the story. I verily believe that Orrery applied a story he had found, to discredit the piety of the Dean.» Mr Swift afterwards found the same story, in the same words, in an old jest-book, printed betwixt 1655 and 1660.

[2] Roger was a man of humour, and merited a master like Swift. When the Doctor remarked that he wore a scarlet waistcoat, he defended himself as being of the church-militant. « Will you not bid for these poultry?

While resident at Laracor, it was Swift's principal care to repair the dilapidations which the church and vicarage had sustained, by the carelessness or avarice of former incumbents. He expressed the utmost indignation at the appearance of the church; and, during the first year of his incumbency, expended a considerable sum in putting it into decent repair. The vicarage he also made comfortably tenantable,[1] and proceeded to improve it, according to the ideas of beauty and taste which were at that time universally received. He formed a pleasant garden; smoothed the banks of a rivulet into a canal, and planted willows in regular ranks by its side. These willows, so often celebrated in the Journal to Stella, are

said Swift to his humble dependant, at a sale of farm-stock. « No, sir; » said Roger, « they're just a-going to *Hatch*. » They were, in fact, on the point of being knocked down to a farmer called Hatch. This humourist was originally a hatter, and died at the age of 90, at Bruky, in the county of Cavan. See *Swiftiana*. Vol. I. page 9.

[1] The house appears, from its present ruins, to have been a comfortable mansion. The present Bishop of Meath (whom the editor is proud to call his friend), with classic feeling, while pressing upon his clergy, at a late visitation, the duty of repairing the glebe-houses, addressed himself particularly to the Vicar of Laracor, and recommended to him, in the necessary improvements of his mansion, to save as far as possible, the walls of the house which had been inhabited by his great predecessor.

now decayed or cut down; the garden cannot be traced; and the canal only resembles a ditch. Yet the parish and the rector continue to derive some advantage, from its having been once the abode of Swift. He increased the glebe from one acre to twenty. The tithes of Effernock, purchased with his own money, at a time when it did not abound, were, by his will, settled for ever on the incumbent of that living.

But Laracor had yet greater charms than its willows and canals, the facetious humours of Roger Coxe, and the applause of the gentry of the neighbourhood. Swift had no sooner found his fortune established in Ireland, than it became his wish that Stella should be an inhabitant of that kingdom. This was easily arranged. She was her own mistress, and the rate of interest being higher in Ireland, furnished her with a plausible excuse for taking up her residence near the friend and instructor of her youth. The company of Mrs Dingley, a woman of narrow income and limited understanding, but of middle age, and a creditable character, obviated, in a great measure, the

[1] This was not without a touch of his peculiar humour. These tithes, by his will, are devised to his successors in the cure, so long as the Established Church lasted; and to the poor, in case it should be exchanged for any other form of the Christian religion, always excepting from the benefit thereof, Jews, Atheists, and Infidels.

inferences which the world must otherwise have necessarily drawn from this step. Some whispers so singular a resolution doubtless occasioned; but the caution of Swift, who was never known to see Stella but in presence of a third party, and the constant attendance of Mrs Dingley, to whom, apparently, he paid equal attention, seem to have put scandal to silence. Their residence was varied with the same anxious regard to Stella's character. When Swift left his parsonage at Laracor, the ladies became its tenants; and when he returned, they regularly retired to their lodgings in the town of Trim, the capital of the diocese, or were received by Dr Raymond, so often mentioned in the Journal, the hospitable vicar of that parish. Every exterior circumstance which could distinguish an union of mere friendship from one of a more tender nature, was carefully observed, and the surprise at first excited by the settlement of Mrs Dingley and Stella in a country to which they were strangers, seems gradually to have subsided.[1] It is, however, highly probable, that

[1] The English acquaintances of the parties expected a different result. Mr Thomas Swift, the Dean's « Parson-Cousin,» in a letter from Puttenham, Feb. 5, 1706, asks « whether Jonathan be married? or whether he has been able to resist the charms of both these gentlewomen that marched quite from Moorpark to Dublin (as they would have marched to the North or anywhere else), with full resolution to engage him?»

between Swift and Stella there was a tacit understanding that their union was to be completed by marriage, when Swift's income, according to the prudential scheme which he had unhappily adopted, should be adequate to the expense of a matrimonial establishment. And here it is impossible to avoid remarking the vanity of that over-prudence, which labours to provide against all possible contingencies. Had Swift, like any ordinary man in his situation, been contented to share his limited income with a deserving object of his affections, the task of his biographers would have been short and cheerful; and we should neither have had to record, nor apologize for, those circumstances which form the most plausible charge against his memory. In the pride of talent and of wisdom, he endeavoured to frame a new path to happiness; and the consequences have rendered him a warning, where the various virtues with which he was endowed ought to have made him a pattern.

Meanwhile, the risk of ill construction being so carefully guarded against, Stella with her beauty and accomplishments was not long without an admirer. She was then about eighteen, her hair of a raven black, her features both beautiful and expressive, and her form of perfect symmetry, though rather inclined to embonpoint. To those outward graces were added good sense, great docility, and uncommon powers both of grave and gay conversation, and a fortune, which, though small, was independent. It is not surprising, therefore, that she should have received an offer of marriage from the Reverend Dr William Tisdal, a clergyman of talents and respectability, with whom Swift lived upon a familiar and friendly footing. The proposals of the lover were made to Swift, as the lady's guardian, by whose wishes and advice she was determined to be guided; and thus he was apparently reduced either to the necessity of stating his own pretensions to Stella's hand, or of resigning her to a rival. Mr Deane Swift has here frankly explained and condemned the conduct of his kinsman, which Mr Sheridan, perhaps for that very reason, has laboured to colour over and justify. According to the former, Swift insisted upon such unreasonable terms for Stella's maintenance and provision, in case of widowhood, that Tisdal was unable to accede to them. Sheridan, on the other hand, assures us, that the refusal came finally from the young lady herself, who, though she shewed at first no repugnance to Tisdal's proposal, perhaps with a view to sound Swift's sentiments, yet could not at length prevail upon herself to abandon the hope of being united to him. Tisdal himself suspected Swift did not warmly befriend his suit, as is evident from a letter, dated 20th April, 1704, in which the latter endeavours, somewhat imperfectly, to justify himself from such an accusation. For considering his express admission, that if his fortune and humour permitted him to think of matrimony, among all persons on earth Stella should be his choice; and, considering the close and intimate union which had so long subsisted between them, it requires strong faith to add implicit credit to Swift's next assertion, that so strong a predilection never operated as an impediment to Tisdal's courtship. Nor is it in nature to suppose that he should have been indifferent to the thoughts of one « whom he loved better than his life, a thousand million of times,»[1] passing into the possession of another. It is also remarkable, that when Tisdal is mentioned in the Journal to Stella, it is always with a slight or sneer, and frequently with allusion to some disgusting imperfection. Yet no open breach took place between the rivals, if we may term them so, for they continued to maintain occasional intercourse down to the year 1740, when Tisdal witnesses the Dean's last will. The coarse epigram attached to the following fragment of one of Swift's letters (never before published), shews that their correspondence was not uniformly of the most friendly nature.

[1] This and similar expressions occur in the Journal.

Dear Sir,—You desired me to finish some lines you wrote at Dunshaglin:—

How can I finish what you have begun?
Can fire to ripen fruit assist the sun?
Should Raphael draw a virgin's blooming face,
Exert his skill to give it every grace,
And leave the rest to some Dutch heavy drone;
Would you not rather see that face alone?
Or should Praxiteles the marble take,
A Venus' head and neck and shoulders make,
And some rude hand attempt the rest from thence,
Would you not think him void of common sense?
These hints I hope will move you to excuse
The first refusal of my humble muse.
The task I must decline, and think it just
Your piece continue as it is, a Bust.
Since want   show,
A golden charm   below.

[Four lines in the original are here erased, and the words here interlined, only could be made out.]

Being in a vein of writing epigrams, I send you the following piece upon Tisdal, which I intend to send to all his acquaintance; for he goes from house to house to shew his wit upon me, for which I think it reasonable he should have something to stare him in the face.

UPON WILLIAM TISDAL, D. D.

When a Roman was dying, the next man of kin
Stood over him gaping to take his breath in.
Were Tisdal the same way to blow out his breath,
Such a whiff to the living were much worse than death
Any man with a nose would much rather die,
So would Jack, so would Dan, so would you, so would I
Without a reproach to the Doctor, I think,
Whenever he dies, he must die with a stink.[1]—(T.)

[1] The original fragment is preserved in the Museum of

From the time that she finally rejected Tisdal's addresses, Stella appears to have considered her destiny as united to that of Swift. She encouraged no other admirer, and never left Ireland, excepting for a visit of five or six months to England, in 1705.

But love or friendship, with its pleasures and embarrassments, were insufficient to occupy Swift's active mind and aspiring disposition. As the *élève* of Sir William Temple, he had been carefully instructed in the principles of the English constitution; as a clergyman of the church of England, he was zealous for the maintenance of her rights and her power. These were the leading principles which governed him through life; nor will it be difficult to shew, that he uniformly acted up to them, unless in addressing those who confound principle with party, and deem that consistence can only be claimed by such as, with blindfold and indiscriminating attachment, follow the banners and leaders of a particular denomination of politicians. Swift, on the contrary, as he carried into the ranks of the Whigs the opinions and scruples of a high-church clergyman, joined, in like manner, the standard of Harley with those sentiments of liberty, and that hatred of arbitrary power, which became

the Dublin Society, Hawkins Street, Dublin. It may have been addressed to Mr Ludlow, whose family seat of Ardsallagh is not far from Dunshaglin.

the pupil of Sir William Temple. Such a distinction between opinions in church and state has not frequently existed, the high-churchmen being usually Tories, and the low-church divines universally Whigs. But in Swift's mind the distinction did exist, and however it might embarrass his political conduct, nothing can be more certain than that he early drew the line, and constantly adhered to it. Even while residing with Sir William Temple, he judged the constancy of Archbishop Sancroft, who refused the oaths to William and Mary, worthy to be celebrated in an ode; while, at the same time, as far as can be safely argued from the Pindaric obscurity of the following stanzas, the poet gave his full approbation to the measure which placed those princes on the throne, so far as it was only a revolution of state:[1]

« Necessity, thou tyrant conscience of the great,
Say, why the church is still led blindfold by the state;
Why should the first be ruin'd and laid waste
To mend dilapidations in the last?
And yet the world, whose eyes are on our mighty prince,
Thinks Heaven has cancell'd all our sins,
And that his subjects share his happy influence;
Follow the model close, for so I'm sure they should,
But wicked kings draw more examples than the good.»

[1] The following severe lines on Dr Sherlock's original refusal to take the oaths, and subsequent compliance with the revolution government, have much of Swift's spirit, and occur in the collection from which so many of his unpublished poems have been retrieved:

With sentiments thus differing from the Whigs in church affairs, and in temporal mat-

From the Lanesborough Manuscript, Trinity College, Dublin, « Whimsical Medley. »

TO DR SHERLOCK, ON HIS NOT TAKING THE OATHS.

Since at the tavern I can't meet you,
With paper embassy I greet you,
T' advise you not yourself t' expose
By a refusal of the oaths;
In spite of fellowship and pupils,
To weigh your conscience out in scruples.
If, as you Queen's-men must believe,
Two nays make one affirmative;
Why, in the name of the predicaments,
And all your analytic sense,
Will you deny poor affirmations
In their turns, too, to make negations?
This postulatum any pate
Will grant, that's not prejudicate.
Nay th' argument, I can assure you,
Appears to some *a fortiori*,
Hoc dato et concesso, thus I
In Baralipton blunderbuss ye.
He who to two things takes an oath,
Is by the last absolved from both;
For each oath being an affirmation,
Both, as 'twas own'd, make a negation.
Thus scientifically you see
The more you re bound, the more you 're free.
As jugglers when they knit one more
Undo the knot they tied before.
I admire that your Smiglesian under-
Standing should make so great a blunder,
As roundly to aver *subjectio*
Wern't cousin-german to *protectio*:
Nay more, they 're relatives, unless I
Mistake Tom Hob's *secundum esse*.
I've hopes that you have slyly taken
The oaths elsewhere, to save your bacon.
So spark, by country clap half undone,
Takes coach and steals a cure at London.

ters from the Tories, Swift was now about to assume the character of a political author. The period was the year 1701, when Lords Somers, Oxford, Halifax, and Portland, were impeached by the House of Commons, on account of their share in the partition-treaty. Swift, who beheld the violence of these proceedings with real apprehension, founded his remonstrance to the public upon the experience to be derived from the history of the civil discords in Athens and Rome, where the noblest citizens, and those who had best deserved of the republic, fell successive victims to popular odium, until liberty itself, after degenerating into licence, was extinguished by tyranny. This discourse on the contests and dissensions between the nobles and commons in Athens and Rome, excited much attention. It was ascribed for some time to Lord Somers, and afterwards to Bishop Burnet, who was

In the « Anthologia Hibernica,» for December 1794, Vol. IV. Mercier, Dublin, page 457, there occurs the following

EPIGRAM ON DR SHERLOCK.

« Regibus obsequium dum binis obligat unum,
Jurat utroque unam, prodit utroque fidem
Quid mirum? Si sit semper jurare paratus;
Cum per quos jurat tres habet ille Deos.

Translated.

« The same allegiance to two kings he pays,
Swears the same faith to both, and both betrays.
No wonder, if to swear he s always free,
That has two Gods to swear by more than we.»

compelled to disown it publicly, in order to avoid the resentment of the House of Commons. Swift, who was probably in London at the time of publication, had again returned to Ireland, and, in a dispute with the Bishop of Kilmore, who twice told him he was a *young man*, when he pretended to deny that Burnet had written the pamphlet, he was induced to mortify his antagonist by owning the publication. Upon his return to England, in 1702, there no longer remained the same prudential reasons for secrecy; and Swift, without hesitation, avowed himself the author of this popular tract, and became at once intimate with Somers and Halifax, and with the Earl of Sunderland, to whom he had been formerly known.

If we can trust Swift's own averment, he made, upon this occasion, a free and candid avowal of his principles, both in church and state, declaring himself in the former to be a high-church man, and in the latter a Whig; a declaration which both Lord Halifax and Somers called to mind years afterwards,[1] at the time of Lord Godolphin's removal from office.

[1] The passage is remarkable, and deserves to be quoted at length. « It was then I began to trouble myself with the differences between the principles of Whig and Tory; having formerly employed myself in other, and I think much better, speculations. I talked often upon this subject with Lord Somers; told him,— that having been long conversant with the Greek and

Thus wore on what may be considered as the happiest term of Swift's life, which was passed in the society of Stella, and the retreat to his willows at Laracor, varied by frequent excursions to England,[1] and a ready reception into the society of the great and of the learned. It was then he formed that invaluable acquaint-

Latin authors, and therefore a lover of liberty, I found myself much inclined to be what they call a Whig in politics; and that besides, I thought it impossible, upon any other principle, to defend or submit to the Revolution; but as to religion, I confessed myself to be a high-churchman, and that I could not conceive how any one, who wore the habit of a clergyman, could be otherwise: That I had observed very well with what insolence and haughtiness some lords of the high-church party treated not only their own chaplains, but all other clergymen whatsoever, and thought this was sufficiently recompensed by their professions of zeal to the church: That I had likewise observed, how the Whig lords took a direct contrary measure, treated the persons of particular clergymen with particular courtesy, but shewed much contempt and ill-will for the order in general: That I knew it was necessary for their party, to make their bottom as wide as they could, by taking all denominations of Protestants to be members of their body: That I would not enter into the mutual reproaches made by the violent men on either side; but that the connivance or encouragement given by the Whigs to those writers of pamphlets who reflected upon the whole body of the clergy, without any exception, would unite the church to one man to oppose them, and that I doubted his lordship's friends did not consider the consequence of this.»

[1] From Swift's Journal these visits appear to have occurred at least once yearly.

ance with Addison, which party-spirit afterwards cooled, though it could not extinguish, with Steele, with Arbuthnot, and with the other wits of the age, who used to assemble at Button's coffee-house. Of the commencement of this intercourse, Sheridan has given a characteristic and whimsical account.[1] It was ce-

[1] Though the greatness of Swift's talents was known to many in private life, and his company and conversation much sought after and admired, yet was his name hitherto little known in the republic of letters. The only pieces which he had then published, were « The Battle of the Books, » and « The Contests and Dissensions in Athens and Rome, » and both without a name. Nor was he personally known to any of the wits of the age, excepting Mr Congreve, and one or two more, with whom he had contracted an acquaintance at Sir William Temple's. The knot of wits used at this time to assemble at Button's coffee-house; and I had a singular account of Swift's first appearance there from Ambrose Philips, who was one of Mr Addison's little senate. He said that they had for several successive days observed a strange clergyman come into the coffee-house, who seemed utterly unacquainted with any of those who frequented it; and whose custom it was to lay his hat down on a table, and walk backward and forward at a good pace for half an hour or an hour, without speaking to any mortal, or seeming in the least to attend to any thing that was going forward there. He then used to take up his hat, pay his money at the bar, and walk away without opening his lips. After having observed this singular behaviour for some time, they concluded him to be out of his senses; and the name that he went by among them, was that of « the mad parson. » This made them more than usually attentive to his motions; and one

mented by the appearance of that celebrated work, The Tale of a Tub, which was first published in 1704.

evening, as Mr Addison and the rest were observing him, they saw him cast his eyes several times on a gentleman in boots, who seemed to be just come out of the country, and at last advanced toward him, as intending to address him. They were all eager to hear what this dumb mad parson had to say, and immediately quitted their seats to get near him. Swift went up to the country gentleman, and in a very abrupt manner, without any previous salute, asked him, « Pray, sir, do you remember any good weather in the world?» The country gentleman, after staring a little at the singularity of his manner, and the oddity of the question, answered, « Yes, sir, I thank God, I remember a great deal of good weather in my time.»—« That is more,» said Swift, « than I can say; I never remember any weather that was not too hot, or too cold; too wet or too dry; but, however God Almighty contrives it, at the end of the year tis all very well.» Upon saying this, he took up his hat, and, without uttering a syllable more, or taking the least notice of any one, walked out of the coffee-house; leaving all those who had been spectators of this odd scene staring after him, and still more confirmed in the opinion of his being mad.—*Sheridan's Life of Swift.*

There follows another anecdote, of which I am happy to give, upon the authority of Dr Wall of Worcester, who had it from Dr Arbuthnot himself, a less coarse edition than that which is generally told. Swift was seated by the fire; there was sand on the floor of the coffee-house, and Arbuthnot, with a design to play upon this original figure, offered him a letter which he had been just addressing, saying, at the same time, « There —sand that:»—« I have got no sand,» answered Swift, « but I can help you to a little *gravel*.» This he said so

This celebrated production is founded upon a simple and obvious allegory, conducted with all the humour of Rabelais, and without his extravagance.[1] The main purpose is to trace

significantly, that Arbuthnot hastily snatched back his letter, to save it from the fate of the capital of Lilliput. Their acquaintance had not then, however, ripened into intimacy; for when Arbuthnot's name first occurs in the Journal to Stella, it is not rightly spelled, and he is mentioned as a stranger.

[1] Among the Dean's books, sold by auction, 1745, was an edition of Rabelais' works, with remarks and annotations in his own hand. This, could it be recovered, would be a work of no little interest, considering that the germ, both of the Tale and of Gulliver's Travels, may be traced in the works of the French Lucian. Swift was not, indeed, under the necessity of disguising his allegory with the buffoonery and mysticism affected by Rabelais; but the sudden and wide digressive excursions, the strain of extraordinary reading and uncouth learning which is assumed, together with the general style of the whole fable, are indisputably derived from the humorous philosopher of Chinon. A strange passage, which Quevedo has put into the mouth of a drunken bully, may, in the opinion of Mr T. Swift, have suggested the noted ridicule on transubstantiation. It occurs in the tenth chapter of the History of Paul the Sharper.

While on this subject, the Editor cannot suppress his opinion, that Swift's commentators have, in some instances, overstrained his allegory, and attempted to extort deep and recondite allusions, from passages where the meaning lay near the surface. Thus, the wars between the Eolists and the monster Moulinavent, appear to mean nothing more than that the fanatics, described under the former denomination, spent their time in combating imaginary spiritual obstacles to their salvation, as the

the gradual corruptions of the Church of Rome, and to exalt the English reformed church at the expense both of the Roman Catholic and Presbyterian establishments. It was written with a view to the interests of the high-church party, and it succeeded in rendering them the most important services; for what is so important to a party in Britain, whether in church or state, as to gain the laughers to their side. But the raillery was considered, not unreasonably, as too light for a subject of such grave importance; and it cannot be denied, that the luxuriance of Swift's wit has, in some parts of the Tale, carried him much beyond the bounds of propriety. Many of the graver clergy, even among the Tories, and particularly Dr Sharpe, the Archbishop of York, were highly scandalized at the freedom of the satire; nor is there any doubt that the offence thus occasioned, proved the real bar to Swift's attaining the highest dignities in the church. King and Wotton, in their answers to the Tale, insisted largely upon the inconsistence between the bold and even profane turn of the satire, and the clerical character of the reputed author. For similar reasons, the Tale of a Tub was hailed by the infidel philosophers on the Continent, as a work well calculated to advance the cause of scepticism; and, as such, was re-

distempered imagination of Don Quixote converted windmills into giants.

commended by Voltaire to his proselytes, because the ludicrous combinations, which are formed in the mind by the perusal, tend to lower the respect due to revelation. Swift's attachment to the real interests of religion are so well known, that he would doubtless rather have burned his manuscript, than incurred the slightest risk of injuring them. But the indirect consequences of ridicule, when applied to subjects of sacred importance, are more extensive, and more prejudicial than can be calculated by the author, who, with his eye fixed on the main purpose of his satire, is apt to overlook its more remote effects.

The Tale of a Tub had for some years attracted the notice of the public, when Dr Thomas Swift, already mentioned as Swift's relation and fellow-student at Trinity College, set up pretensions to a share in that humorous composition. These he promulgated, in what he was pleased to entitle, « A Complete Key to the Tale of a Tub,» printed in 1710, containing a flimsy explanation of the prominent points of the allegory, and averring the author to be « Thomas Swift, grandson to Sir William Davenant, and Jonathan Swift, cousin-german to Thomas Swift, both retainers to Sir William Temple.» *Our* Swift, it may be easily imagined, was not greatly pleased by an arrangement, in which his cousin is distinguished as a wit, and an author by descent, and he himself only introduced as his relative; and still less could he endure his arrogating the principal share of the composition, and the corresponding insinuation, that the work had suffered by his cousin Jonathan's inability to support the original plan. The real author, who, at the time the Key appeared, was busied in revising a new edition of the book, wrote a letter to his bookseller, Benjamin Tooke, sufficiently expressive of his feelings.[1] «I have just now your last,

[1] Dr Thomas Swift's pretensions are thus arrogantly set forth in a sort of preface to the Key, on the occasion of writing the Tale of a Tub.

« A preface of the bookseller to the reader, before the Battle of the Books, shews the cause and design of the whole work, which was performed by a couple of young clergymen in the year 1697; who, having been domestic chaplains to Sir William Temple, thought themselves obliged to take up his quarrel, in relation to the controversy then in dispute between him and Mr Wotton, concerning Ancient and Modern Learning.

«The one of them began a defence of Sir William under the title of the Tale of a Tub; wherein he intended to couch the general history of Christianity, shewing the rise of all the remarkable errors of the Roman church, in the same order they entered, and how the Reformation endeavoured to root them out again, with the different temper of Luther from Calvin, (and those more violent spirits) in the way of his reforming. His aim was to ridicule the stubborn errors of the Romish church, and the humours of the fanatic party; and to shew that their superstition has somewhat very fantastical in it, which is common to both of them, notwithstanding the abhorrence they seem to have for one another.

«The author intended to have it very regular, and

with the complete Key. I believe it so perfect a Grub-Street piece, it will be forgotten in a week. But it is strange that there can be no satisfaction against a bookseller for publishing names in so bold a manner. I wish some

withal so particular, that he thought not to pass by the rise of any one single error, or its reformation. He designed at last to shew the purity of the church in the primitive times; and consequently how weakly Mr Wotton passed his judgment, and how partially, in preferring the modern divinity before the ancient, with the confutation of whose book he intended to conclude. But when he had not yet gone half way, his companion, borrowing the manuscript to peruse, carried it with him to Ireland, and, having kept it seven years, at last published it imperfect; for indeed he was not able to carry it on after the intended method: for divinity, though it chanced to be his profession, had been the least of his study. However, he added to it the Battle of the Books, wherein he effectually pursues the main design of lashing Mr Wotton; and having added a jocose epistle dedicatory to my Lord Somers, and another to Prince Posterity, with a pleasant preface, and interlarded with four digressions:—1. Concerning critics;—2. In the modern kind;—3. In praise of digressions;—4. Concerning the use and improvement of madness (with which he was not unacquainted) in a commonwealth; concludes the book with a fragment of the first author s, being a Mechanical Account of the Operation of the Spirit, and which he intended should have come in about the middle of the Tale, as a preliminary to Jack's character.

"Having thus shewn the reasons of the little order observed in the book, and the imperfectness of the Tale, it is so submitted to the reader's censure."—*A Complete Key to the Tale of a Tub.* London, 1714, 12mo. 3d edit.

lawyer could advise you how I might have satisfaction; for at this rate there is no book, however vile, which may not be fastened on me. I cannot but think that little parson-cousin of mine is at the bottom of this; for having lent him a copy of some part of, etc. and, he shewing it, after I was gone for Ireland, and the thing abroad, he affected to talk suspiciously, as if he had some share in it. If he should happen to be in town, and you light on him, I think you ought to tell him gravely, 'That, if he be the author, he should set his name to the,' etc., and rally him a little upon it; and tell him, 'if he can explain some things, you will, if he pleases, set his name to the next edition.' I should be glad to see how far the foolish impudence of a dunce would go.»

After all, as there is seldom any falsehood without some slight tincture of sophisticated truth, it is possible that Swift, who was neither a polemical divine nor a logician, may have used his parson-cousin's accomplishments in these sciences, to save him some labour and research, and on such communication the conceited pedant may have rested his claim to a share in composing this satirical master-piece.[1]

[1] Thomas Swift was afterwards Rector of Puttenham in Surrey, and published a sermon in 1710, entitled «Noah's Dove, an Exhortation to Peace.» This sermon some knavish bookseller reprinted under the title of Dr Swift's sermon, that it might be attributed to the real

But, although Swift resented his cousin's presumption, he was himself far from openly avowing the production. From Tooke the bookseller, to whom he was transmitting the additions made in the edition 1711, it was, of course, impossible to conceal it; and Faulkner pretended, that in the latter part of Swift's life, he owned it to him also, in direct terms. But, as the Dean maintained the strictest reserve upon the subject with his intimate friends, it can scarce be supposed he should be unnecessarily communicative to a person in Faulkner's situation. The following anecdote may be depended upon. Mrs Whiteway observed the Dean, in the latter years of his life, looking over the Tale, when suddenly closing the book, he muttered, in an unconscious soliloquy, « Good God! wl at a genius I had when I wrote that book! »—an exclamation which resembles that of Marlborough, in a similar declension of faculties, when, gazing on his own portrait, he uttered the pathetic reflection, « That was once a man. » Mrs Whiteway begged the volume of the Dean, who made some excuse at the moment, but, on recurrence of her birthday, he presented her with the book, inscribed « From her affectionate cousin. » On observing

author's illustrious relative. This confusion of persons and productions gave occasion to the Earl of Oxford's raillery, who used to teaze Swift, by calling him Dr Thomas.

the inscription, she ventured to say, «I wish, sir, you had said, 'the gift of the author'» The Dean bowed, smiled good-humouredly, and answered, «No, I thank you,» in a very significant manner.[1]

Notwithstanding the silence of the real author, and the usurped title of Dr Thomas Swift, no one appears to have entertained any doubt upon the subject; and the society of the vicar of Laracor was assiduously cultivated by men of the first distinction for birth and talents. Of its effect in this respect, Swift was himself sufficiently conscious, and points it out to Stella, though with the ambiguity he generally used in writing concerning his own publications, as the source of his favourable reception with Lord Oxford's ministry. «They may talk of the *you know what*, but, Gad, if it had not been for that, I should never have been able to get the success I have had; and if that helps me to succeed, then that *same thing* will be serviceable to the church.» But long before

[1] This anecdote is given on the authority of Mr Theophilus Swift. The volume was in Mr T. Swift's possession till very lately. The Dean had corrected, with his pen, all the abbreviations and elisions which were ordinary in the beginning of the century, by replacing *it is* for *'tis, the end* for *th' end,* and the like, but without any other alterations. On the blank leaf was written, «To Mrs Martha Whiteway, a present on her birth-day, May 29, 1735, from her affectionate cousin, JONATH. SWIFT.»

high-churchmen acknowledged its merit, the author of this extraordinary performance had been caressed by those of the opposite party, with whom he coincided in temporal though not in ecclesiastical politics. These were Lord Somers, Lord Halifax, the Earl of Pembroke, and Bishop Burnet, among the statesmen; and among the learned and witty, Addison, Steele, Philips, Anthony Henley,[1] and Tickell.

Among the friendships thus acquired, the love and intimacy of Addison were particularly valued by Swift; and when they spent their hours together, they never wished for the entrance of a third person. A copy of Addison's travels, presented by him to our author, is inscribed « To Doctor Jonathan Swift, the most agreeable companion, the truest friend, and the greatest genius of his age, this book is presented by his most humble servant, the au-

The proprietor of the Grange in Hampshire, to whom Garth dedicated the Dispensary. Several of his letters occur in the early part of Swift's correspondence He was a man of great wit and humour, and was distinguished as the author of a letter to the Tatler, under the character of old Downes the prompter, in which he ridicules the administration which was just formed by the Earl of Oxford, under the allegory of a change of managers at the theatre. About this Swift and he probably differed, when Henley, whose wit sometimes bordered on profanenesss, pronounced « that Jonathan would be a beast for ever, after the order of Melchisedec. »

thor." [1] Nor was Swift backward in expressing similar sentiments towards his distinguished contemporary. He mentions him repeatedly in his correspondence, as a most excellent person, and his own most intimate friend. It is painful to reflect, that friendship between two men of such eminent talents should have been chilled by their difference in political opinions. But the placid and gentle temper of Addison appears to have avoided those extremities which took place between Swift and Steele, and thus there was an opening for the revival of their intercourse at a subsequent period, a circumstance hitherto unnoticed by Swift's biographers.

The powers which had acquired for Swift these friends and this station in society, were taxed for the support and extent of his fame. He appears to have designed, about this time, to engage in the controversy concerning the deistical opinions expressed in Dr Tindal's Rights of the Christian Church, and had collected materials for a severe and scalping answer to that once famous publication. Swift was afterwards not unwilling to have it thought that these remarks (which were never finished) were not only levelled against the opinions of infidels and latitudinarians, but involved an indirect attack upon the state Whigs, among

[1] From the obliging information of Mr Theophilus Swift.

whom these latitudinarians chiefly sheltered their heretical opinions. But he has at this period recorded himself, in the conclusion of his verses to Ardelia, as « a Whig, and one who wears a gown; » a memorable line, expressive that the principles which then ruled his mind were an attachment to the liberties of his country in state politics, and to the rights of his order in those of the church. These points, however reconcilable in themselves, were, in general estimation, usually regarded as in opposition to each other; a high-church Whig was a political character, of which all parties refused to recognize the existence. Swift saw and felt the difficulty of preserving consistency in the eyes of the public, and busied himself, according to his own account, with projects for the uniting of parties, which he perfected over night, and destroyed in the morning. One tract, however, the « Sentiments of a Church of England Man, with respect to Religion, and Government, » escaped this condemnation, and was published in 1708. It contains a statement concerning the national religious establishment, fair, temperate, and manly, unless where it may be thought too strongly to favour the penal laws against non-conformity. In civil politics, the revolution principles are strongly advocated; and the final conclusion is, that, « in order to preserve the constitution entire in church and state, whoever has a true value for both, would be sure to avoid the extremes of Whig, for the sake of the former, and the extremes of Tory, on account of the latter.» But moderation in politics, however reasonable in itself, and though recommended by the powers of Swift, has been always too cold for the temper of the English nation. All that they could or would understand from the sentiment above expressed, was, that the author was disposed to leave the political party with which he had hitherto acted, and was anticipating an apology for uniting with the Tories. And these suspicions were confirmed in the eyes of the party which entertained them, when he published, in 1708-9, the «Letter upon the Sacramental Test,» opposing, by every argument of reason and ridicule, which his prompt imagination should supply, any relaxation of this important legal disability. The author, indeed, for some time remained unknown; and Swift, in a letter to Archbishop King, even affects to complain of the misrepresentation which he himself undergoes in that celebrated tract. But the world was not long deceived. The chaplain of Lord Wharton, and others, soon discovered the real author; and to this circumstance he traces the commencement of the coolness betwixt him and his friends of the Whig party.

Memoirs relative to the change of ministry.

Meanwhile Swift displayed his zeal for the interest of the church of England, by his actions, as well as by his writings. Queen Anne, upon the motion, it is said, of Bishop Burnet, had made, in 1703-4, a grant of the first fruits and tenths,[1] to augment the maintenance of the poor clergy of England. The clergy of Ireland were naturally desirous to obtain the same boon; but hitherto their various applications had been rejected. In 1708, Swift, who had been an active member of the Irish convocation in the preceding year, was employed by Archbishop King, and the rest of the Irish prelacy, to solicit the remission of the first-fruits. He made his application to Lord Godolphin, by the encouragement of Lord Sunderland, Lord Somers, Mr Southwell, and other leading members among the ministry. But it was ineffectual. The grant of the first-fruits and tenths in England had not been attended with the expected consequences of reconciling the clergy to the ministers, by whom the favour

[1] This was a tax imposed originally upon church-livings, for maintenance of the crusade: it continued to be levied as a branch of the papal revenue, until the time of Henry VIII., when it was seized upon by that monarch, and settled by Parliament as a part of the income of the crown for ever. The tenths averaged near *l.*11,000 yearly; and the first-fruits about *l.*5,000. This fund, though so considerable, was never applied to any national purpose, but usually employed to gratify the court-favourites of the day.

was bestowed, and the lord treasurer shewed little inclination to repeat so expensive an experiment. Yet he intimated to Swift, that the grant *might* be obtained, on condition the Irish clergy were disposed to make such acknowledgments «as they ought;» or, as he reluctantly explained the phrase, better acknowledgments than had been made by the church of England. Swift's inference was, that Godolphin suspected the clergy to be *Tories* in the English sense, that is, hostile to the revolution and settlement of the crown; a prepossession which rendered his commission desperate. And though he afterwards was put into better hopes by Lord Pembroke, yet his first opinion proved just, and nothing was done in the matter till the administration of Harley. While acting as solicitor in this business, Swift appears, from his correspondence, to have resided in England from February 1707-8, until the end of April 1709.

During his residence at London, Swift was not altogether negligent of his own interest. Considering himself as useless in Ireland, « in a parish with an audience of half a score,» he was willing to have accepted the office of secretary of embassy, had Lord Berkeley gone as ambassador to Vienna. But this purpose was disappointed by Lord Berkeley's age and infirmities, which did not permit him to undertake the office. There was also a plan suggested, perhaps, by Colonel Hunter, governor of Virginia, to send out Dr Swift as bishop of that province, to exercise a sort of metropolitan authority over the colonial clergy. But neither did this appointment take place. Thus disappointed, Swift was still entitled to look for preferment, through the interest of those powerful persons who had professed themselves his friends, and who, about this time, had themselves received promotion. Lord Pembroke was named high admiral, Lord Somers president of the council, and Lord Wharton lord-lieutenant of Ireland, with whom Addison went over as secretary. Some hopes, accordingly, Swift seems to have entertained; for he takes the pains about this time to assure Archbishop King, that no preferment which he might receive from the government should lead him to flinch in his attachment to the interests of the established church. From a letter to Addison also, to be quoted in the next section, it seems that Swift expected, either the prebendary of Dr South, then supposed to be dying, for which Halifax deeply pledges his interest, or some such sinecure as the post of historiographer. But it is one thing to expect promotion on fair and honourable terms, and another to supplicate for it in a mean and abject manner. And to suppose, as has been insinuated by one writer, that Swift mendicated from Lord Somers a recommendation to Lord Wharton, to be his chaplain, and that his subsequent union with the Tories, was owing to Wharton's scornful refusal to countenance a fellow of no character,'

This strange account is given in the curious and excellent edition of the Tatler, already quoted in p. 39, and rests on the sole authority of Dr Salter of the Charter House. It is in these words: « Lord Somers recommended Swift, at his own very earnest request, to Lord Wharton, when that earl went lieutenant to Ireland, in 1708, but without success, and the answer Wharton is said to have given, was never forgotten or forgiven by Swift, but seems to have laid the foundation of that peculiar rancour, with which he always mentions Lord Wharton. I saw and read two letters of Jonathan Swift, then Prebendary of St Patrick, Dublin, to Lord Somers; the first, earnestly entreating his favour, pleading his poverty, and professing the most ardent attachment to his lordship's person, friends, and cause; the second acknowledging Lord Somers's kindness, in having recommended him, and concluding with the like professions; not more than a year before Swift deserted Lord Somers and all his friends, writing avowedly on the contrary side, and, as he boasts himself, libelling all the junto round. I saw also the very letters which Lord Somers wrote to Lord Wharton, in which Swift is very heartily and warmly recommended, and I well remember the short and very smart answer Lord Wharton is said to have given, which, as I observed, Swift never forgave or forgot. It was to this purpose, 'Oh! my lord, we must not prefer or countenance these fellows; we have not character enough ourselves.' »

Such are the words of a letter by Dr Salter, addressed to the Editor of the Gentleman's Magazine, then conducted by Mr Calder, a zealous Presbyterian, and in no degree friendly to the memory of Swift; and by whom it would require very different proof from the assertion of an individual, that he had seen letters, which in his opinion warranted the conclusion. The allegation which charges such a character with meanness and servility,

seems to have been coupled with the story of the rape at Kilroot, mentioned in the last section. A note avowed, that any explanation from a friend of Swift's would be received and inserted. A defence, founded upon the circumstances of evidence already noticed, was transmitted to the Magazine by Mr Theophilus Swift, but refused admittance, as being too long. Both stories were then inserted in the elaborate and curious edition of the Tatler, in the notes to which they may be found, vol. V. p. 145. Mr George Monck Berkeley makes the following pertinent queries on the sort of evidence here produced: « We are told, Dr Salter saw these letters. But where did he see them? In whose possession were they? How did he know they were genuine, etc.? Was he sure Lord Wharton made the reply ascribed to him? Did he see that in writing, or did he take it on report? » To these questions, which occur in the Literary Reliques, p. 41, no answer has been made, though the date of the second edition is 1792. It has, however, been pointed out to the present editor, by a person of high rank, that Dr Salter, having been college tutor to the Earl of Hardwicke, son to the chancellor, may have seen such a correspondence as he pretends to quote, among Lord Somers's papers, which came into the chancellor's hands by his marriage with a niece of Lord Somers. These papers were lent to the Honourable Philip Yorke, and destroyed by a fire at Lincoln's Inn, from which he himself narrowly escaped. But this, it is obvious, must be a matter of mere supposition, and Dr Salter's silence to Mr Monck Berkeley's challenge has still its full weight.

inconsistent with the whole tenor of his life, requires better evidence than a reference to vouchers, neither quoted nor produced; for there are few who will not rather believe the reporter to have been misguided by prejudice, or mistaken in judgment, than that Swift should, in this instance, have departed from the proud and stern tone of independence, which rejected the patronage of Temple in his youth, and vindicated in his age the liberties of Ireland.

Mr Monck Berkeley thus sums and refutes the evidence which is advanced from Swift's own correspondence, to support the legend of Dr Salter:

« Swift says, » according to the note in the Tatler, « that, at the request of Archbishop Tennison, and several Irish bishops, the chaplaincy was refused to him, and given to Dr Lambert. He says that Lord Somers wrote to Lord Wharton. He says that he expects the chaplaincy; seems displeased at the preference shown to Dr Lambert; positively denies to Archbishop King having made any application for the chaplaincy. He does the same to Dr Sterne. Lastly, he calls Lord Somers a false, deceitful rascal. »

« As I readily admit, » says Mr M. Berkeley, in reply, « the exactness of these quotations, I shall proceed to inquire what they prove. The first extract proves nothing but that Swift was persecuted by a parcel of right reverend blockheads. The second extract proves, that Lord Somers applied for the chaplaincy, but no mention is made of its having been done at the request of Swift. The third extract proves, that he expected the chaplaincy, which, after the recommendation of Lord Somers, he might very reasonably do The fourth extract proves, that to Swift, as to the rest of the world, a disappoint-

Swift himself, indeed, informs us, that Lord Somers pressed upon him a letter to be carried by him to the Earl of Wharton, which he long declined to receive, and for some time delayed to deliver, and that, when he did deliver it, no consequence followed in his favour. Thus far, therefore, parties are at one; and it only remains to inquire, whether the favour of Lord Somers's intercession was asked with servility, or so granted, that, notwithstanding its proving totally ineffectual, the circumstance of its existence is sufficient to fix the brand of ingratitude upon Swift's character,

ment was unpleasant. The fifth extract proves, that he never did apply for the chaplaincy. The sixth extract also proves, that no application was made for the chaplaincy. The seventh extract proves, that he thought of Lord Somers as most people did who knew him."—*Literary Reliques, Introduction,* p. 43. With exception of the disparagement thrown on the character of Somers, which few readers will readily admit, it seems difficult to draw any other conclusion from the correspondence of Swift, than that of Mr Monck Berkeley. Certainly it is not sufficient to establish a story destructive of any individual's reputation, that the accused party has given a different relation of the transaction, altogether inconsistent with the defamatory and malignant inferences of the accuser. And since it becomes necessary to balance the reputation of the reporters of these various editions of the same story, the editor is compelled to add, upon the authority of the late excellent Dr Percy, Bishop of Dromore, that the assertion of Dr Salter, by itself, was by no means fit to support an anecdote otherwise deficient in evidence.

for the reflections he has cast upon Lord Somers in the Examiner. On the first point, the reader may look at a letter of Lord Halifax, on the subject of Swift's promotion in the church, and consider whether the individual, whose lack of preferment is stated by that nobleman to be a shame to himself and his whole party, and who is there expressly promised the survivance of Dr South's prebendary, was likely to have occasion to apply to Lord Somers in the degrading manner which Dr Salter has intimated. Whether Swift acted justly in doubting the sincerity of Lord Somers, we have no means of determining; but we know that his lordship's intercession was totally ineffectual; and that is a circumstance which seems strange, if it were indeed as earnest as Dr Salter informs us. That Swift should have expected the chaplaincy from Lord Wharton, through the mediation of Lord Somers, argues no unreasonable confidence in the friendship of that great statesman, who had sought him out and courted his company; and that, when disappointed of those hopes, he was angry both with Somers and Wharton, and considered it as owing to a juggle betwixt them, only proves that, like the rest of mankind, he was irritated by disappointment and by the neglect of those friends who could certainly have served him, had their intentions been as serious as their professions were fair.

And if mere promises, whether fulfilled or neglected, bind to gratitude those in whose favour they are made, it is a better reason for their being liberally dispensed by courtiers and statesmen, than any which has been assigned for so general a practice. Upon the whole, we do no injustice to the relaters of this tale, in refusing credence to allegations unsupported by evidence,—brought forward so many years after Swift's death,—inconsistent with the whole tenor of his life and character,[1] and depending merely upon the report of a self constituted and prejudiced reporter.

The publications of Swift, during this period, were not entirely confined to the feverish subject of politics. His Project for the Advancement of Religion, published in 1709, made a deep and powerful sensation on all who considered national prosperity as connected with national morals. It may in some respects be considered as a sequel of the humorous Argument against abolishing Christianity. Several of Swift's biographers affect to discover a political tendency in the treatise;

[1] Oldmixon's authority might indeed be quoted in support of the figment. But that willing evidence goes a little too far, since he informs us in his history, p. 426, that Jonathan Swift was actually preferred by Lord Wharton to be one of his chaplains, which he repaid by libelling his benefactor in the Examiner, under the character of Verres.

but excepting the complaint against the contempt of the clergy, which circumstances had then rendered more common from their very generally entertaining Tory principles, it is difficult to trace any opinion which could give offence, even to the spleen of faction. The main argument of taking away the wicked from before the throne, that it might be established in righteousness, is obviously more laudable than capable of application to practical use; and Swift's plan of censors or inspectors, who should annually make circuits of the kingdom, and report, upon oath, to the court or ministry, the state of public morals, would, from the natural frailty of human nature, be gradually converted into a most oppressive abuse. With better chance of practical and effectual reform, the author recommends to the court, to discourage characters of marked and notorious impiety; to revise, with more attention to moral and religious qualifications, the lists of justices of peace; to suppress the gross indecency and profaneness of the stage; and to increase the number of churches in the city of London. The last of these useful and practical hints alone was attended to; for, in the subsequent administration of Harley, fifty new churches were erected in the city of London, almost avowedly upon the suggestion of this pamphlet. The treatise was dedicated in an elegant, yet manly and independent style of eulogy, to Lady Berkeley, whose character, as we have already noticed, was justly venerated by the author. It was very favourably received by the public, and appears to have been laid before Queen Anne by the Archbishop of York, the very prelate who had denounced to her private ear the author of the Tale of a Tub, as a divine unworthy of church-preferment. The work was also commended in the Tatler, as that of a man whose virtue sits easy about him, and to whom vice is thoroughly contemptible,—who writes very much like a gentleman, and goes to heaven with a very good mien.

A lighter species of literary amusement occasionally occupied Swift's time during this part of his life, and gave exercise to his peculiar talent of humour. Astrologers, though no longer consulted by princes and nobles, as was the case but a century before, retained still a sort of empire over the minds of the middling and lower classes, whom their almanacks instructed, not only in the stated revolutions of the planetary system, but in the fit times of physic and blood-letting,—the weather to be expected in particular months,—and, though expressed with due and prophetic ambiguity, in the public events which should occur in the course of the year. Among these empirics, one John Partridge, (if that was indeed his real name,)[1] had the fortune to procure a ludicrous immortality, by attracting the satire of Swift. This fellow, who was as

[1] Little is known of Partridge's private history, except from an altercation betwixt him and one Parker, which, of course involved much personal abuse. According to his adversary, Partridge's real name was Hewson, a shoemaker by trade, (which particular at least is undoubted,) but by choice a confederate and dependant of Old Gadbury, one of the greatest knaves who followed the knavish trade of astrology. In 1679, Partridge commenced business for himself, publishing two or three nonsensical works upon his imaginary science. He also practised physic, and styled himself Physician to his Majesty. But in King James's time, his almanacks grew so smart on Popery, that England became too hot for him; and, accordingly, John Dunton found him, with other refugees, in Holland. He returned at the Revolution, and married the widow of the Duke of Monmouth's tailor, who finally deposited him in the grave, which had so long gaped for him, in the year 1715, and adorned his monument, at Mortlake in Surrey, with the following epitaph:—« *Johannes Partridge, astrologus, et medicinæ doctor, natus est apud East Sheen, in comitatu Surry*, 18 *die Januarii, anno* 1644, *et mortuus est Londini*, 24 *die Junii, anno* 1715. *Medicinam fecit duobus regibus unique Reginæ; Carolo scilicet Secundo, Willielmo Tertio, Reginæque Mariæ; Creatus Medicinæ Doctor Lugduni Batavorum.*» GRANGER, vol, IV. p. 105, Ed. 1804. Granger farther acquaints us, that, in the Miscellanea Lipsiensia, Tom. II. p. 763, the obituary for 1715 distinguishes, among other deaths, ex ordine philosophorum, « Joannes Partridge, Astronomus et Astrologus in Anglia famigeritissimus.»

ignorant and impudent as any of his canting fraternity, besides having published various astrological treatises, was the editor of an almanack, under the title of Merlinus Liberatus. Swift, in ridicule of the whole class of impostors, and of this man in particular, published his celebrated « Predictions for the year 1708, by Isaac Bickerstaff, Esq.» which, amongst other prognostications, announced[1], with the most happy assumption of the mixture of caution and precision affected by these annual soothsayers, an event of no less importance than the death of John Partridge himself, which he fixed to the 29th of March about eleven at night. The wrath of the astrologer was, of course, extreme, and in his almanack for 1709, he was at great pains to inform his loving countrymen, that Squire Bickerstaff was a sham name, assumed by a lying, impudent fellow, and that, « blessed be God, John Partridge was still living, and in health, and all were knaves who reported otherwise.» This round denial did not save him from further persecution. The Vindication of Isaac

[1] The secret of Bickerstaff's real name was probably for a time well kept, for poor Partridge, unwilling, as an astrologer, to appear ignorant of any thing, thus opens manfully on a false scent, in a letter, dated London, 2d April, 1708, addressed to Isaac Manley, post-master of Ireland, who, to add to the jest, was a particular friend of Swift, his real tormentor. The letter is preserved in the valuable edition of the Tatler, 1786, vol. V. where

Bickerstaff appeared, with several other treatises upon a subject which seems greatly to have amused the public. At length poor Partridge, despairing, by mere dint of his own assertions, to maintain the fact of his life and identity, had recourse, in an evil hour, to his neighbour, Dr Yalden, who stated his grievances to the public in a pamphlet, called « Bickerstaff Detected, or the Astrological Impostor convicted, » in which, under Partridge's name, he gave such a burlesque account of

the appendix contains a very full account of the unlucky astrologer.

« Old Frirnd,

« I dont doubt but you are imposed upon in Ireland also, by a pack of rogues, about my being dead; the principal author of it is one in Newgate, lately in the pillory for a libel against the state. There is no such man as Bickerstaff; it is a sham name, but his true name is Pettie; he is always in a garret, a cellar, or a jail; and therefore you may by that judge what kind of reputation this fellow hath to be credited in the world. In a word, he is a poor, scandalous, necessitous creature, and would do as much by his own father, if living, to get a crown; but enough of such a rascal. I thank God I am very well in health; and at the time he had doomed me to death I was not in the least out of order. The truth is, it was a high flight at a venture, hit or miss. He knows nothing of astrology, but hath a good stock of impudence and lying. Pray, sir, excuse this trouble, for no man can better tell you I am well than myself; and this is to undeceive your credulous friends that may yet believe the death of your real humble servant,

« John Partridge. »

his sufferings, through the prediction of Bickerstaff, as makes one of the most humorous tracts in this memorable controversy. In 1710, Swift published a famous prediction of Merlin, the British wizard, giving, in a happy imitation of the style of Lily, a commentary on some black-letter verses, most ingeniously composed in enigmatical reference to the occurrences of the time. There were two incidental circumstances worthy of notice in this ludicrous debate: *1st*, The Inquisition of the kingdom of Portugal took the matter as seriously as John Partridge, and gravely condemned to the flames the predictions of the imaginary Isaac Bickerstaff. *2dly*, By an odd coincidence, the company of stationers obtained, in 1709, an injunction against any almanack published under the name of John Partridge, as if the poor man had been dead in sad earnest. Swift appears to have been the inventor of the jest, and the soul of the confederacy under whose attacks Partridge suffered for about two years; but Prior, Rowe, Steele, Yalden, and other wits of the time, were concerned in the conspiracy, which might well have overwhelmed a brighter genius than the ill-fated Philo-math.

But the most memorable consequence of the predictions of Isaac Bickerstaff,[1] was the

[1] Swift is said to have taken the name of Bickerstaff

establishment of the Tatler, the first of that long series of periodical works, which, from the days of Addison to those of Mackenzie, have enriched our literature with so many effusions of genius, humour, wit, and learning. It appears that Swift was in the secret of Steele's undertaking from the beginning, though Addison only discovered it after the publication of the sixth number. By the assumption of the name of Isaac Bickerstaff, which an inimitable spirit of wit and humour had already made so famous, the new publication gained audience with the public, and obtained under its authority, a sudden and general acceptance. Swift contributed several papers and numerous hints to carrying on the undertaking, until the demon of politics disturbed his friendship with the editor

These literary amusements, with the lines on Partridge's supposed death, the verses on Baucis and Philemon, those on Vanbrugh's house at Whitehall, with some other light pieces of occasional humour, seem chiefly to have occupied Swift's leisure about this period. Yet the controversy with Partridge, and these other levities, are better known to the general reader, than the laboured political

from a smith's sign, and added that of Isaac, as a Christian appellation of uncommon occurrence. Yet it was said a living person was actually found who owned both names.

treatises which we shall have occasion to mention in the next section.

To conclude the present chapter, it is only necessary to resume, that Dr Swift, dissatisfied with the inefficient patronage of those ministerial friends from whom he had only received compliments, promises, and personal attentions, returned to Ireland early in summer 1709, and, estranging himself from the court of the lord-lieutenant, resumed his wonted mode of life at Laracor. The corrections and additions intended for his new edition of the Tale of a Tub, probably, occupied great part of his leisure, as we find him corresponding upon that subject with Tooke, the bookseller. He seems also to have meditated the publication of a volume of miscellanies.[1] But his literary

[1] See his correspondence on this subject. On the subject of his Miscellanies, he had, so far back as 1708, made the following memorandum:—

SUBJECTS FOR A VOLUME.

Discourse on Athens and Rome.	Vanbrugh's House.
Bickerstaff's Predictions.	The Salamander.
Elegy on Partridge.	Epigram on Mrs Floyd.
Letter to Bishop of K[illala].	Meditation on a Broomstick.
Harris's Petition.	Sentiments of a Church of England Man.
Baucis and Philemon.	Part of an Answer to Tindal.
Reasons against abolishing Christianity.	History of Van's House.
Essay on Conversation.	Apollo outwitted. To Ardelia.

occupations were broken in upon by domestic affliction, for, in May 1710, he received the news of his affectionate mother's death, after long illness. « I have now,» he pathetically remarks, « lost my barrier between me and death. God grant I may live to be as well prepared for it as I confidently believe her to have been! If the way to heaven be through piety, truth, justice, and charity, she is there.»

Conjectures on the Thoughts of Posterity about me.
On the present Taste of Reading.
Apology for the Tale, etc.
Project for Reformation of Manners.
A Lady's Table-book.
Critical Essay.—N.

SECTION III.

Swift's Journey to England, in 1710—His quarrel with the Whigs, and union with Harley and the Administration—He writes the Examiner—The character of Lord Wharton—And other political tracts—Obtains the First-Fruits and Twentieth-Parts for the Irish Clergy—His correspondence with Archbishop King—His intimacy with the Ministers—The services which he renders to them—Project for improving the English Language—His protection of Literary Characters—Difficulties attending his church preferment—He is made Dean of St Patrick's—And returns to Ireland.

SWIFT had now become more than doubtful of those well grounded views of preferment, which his interest with the great Whig leaders naturally offered. He resided at Laracor during the greater part of Lord Wharton's administration; saw the lieutenant very seldom when he came to Dublin, and entered into no degree of intimacy with him or his friends, excepting only with Addison. Such is his own account of his conduct, which he prepared for publication at a time when hundreds were alive and upon the watch to confute any inaccuracy in his statement.[1] He adds, that upon an approaching change in the political administration, Lord Wharton affected of a sudden greatly to caress him, which he imputes to a wish of rendering him odious to the church party.

The fall of that ministry, which had conducted with so much glory the war upon the Continent, was caused, or at least greatly accelerated by one of those explosions of popular feeling peculiar to the English nation. Swift, with all his genius, had in vain taught the doctrine of moderation; but Sacheverell, with as little talent as principle, at once roused the whole nation, and became himself elevated into a saint and a martyr, by a single inflammatory sermon. He was carried in procession through the land,

> Per Graium populos, mediæque per Elidis urbem
> Ibat ovans——

and wherever the doctor appeared, arose a popular spirit of aversion to the Whig administration, and all who favoured the dissenters. Swift was probably no indifferent spec-

[1] Memoirs relating to the change in the Queen's ministry. There is also an appeal to Stella on this subject, in his Journal. "I am resolved, when I come, (to Ireland, namely,) to keep no other company, but M. D. You know I kept my resolution last time; and, except Mr Addison, conversed with none but you and your club of Deans and Stoytes."

tator, while the interests of the high-church party began to predominate over the power of those whose opinions in state policy had been avowedly his own. He did not, however, interfere in the controversy; and we learn from a passage in his Journal, that although he afterwards interceded for Sacheverell with Harley's administration, it was without esteem for the man, or favour to those principles of which the doctor was the champion.[1] The

[1] See an account of his solicitation in behalf of Sacheverell's brother; and the following characteristic story told by Sheridan: « Afterwards, in the year 1713, soon after the three years' silence imposed upon the doctor by the House of Lords, in consequence of his impeachment, had expired, Swift procured for him the Rectory of St Andrew's, Holborn, in the following whimsical manner:—Upon that living's becoming vacant, he applied for it in behalf of Sacheverell, to Lord Bolingbroke, who seemed not at all disposed in his favour, calling him 'a busy, meddling, factious fellow, one who had set the kingdom in a flame.' To which Swift replied, It is all true, my lord; but let me tell you a story. 'In a sea-fight, in the reign of Charles II., there was a very bloody engagement between the English and Dutch fleets; in the heat of which, a Scotch seaman was very severely bit by a louse on his neck, which he caught, and stooping down to crack it, just as he had put himself in that posture, a chain-shot came and took off the heads of several sailors that were about him; on which he had compassion on the poor louse, returned him to his place, and bid him live there at discretion; for, said he, as thou hast been the means of saving my life, it is but just I should save yours.' Lord Bolingbroke laughed

following letter,[1] which was written by Swift to Addison, upon the impending change of administration, seems to indicate that his slight expectations of promotion still rested upon the Whigs, and upon Lord Somers in particular. There is, however, to use a phrase of his own, some refinement in the epistle; for while Swift asks Addison's advice whether he should come to London, he had, in all probability, already determined on his journey, as he set out upon the first day of September following.

« Dublin, August 2, 1710.

"I looked long enough at the wind to set you safe at the other side, and then ***** our conduct, very unwilling for fear you [*about two lines are effaced*] up to a post-horse, and hazard your limbs to be made a member. I believe you had the displeasure of much ill news almost as soon as you landed. Even the moderate Tories here are in pain at these revolutions, being what will certainly affect the Duke of Marlborough, and consequently the success of the war. My lord-lieutenant asked me yesterday, when I intended for England? I said I had no business there now,

heartily, and said, 'Well then, the louse shall have the living for your story.' And accordingly he was soon after presented to it.»—*Sheridan's Life of Swift.*

[1] The original is among Mr Tickell's manuscripts. The words in Italics are filled up from conjecture.

since I supposed in a little time I should not have one friend left that had any credit; and his excellency was of my opinion.[1] I never once began your [*task*] since you [*left this*,] being perpetually prevented by all the company I kept, and especially Captain Pratt, to whom I am almost a domestic upon your account. I am convinced that, whatever Government come over, you will all find marks of kindness from any Parliament here, with respect to your employment;[2] the Tories contending with the Whigs which should speak best of you. Mr Pratt says, he has received such marks of your sincerity and friendship, as he never can forget; and, in short, if you will come over again, when you are at leisure we will raise an army and make you king of Ireland.[3] Can you think so meanly of a kingdom, as not to be pleased that every creature in it, who hath one grain of worth, has a veneration for you? I know there is nothing in this to make you add any value to yourself;

[1] Yet Swift must have then expected the commission from the bishops, which was granted a week afterwards. His answer to Lord Wharton must therefore be considered as evasive.

[2] Addison had been recently made keeper of the records in Ireland, with an augmented salary.

[3] This reminds us of an expression in the Journal to Stella. « Mr Addison's election has past easy and undisputed; and, I believe, if he had a mind to be chosen king, he would hardly be refused. »

but it ought to put you on valuing them, and to convince you that they are not an undistinguishing people. On Thursday, the Bishop of Clogher, the two Pratts, and I, are to be as happy as Ireland will now give us leave, we are to dine with Mr Paget at the Castle, and drink your health. The Bishop showed me the first volume of the small edition of the Tatler, where there is a very handsome compliment to me; but I can never pardon the printing the news of every Tatler—I think he might as well have printed the advertisements. I knew it was a bookseller's piece of craft, to increase the bulk and price of what he was sure would sell; but I utterly disapprove it. I beg you would freely tell me whether it will be of any account for me to come to England. I would not trouble you for advice, if I knew where else to ask it. We expect every day to hear of my lord-president's[1] removal; if he were to continue, I might, perhaps, hope for some of his good offices. You ordered me to give you a memorial of what I had in my thoughts. There were two things, Dr So—th's prebend[2] and sinecure,

[1] Somers.

[2] The celebrated Dr South, Prebendary of Westminster, was then very infirm, and far advanced in years. He survived, however, until 1716, and died aged 83. On the subject of Swift's expectations, see Halifax's letter.

or the place of historiographer. But if things go on in the train they are now, I shall only beg you, when there is an account to be depended on for a new government here, that you will give me early notice, to procure an addition to my fortunes. And, with saying so, I take my leave of troubling you with myself.

« I do not desire to hear from you till you are out of [*the*] hurry at Malmsbury.[1] I long till you have some good account of your Indian affairs, so as to make public business depend upon you, and not you upon that. I read your character in Mrs Manly's noble Memoirs of Europe.[2] It seems to me, as if she had about two thousand epithets and fine words packed up in a bag; and that she pulled them out by handfu s, and strewed them on her paper, where about once in five hundred times they happen to be right.

« My lord-lieutenant, I reckon, will leave us in a fortnight; I led him, by a question, to tell me he did not expect to continue in the government, nor would, when all his friends were out. Pray take some occasion to let my

[1] For which borough Addison was a candidate.

[2] « Memoirs of Europe towards the close of the eighth century, written by Eginardus, secretary and favourite of Charlemagne, and done into English by the translator of the New Atalantis.» In this scandalous lampoon, Addison is introduced under the name of Maro.

[*Lord*] Halifax know the sense I have of the favour he intended me.»

Swift's departure for England was, however, nearer than this letter announces. The hopes which were now entertained that Queen Anne would once more favour the High interest, had already extended themselves to Ireland, and it was thought by the clergy of that kingdom a propitious season for renewing their suit for remission of the first-fruits and twentieth-parts, in which they had formerly been unsuccessful. The Bishops of Ossory and Killaloe were employed to solicit a favourable answer to this supplication, and, by a letter from the prelates of Ireland, dated 31st August, 1710, Swift was united with them in commission, with a provision that, in case the bishops should leave London before bringing the business to effect, the charge of further solicitation should entirely devolve upon him.[1] On the 1st September, therefore

[1] Swift has been injuriously charged with having intruded himself into the management of this matter, less from any real concern for its success, than to serve his own interested purposes of self-aggrandizement. The leading fact, on which this accusation is founded, is, that, whereas the Bishops of Ossory and Killaloe had their expenses defrayed while engaged in this solicitation, Swift was, on the contrary, left to carry on the warfare on his own charges. And hence it is shrewdly concluded that he must have had some interested purpose of his own to serve, by undertaking an office which could be

Swift left Ireland, and on the 9th of the same month reached London, where he was at once plunged into that tide of public business, of which his Journal to Stella affords such a singular record.

This extraordinary diary is addressed ostensibly to Mrs Dingley, as well as Stella; but there is no doubt that all the unbounded confidence and tenderness which it exhibits were addressed to the latter alone. It is a wonder-

attended with no other direct reward than the pleasure of advancing his character among his brethren, and essentially serving the church establishment, of which he was a zealous member. To this argument, it seems unnecessary to reply, especially as Swift's nomination appeared natural and proper on so many accounts. His talents could not surely be doubted, nor his zeal, nor his opportunities of obtaining access to the great, nor his acquaintance with the business in which he had formerly been agent.

Indeed, the state of the affair obviously required different management, and more earnest attention than it had yet received. The grant had been first unsuccessfully solicited from Godolphin. It was then submitted to Lord Wharton, while lord-lieutenant of Ireland, in the form of an address and memorial from the Irish convocation. But Wharton, irritated at a dispute which occurred in the lower House of Convocation, in which he conceived himself to be insulted in the person of his chaplain, refused to interest himself in the petition submitted to him, and thus the matter was given up as desperate. Here, therefore, the matter rested, and it required both attention and dexterity to put it once more in motion.

ful medley, in which grave reflections and important facts are at random intermingled with trivial occurrences and the puerile jargon of the most intimate tenderness. From Stella, nothing is to be either concealed or disguised; and as the Journal is written during the hurry of every day's occurrences, it rather resembles the author's thoughts expressed aloud, as they passed through his mind, than a connected register of his opinions. What it wants, however, in system and gravity, it gains in authenticity and interest, for the readiness with which the author's pen expresses, in the « little language,» every whim which crossed his brain, vouches for his ample and unreserved confidence:—a circumstance which ought to propitiate the offended gravity of those deep critics, who deem the publication of these frolicsome expansions of the heart and spirits derogatory to the charatcer of a great and distinguished author. With gratitude, therefore, for the light afforded upon our author's habits, opinions, and actions, by a record at once so minute and so authentic, we proceed to trace, by its assistance, the principal events of his life during this its most busy period.

Swift arrived in London, already prepossessed with a strong feeling of the neglect which he had experienced from the Whig administration. His old friends, however, appeared ravished to see him ; offered apologies for the mode in which he had been treated, and caught at him as at a twig when they were drowning. The influence of Swift's talents upon the public opinion had already been manifested, and the Whigs were doubtless unwilling that their weight should be cast into the opposite scale. Godolphin alone despised to court in his fall the genius which he had neglected while possessed of power. His reception of Swift was short, dry, and morose; and he, who thought he deserved the contrary from a minister whose principles he had professed and supported, departed almost vowing revenge. With Somers also he seems at this juncture to have quarrelled. He saw him on his arrival in London, but it was for the last time. This great statesman used some efforts to convince him, that he was serious in his recommending him to Lord Wharton's favour, and had written twice to that nobleman on the subject without receiving an answer. To this Swift answered, that he never expected any thing from Lord Wharton, and that Wharton knew he understood it so. In short, he retained his opinion that he had been treated with duplicity by Lord Somers, nor does he ever appear to have retracted it. To his literary friends his arrival was as acceptable as ever. He resumed his intimacy with Addison and Steele but refused to pledge

Lord Halifax, when he proposed as a toast the Resurrection of the Whigs, unless he would add « and their Reformation.» Thus indifferent to the interests of the falling ministry, Swift was still astonished and shocked at the bold steps taken by the court, in removing so many great statesmen from employment, and promised himself to be an unconcerned spectator of the struggles which such measures were likely to occasion. But let no man promise on his own neutrality. By 1st October, he had written a lampoon on Lord Godolphin,[1] and on the 4th, he was for the first time presented to Harley; and it is remarkable, that, on the very same day, he refused an invitation from Lord Halifax, thus making his option between those distinguished statesmen.[2]

Harley had been prepared to meet Swift as

Sid Hamet's Rod; composed on occasion of Godolphin's breaking his treasurer's staff, in a manner not very respectful to the queen, his mistress.

[2] Mr Deane Swift has the following note upon Swift's connexion with Lord Halifax:—« What obligation Swift had to that lord, and his party, may be seen by his indorsement on a letter, dated Oct 6, 1709. 'I kept this letter as a true original of courtiers, and court promises.' And in the first leaf of a small printed book, entitled, 'Poésies Chrétiennes de Mons. Jolivet,' he wrote these words, 'Given me by my Lord Halifax, May 3, 1709. I begged it of him, and desired him to remember, it was the only favour I ever received from him or his party.'»—S.

one whose political tenets resembled his own (for he also had been bred up in revolution principles), but who was now a discontented person, ill used, for not being « Whig enough, » by the last administration. He was received accordingly, with all that kindness and respect which statesmen know so well how to show towards those whose attachment they deem worth securing. In the same paragraph which acquaints Stella with this first interview with the new prime minister, Swift announces that he has given his lampoon against Godolphin to the press, and already threatens « to go round with them all. » They met, therefore, with mutual views of union, Swift anxious to avenge the neglect with which he had been treated by the Whigs, and to advance the mission of which he was the solicitor, and Harley desirous of bringing to the support of the new administration an author of talents so formidable and so popular. By Harley Swift was introduced to St John (afterwards Lord Bolingbroke), and the intercourse which he enjoyed with these ministers approached to intimacy with a progress more rapid than can well be conceived in such circumstances.[1]

[1] The following passages in the Journal to Stella, with the dates, mark how rapidly Swift passed from acquaintance to intimate friendship, and a conformity of views and interests :—

But the assistance of Swift was essential to the existence of the ministry, and ample confidence was the only terms on which it could be procured. That which might be called

« Oct. 4, 1710.—Mr Harley received me with the greatest respect and kindness imaginable, and appointed me an hour, two or three days after, to open my business to him.»

« Oct. 7.—I had no sooner told him my business, but he entered into it with all kindness; asked me for my powers, and read them; and read likewise the memorial I had drawn up, and put it into his pocket to show the queen: told me the measures he would take; and, in short, said every thing I could wish. Told me he must bring Mr St John and me acquainted; and spoke so many things of personal kindness and esteem, that I am inclined to believe what some friends had told me, that he would do every thing to bring me over. He desired me to dine with him on Tuesday; and, after four hours being with him, set me down at St James's coffee-house in a hackney-coach.

« I must tell you a great piece of refinement in Harley. He charged me to come and see him often; I told him I was loth to trouble him, in so much business as he had, and desired I might have leave to come at his levee; which he immediately refused, and said, 'That was no place for friends.' »

« Oct. 10.—Harley tells me he has shewn my memorial to the queen, and seconded it very heartily; because, said he, the queen designs to signify it to the bishops of Ireland in form, and take notice that it was done upon a memorial from you; which he said he did to make it look more respectful to me. I believe never was any thing compassed so soon: and purely done by my personal credit with Mr Harley; who is so excessively obliging, that I know not what to make of it, unless to properly the Tory party, by whose influence the new ministers had obtained and now held their station, differed in many essential points of doctrine, both from Harley and St John, in so far, at least, as the principles of the latter were then understood. Both these statesmen had been members of Godolphin's administration, from which they had seceded in 1708, yet, having once belonged to it, they could not be supposed at once to rush to the opposite extremes of passive obedience and divine hereditary right. Still they were under the necessity of availing themselves of the drift of popular opinion, as a boatman benefits by the current which bears him towards his haven, managing meanwhile by sail and oar, so to moderate and controul its impulse, that it shall neither hurry him beyond the point proposed, nor dash him against the adjacent cliffs. Under such difficulties the talents of Swift, to mould and moderate the tone of public feeling, became of the last importance to the new rulers; and hence Harley laid aside his reserve, and St John his levity, to vie in courtesy towards an author, whose principles in church and state had hitherto

show the rascals of the other party that they used a man unworthily who had deserved better. He speaks all the kind things to me in the world.—Oct. 14. I stand with the new people ten times better than ever I did with the old, and forty times more caressed.»

been those of moderation, and who combined the power of expressing and supporting his sentiments in a manner at once forcible and adapted to the capacity of the public. Swift, on the other hand, beheld the triumph of the church establishment, and saw, with pleasure that the affairs of state were to be conducted, by men, whose tenets were ostensibly as favourable to liberty as his own. He saw, besides, an opportunity of reaking his vengence on those by whom he had been overlooked in the plenitude of their power; and, from the influence of those mixed motives, enlisted himself, with heart and hand, under the banners of the new ministers.

The first and most urgent point in which they required his assistance, was the conduct of the « Examiner,» a periodical paper which St John himself, Prior, Dr Freind, King, and other Tory writers, had already commenced as the organ of the new rulers. Thirteen numbers had been published, and the want of a regular and responsible editor was already visible. The thirteenth number was an avowed and violent defence of the doctrine of hereditary right, in its most absurd extent.[1] This was a subject on which they were

[1] This was No. XIII. of the original edition of the Examiners. But being omitted in the republication of that paper, the first number composed by Swift came to rank as No. XIII., which had originally been No. XIV.

willing to avoid committing themselves and caution was the more necessary, as Addison had already, in a paper called the « Whig Examiner, » assumed the task of replying to and exposing the argument of their Coryphæus. But three weeks ere Swift entered the field of controversy, it was relinquished by his illustrious contemporary.[1] The moderate and gentle disposition of Addison was ill suited for the virulence of personal debate; and if he withdrew from it when he learned that Swift was about to take the field, it is neither an imputation on his talents nor his courage that he should have avoided a contest at once doubtful, harassing, and invidious. It was the avowed purpose of this publication, « to censure the writings of others and to give all persons a re-hearing, who had suffered under any unjust sentence of the Examiner, » and, during the existence of the work, the task was accomplished with great energy and little mercy. Not only Sacheverell, but Prior and St John himself, were attacked, and severely satirized. The Whig Examiner was succeeded by the Medley, on the same side of the question,

[1] Dr Johnson overlooked this circumstance when he represented the controversy as conducted between Swift and Addison personally. The last Whig Examiner is dated 12th October, 1710, and No. XIII. of the Examiner, the first written by Swift, is dated 2d November, at the distance of about three weeks.

a periodical paper composed by Oldmixon, and revised by Mainwaring. The first number appeared 5th October, 1710, and the last, being Number XLV., is dated 6th August, 1711, during which period the authors maintained a constant warfare with the Examiners.[1] This last publication was conducted by Swift, from the 13th to the 45th and 46th Numbers, or from 10th November, 1710, to 14th June, 1711, a space of seven months, during which time, in the language of Homer, he bore the battle upon his single shield, and by the vigour of his attack, and dexterity of his defence, inspired his own party with courage, and terrified or discomfited those champions who stept from the enemy's ranks for the purpose of assailing him. Unrestrained by those considerations which probably influenced the gentler mind of Addison, he engaged in direct personal controversy, and, not satisfied with directing his artillery on the main body of the enemy, he singled out for his aim, particular and well-known individuals. Wharton, whose character laid him too open to such an attack, was the first of those victims; Sunderland, Godolphin, Cowper, Walpole, and Marlborough himself, be-

[1] Oldmixon himself states, that the Medley was proposed by Mr Mainwaring, and was written by that gentleman, Steele, Henley, Kennet, and himself, who had upon his hands the chief labour.—*History of England*, p, 456.

came the butts of his satire; but he is least justifiable where it is exerted against Lord Somers, whose services to his country, independent of ancient friendship and undeniable virtues, ought to have silenced such reproaches as had no better foundation than private scandal.[1]

It was not, however, in the Examiner alone, that Swift manifested his zeal for Harley's administration: with a readiness and versatility almost inconceivable, he assumed every shape which could give courage to his friends, and perplex or annoy their opponents. His ready talent for popular poetry was laid under liberal contribution; and Sid Hamet's Rod was succeeded by a variety of pamphlets and lampoons, composed or corrected by Swift, whose effect upon the public mind, while they had all the raciness of fresh and current personal satire, may be guessed by the amusement which they continue to afford the reader, when many innnendoes are lost, and others can only be understood through the labour of the commentator. His resentment against Lord Wharton he again indulged, in the «Short Character» of that nobleman, with some account of his government. The character was drawn in the keenest strokes of satire; and it seems only to have grieved the writer, that the facts imputed to the lord-lieutenant, being

[1] See Examiner, No. 26.

rather morally flagitious than legally criminal, afforded no grounds for the impeachment with which Wharton had been threatened by the predominant Tories. He also published «Remarks upon a Letter to the seven Lords who examined Greg,» a tract designed to vindicate Harley's character, whom the spirit of party endeavoured to implicate in a treasonable correspondence, which that person, a clerk in his office, had maintained with the public enemy.

While thus actively engaged in political controversy, Swift did not omit to solicit the cause for which he had been deputed from Ireland. The interest which he enjoyed with the new ministers, together with their wish to be considered as benefactors to the church, soon obtained for the Irish clergy the long-solicited grant of the first-fruits. But before this satisfactory result of Swift's mission was known in Ireland, the bishops (slow, it would seem, in political intelligence) had adopted an idea, that, from his former intimacy with the Whig party, he would be no agreeable intercessor with those now in power, and therefore recalled his commission, under the pretext of putting the whole affair into the hands of the Duke of Ormond. Swift was naturally offended and disgusted at being encountered with such a requital, at the very moment when he had achieved the object of his mission, and had a right to expect the thanks of the convocation.

It is the subject of a correspondence with Archbishop King, in which that prelate makes some reluctant and awkward excuses for the treatment which Swift had received from his brethren. Indeed, all the letters which pass between these distinguished men exhibit much more formality and respect, than real friendship and kindness.[1] And, finally, when Swift expected that the archbishop would propose some mode of requiting the services which the church owed him upon this occasion, he received a curious letter of advice, in which King recommends to him (needlessly, surely), first, to push his present interest with govern-

[1] There are many indications of this want of cordiality. King attacks, with great vehemence, the short character of the Earl of Wharton, which he probably suspected to be Swift's. He appears to have regarded our author's character as too volatile, nor did he (though of high-church principles) heartily approve of Harley's administration. He was accused of maliciously applying a quotation from the story of Piso, in Tacitus, to the wound which Harley received from Guiscard. And although Swift, upon that occasion, stifled the report, and vindicated the archbishop, yet it appears from his journal that he, in some degree, believed it. While Swift also was anxious to press upon King the services which Harley, at Swift's intercession, had rendered the church, in the matter of the first-fruits, the archbishop endeavours to escape from his conclusion, and to transfer great part of the merit to the Duke of Ormond. Afterwards Swift had several debates with King on the subject of his jurisdiction over the deanery of St Patrick's, and on other subjects.

ment into obtaining some preferment that might make him easy; and, secondly, after an oblique hint that his literary hours had been hitherto but idly employed, he advises his correspondent to look into Dr Wilkin's « Heads of Matters,» contained in his «.Gift of Preaching,» and thence select some serious and useful theological subject, and so to manage it as to be of use to the world. Swift considered this letter as a sort of covered insult; and replied to the first part, that though his interest was as great at court as ever belonged to one of his level, he would never solicit for himself, whatever he had done for others; to the second, that to advise him to become useful to the church, by his writings, while his own fate was totally uncertain, was to ask a man, floating at sea, what he meant to do when he came ashore. But, notwithstanding these petty feuds, the archbishop and Swift continued on terms of civility, and occasional correspondence, until the death of the prelate; and King is mentioned with high commendation in an « Essay on the use of Irish manufactures,» and other treatises of the author.

Swift was now the constant friend and associate of Harley and St John; the moderator in their disputes; the assistant of their counsels; the sharer and enlivener of their social moments,—and that upon a footing of freedom and independence usually unknown in such relations. He not only spurned at the proposal of pecuniary remuneration for his literary labours, but made the offer itself a cause of quarrel with Mr Harley.[1] He even rejected the situation of chaplain, when offered to him by the same statesman.[2] And he assumed and

[1] Feb. 6, 1710. «Mr Harley desired me to dine with him again to-day, but I refused him; for I fell out with him yesterday, and will not see him again till he makes me amends.

Feb. 7. «I was this morning early with Mr Lewis, of the secretary's office, and saw a letter Mr Harley had sent him, desiring to be reconciled; but I was deaf to all entreaties, and have desired Lewis to go to him, and let him know that I expected farther satisfaction. If we let these great ministers pretend too much, there will be no governing them. He promises to make me easy, if I would but come and see him; but I won't, and he shall do it by message, or I will cast him off. I will tell you the cause of our quarrel when I see you, and refer it to yourselves. In that he did something, which he intended for a favour, and I have taken it quite otherwise, disliking both the thing and the manner, and it has heartily vexed me; and all I have said is truth, though it looks like jest: and I absolutely refused to submit to his intended favour, and expect farther satisfaction.»

In a subsequent part of the Journal he acquaints Stella with the cause of quarrel, which was the offer of a bank note of fifty pounds.

[2] «My Lord Oxford,—— by a second hand, proposed my being his chaplain, which I, by a second hand, excused. I will be no man's chaplain alive.» And he elsewhere declares his reason for refusing was, that it did not become him to engage in a state of dependence.

Journal to Stella, April 1, 1711. «I dined with the

maintained the right of an independent friend, to take umbrage at the slightest shadow of caprice in those to whom he was so ardently attached. Indeed it was probably the exercise of this intimacy, and the display of power which it implied, which were the chief gratifications received by Swift, from the high situation which he occupied during this admi-

secretary, who seemed terribly down and melancholy; which Mr Prior and Lewis observed as well as I; perhaps something is gone wrong; perhaps there is nothing in it.»

April 3. «I called at Mr Secretary's to see what the d—— ailed him on Sunday; I made him a very proper speech, told him I observed he was much out of temper; that I did not expect he would tell me the cause, but would be glad to see he was in better; and one thing I warned him of, never to appear cold to me, for I would not be treated like a school-boy; that I had felt too much of that in my life already (meaning from Sir William Temple); that I expected every great minister who honoured me with his acquaintance, if he heard or saw any thing to my disadvantage, would let me know in plain words, and not put me in pain to guess by the change or coldness of his countenance or behaviour; for it was what I would hardly bear from a crowned head; and I thought no subject's favour was worth it; and that I designed to let my lord keeper and Mr Harley know the same thing, that they might use me accordingly. He took all right; said I had reason; vowed nothing ailed him, but sitting up whole nights at business, and one night at drinking; would have had me dine with him and Mrs Masham's brother, to make up matters; but I would not: I don't know, but I would not. But indeed I was engaged with my old friend Rollinson; you never heard of him before.

nistration; for a contempt of rank, and a marked neglect of the ceremonials it requires, were carried by him to the verge of affectation. This was doubtless an error, and one which leaves room to suspect, that the advantages which he studiously undervalued held, in truth, more than their just proportion in his estimate. The whim of publicly sending the prime-minister into the House of Commons, to call out the first secretary of state, only to let him know that he would not dine with him if he dined late; the insisting that a duke should make him the first visit, merely because he was a duke;—these, and other capricious exertions of despotic authority over the usual customs of society, are unworthy of Swift's good sense and penetration. In a free country, the barriers of etiquette between the ranks of society are but frail and low, the regular gate is open, and the tax of admittance a trifle; and he who, out of mere wantonness, overleaps the fence, may be justly supposed not to have attained a philosophical indifference to the circumstance of being born in the excluded district. The conduct of Swift, in this particular, did not escape the satirists of the opposite party,[1] who scrutinized, with a jealous

[1] Among these is the author of a rare tract, who, in the preface, thus enlarges upon Swift's habit of reversing the usual ceremonials of society, and gives, probably, no inaccurate account of his levee:—« Charging Patrick,

and unfriendly eye, both his life, habits, and manners. The most curious of these speci-

his footman, never to present any service; giving notice that all petitions be delivered to him on the knee; sitting to receive them like a triton in a scene of wreck, where, at one view, according to Patrick's fancy in disposing of them, you might have seen half shirts and shams, rowlers, decayed night-gowns, snuff swimming upon gruel, and bottles with candles stuck in them, ballads to be sung in the street, and speeches to be made from the throne; making rules of his own to distinguish his company, which shewed that he was greater than any of them himself. For, if a lord in place came to his levee, he would say, 'Preeth'y, lord, take away that damn'd chamber-pot, and sit down.' But, if it were a commoner only, or an Irish lord, he would remove the implement himself, and perhaps ask pardon for the disorder of the room, swearing that he would send Patrick to the devil, if the dog did not seem to be willing to go to him of himself.

"'Twas after the invention of this art that he had the quarrel with the ambassador about place, and that he quitted the quarrel (as one would have thought) to discourse upon the virtue of new-laid eggs.

"A new-laid egg is better for the stomach than dates, or Daffy's elixir, or saffron; tis a very fit diet to be used in drawing up a manifesto; 'tis as good as opium in causing pleasant dreams; Lord Bacon saith it nourisheth as it passes the œsophagor; and Pythagoras proposed it might be worshipped as a god. In the end, after many flights of this kind, he concluded with a bitter and hearty curse upon all the various and different species of weasels.

"About a year and a month after this, he was heard to make some self-denying promises in prayer, that, for the time to come, he would stint himself to two or three bottles in an evening; that he would keep himself clean, mens of dislike and apprehension occurs in the diary of Bishop Kennet, a zealous Whig, who, in the state and patronage assumed by Swift, as well as in his favour for the poetry of *one Mr Pope, a papist*, saw little else than the speedy introduction of Popery and the Pretender. The picture is powerfully drawn, though with a coarse and invidious pencil:— « 1713. Dr Swift came into the coffee-house, and had a bow from every body but me. When I came to the antichamber to wait before prayers, Dr Swift was the principal man of talk and business, and acted as a master of requests. He was soliciting the Earl of Arran to speak to his brother the Duke of Ormond, to get a chaplain's place established in the garrison of Hull for Mr Fiddes, a clergyman in that neighbourhood, who had lately been in jail, and published sermons to pay fees. He was promising Mr Thorold to undertake with my lord-

changing his shirt often as other good men do; that he would never play at ombre, or make songs again upon a Sunday, if his prayers were immediately granted. But, on the other hand, he threatened, that, if ever there were any delay made in it, he would never pray again as long as he lived. No! he vowed to God that he would not.

« It is not known what it was that he desired, nor can there be any conjecture made of it. But this has been taken notice of, that within some time after he left the town, and that he has not been heard of since.»

Preface to « A Treatise upon the Modes, or a Farewell to French Kicks. London, 1715.»

treasurer, that, according to his petition, he should obtain a salary of 200 *l. per annum*, as minister of the English church at Rotterdam. He stopped F. Gwynne, Esq., going in with the red bag to the Queen, and told him aloud he had something to say to him from my lord-treasurer. He talked with the son of Dr Davenant to be sent abroad, and took out his pocket-book and wrote down several things, as *memoranda*, to do for him. He turned to the fire, and took out his gold watch, and telling him the time of the day, complained it was very late. A gentleman said, he was too fast.'—'How can I help it,' says the doctor, 'if the courtiers give me a watch that won't go right?' Then he instructed a young nobleman, that the best poet in England was Mr Pope, (a papist,) who had begun a translation of Homer into English verse, for which 'he must have them all subscribe; for,' says he, 'the author *shall not* begin to print till *I have* a thousand guineas for him.' Lord-treasurer, after leaving the Queen, came through the room, beckoning Dr Swift to follow him: both went off just before prayers.»

«Nov. 3.—I see and hear a great deal to confirm a doubt, that the Pretender's interest is much at the bottom of some hearts: a whisper that Mr Nelson had a prime hand in the late book for hereditary right; and that one of them was presented to majesty itself, whom

God preserve from the effect of such principles and such intrigues!»

It has been suggested by Swift's noble biographer, that this humour of predominating over those whose rank was superior to his own, impeded his rise in the church, and even limited his intercourse with the administration of 1710 to a seeming rather than a real confidence. «His spirit,» says Lord Orrery, «for I would give it the softest name, was ever untractable. The motions of his genius were often irregular. He assumed more the air of a patron than of a friend. He affected rather to dictate than advise.» This is the language of one who felt that the adventitious distinctions of rank sunk before the genius of Swift; and who, though submitting to the degradation during the Dean's life, in order to enjoy the honour of calling himself his friend, was not unwilling, after the death of that friend, to indemnify himself for the humiliation which he had sustained in the course of their intercourse. The following passage, when it is considered, that Swift, of whom it treats, was one of the most keen and penetrating of mankind, jealous even to punctilio of frank and cordial reciprocity of confidence in the friendships which he formed with the great, appears yet more fantastical and groundless. «He was elated with the appearance of enjoying ministerial confidence. He enjoyed the shadow;

the substance was detained from him. He was employed, not trusted; and at the same time he imagined himself a subtile diver, who dexterously shot down into the profoundest regions of politics; he was suffered only to sound the shallows nearest the shore, and was scarce admitted to descend below the froth at the top. Perhaps the deeper bottoms were too muddy for his inspection.»[1] It had been kind of his lordship, in elucidation of this metaphorical tirade, to have given us some glimpse into those profound regions of state policy, which the sagacity of Swift did not enable him to fathom. Without such light we can only attach one interpretation to these expressions, namely, that the ministry of Queen Anne had determined upon the restoration of the line of Stuart, as the ultimate purpose of their government. In this supposed case, certainly Swift was not of their counsel. But if a scheme so desperate was ever meditated, it could be by St John alone, when, placing himself at the head of the violent Tory and Jacobite party, he broke off all friendship with Harley; and such a plan could only have been formed after Swift had retired to Letcombe, where there was no opportunity of intrusting it to him, if, indeed, his acquiescence could have been expected, in a project so contrary to his well-known principles. As for the other depths of

[1] Orrery's remarks on the Life of Swift, 1753. p. 30.

state policy, pure or muddy, deep or shallow, which were sounded by Queen Anne's last ministry, they are now well known to history; and a short deduction of Swift's labours, in the cause of that government, will plainly show how intimately they were then known to him.

The first and most pressing danger of the new ministers, arose from the difficulty they experienced in restraining the impetuosity of the Tory party, who had, indeed, borne them into power, but who watched, with an eye of doubt and jealousy, ministers whom their superior talents for public business, rather than ardent party zeal, had recommended to the situations they held Hence a schism arose among the majority of the House of Commons, and a numerous body of country members, under the title of the October Club, formed themselves into an association for controlling the government and hurrying matters to extremity against the obnoxious members of the opposite party. The talents of Swift were employed to appease a discontent which was hastily ripening into mutiny, and his « Advice humbly offered to the members of the October Club, » had the desired effect of softening some, and convincing others, until the whole body of malcontents was first divided and finally dissolved. The treatise is a masterpiece of Swift's political skill, judiciously palliating those ministerial errors which could not be denied, and artfully intimating those excuses, which, resting upon the disposition of Queen Anne herself, could not, in policy or decency, be openly pleaded. Such were his services during this first crisis in the new administration. But another still more perilous was rapidly approaching.

The very existence of Harley's administration rested upon the possibility of making a peace with France; and as such necessity was but too obvious to that wily nation, she seized the opportunity of endeavouring to regain by negotiation, what she had lost by the victorious arms of Marlborough. The mind of the public, therefore, was to be prepared, not for such a peace as might have justly been expected to conclude a war of distinguished success; but for such terms as France might be induced to grant from the dread of overplaying her own game, and so becoming the means of destroying the very administration on whose continuance the prospect of peace depended. For this purpose, Prior was dispatched to Paris, and Swift undertook to pave the way for peace, by representing that England was the dupe of her allies, and bore almost the whole burden of the war, of which they reaped the exclusive advantage. A light and humorous pamphlet, professing to give an account of Prior's journey, but in truth a mere fiction from beginning to end, was first published to amuse the credulous, and perhaps gradually to reconcile the public mind to the possibility of a peace with France. But the design was more gravely prosecuted in the celebrated treatise upon the «Conduct of the Allies,» and in the «Remarks upon the Barrier Treaty.» The reasoning in these pieces was most judiciously adapted to the prejudices of the English people. Neither the pride nor the good sense of the nation would have endured any arguments drawn from the uncertain fortunes of war, or from the state of the present campaign. But they listened with greedy ear to reasoning which assured them that the triumphs of English valour brought only honour to the country, while the Whig ministry at home exhausted the finances of Britain, and the Dutch and Germans abroad, by a train of gross encroachment and imposition, broke every article of the treaty, and treated England with insolence and contempt, at the very time she was gaining towns, provinces, and kingdoms for them, at the price of her own ruin, and without the slightest prospect of national interest. The treatise on the Conduct of the Allies, appeared on the 27th November, 1711, while the question of peace and war was depending before Parliament. Four editions were devoured by the public in the space of a week, and perhaps no production of the kind ever produced so strong an effect upon general opinion. It was the text-book from which the ministerial members in the House of Commons quoted their facts, and drew their arguments; while the Whigs, on the contrary, threatened to bring the author to the bar of the House of Lords, where by the junction of Lord Nottingham, that party had acquired a temporary superiority. But Swift did not upon this occasion gain the painful distinction of proscription, to which he was afterwards repeatedly subjected. While Walpole and Aislabie harangued against him, the ministers employed the pen which they had found so forcible, in drawing up the celebrated Representation of the House of Commons on the State of the Nation, and the subsequent Address of Thanks to the Queen, two state-papers of the utmost importance.

While thus extending and confirming his interest with the party which was in power, it followed, almost necessarily, that Swift became gradually estranged from those friends with whom he had formerly been familiar. The coldness which arose between him and Addison may be traced from passages in the Journal, and seems to have commenced on the part of the latter. Indeed, when politics occasion dissension between two men of generous spirit, he who is opposed to the party in power is for that single reason the most ready to take offence. Swift had used every effort consistent with the line of political conduct which he had adopted, to propitiate his friends of the Whig party. Congreve, Rowe, and Philips, experienced in their turn the benefits of his intercession, and it appears that he was really anxious to have been of service to Steele. Against this ardent and ready writer the ministers entertained a deep antipathy. He had published in his Tatler a very poignant satire against the new administration (written by Henley), in which, under the allegory of a change of management at a theatre, Harley is represented as a deep intriguer, who had worked himself into the direction of the stage, to the extirpation of the good old British actors, and the introduction of foreign pretenders. This and similar attacks upon government occasioned Steele being deprived of his office of Gazetteer. It is stated by Swift, and I have found it nowhere contradicted, that he interceded with ministers at this crisis in behalf of Steele, who, through his intercession, was permitted to retain his other post of commissioner of stamp-duties. So far, therefore, the balance of obligation was against Steele. But, as usually happens in such cases, that author's warm interference in politics drew upon him personal abuse in several papers of the Examiner, which was then the official organ of the ministerial party. These Steele seems to have imputed, in part at least, to the influence of his alienated friend; and in the Guardian, No. 53, he alludes to Swift with assumed contempt, and classes him as a reputed author of the Examiner along with Mrs Manley, of whose character, in the same sentence, he pronounces the infamy: Swift adds, that he charged him with infidelity, but the passage was afterwards softened or omitted. This was the first open blow, —a blow for which no occasion was given, unless we suppose, with the annotator on the Tatlers, that Swift, although not at that time the editor of the Examiners, either countenanced or failed to expunge those personal reflections of which Steele complained. Swift, who appears keenly to have felt the insult, wrote a letter of exculpation to Addison, in which he disclaimed all concern with the Examiner; declared himself a stranger to the author, and charged Steele with injustice and ingratitude in attacking, without any previous request of explanation, a friend, at whose entreaty and intercession he had been suffered to retain his office. This produced a petulant reply from Steele, in which he told Swift that the ministers « laughed at him, » if they made him believe they had kept Steele in his office at his intercession; that if Swift had ever spoken in his favour, he was glad he had treated him with respect, although he still believed he was an accomplice of the Examiner; and he accuses Swift of duplicity and evasion, in his mode of denying that connexion. To this Swift returned a very angry vindication, in which he alleged, that, through his interest, the lord-treasurer had appointed a meeting with Steele, without requiring him to sacrifice any friend or principle, but that Steele had broken his appointment; and he adds, that he himself had not the least hand in writing any of the Examiners; had never exchanged a syllable with the supposed author (Oldisworth) in his life, nor ever seen him above twice, and that in mixed company Under this explanation, the blame of the open breach must remain with Steele, who, excited by a groundless suspicion, attacked in public the friend who had struggled in private to protect his interests, and that without soliciting either amicable explanation or apology. Modern editors have indeed doubted, with Steele, the truth of Swift's assertions, of his being totally unconnected with the Examiner; and an attempt has been made to glean evidence to the contrary, from his Journal to Stella, in which he mentions, upon different occasions, cor-

This is confirmed by what he tells Stella, whom he was under no temptation to deceive:—« He (Oldisworth) is an ingenious fellow, but the most confounded vain coxcomb in the world, so that I dare not let him see me, nor am acquainted with him.»—This was on the 12th March, 1712-13, just before his breach with Steele.

recting the pieces of inferior agents, and conducting in secret the subordinate paper warfare which was maintained between the parties. But the admittance of such reasoning would make Swift as justly liable for the whole scurrility, without exception (and it was no small quantity), with which the Tory pamphleteers of the time bespattered the opposite party. Besides, if the Journal be taken for evidence, it will appear from that authority, that the Examiners were not under Swift's control, for he regrets not being able to soften the reflections which they cast upon Marlborough. A suspicion, therefore, of so vague a nature, furnishes no ground for disputing the solemn averment of Swift himself, who, as he lay under no obligation to Steele, was not surely under temptation to pledge himself unnecessarily to a direct and positive falsehood. That he interceded for Steele is certain; and why he should be suspected of privately injuring by libels the man whom he had endeavoured to serve, will require both proof and explanation, ere it can be recorded to the prejudice of Swift's character. It is, however, deeply to be regretted, that, in their subsequent controversy, Swift should have so totally forgotten their former friendship in their present animosity.

Meantime, if, in one instance, a friend had misconstrued his attempts to serve him, he was successful in the acquisition of others, who united with him in their sentiments on public affairs. The formation of the Society of Brothers, consisting of men of the first rank and most eminent talents among the Tories, who agreed to call themselves by the fraternal title, was accomplished under his auspices. It was by their assistance that, in the midst of political faction, and during much business, more or less dependent upon his personal labour, Swift meditated a task so gigantic as to limit and fix the English tongue by a general standard, to be ascertained by a society resembling the French Academy. The antiquities of our language had been no part of Swift's study; and he obviously shews an ignorance of the leading fact, that the present speech of England did not, properly speaking, exist as a language until about the time of Edward III., when mutual convenience had accomplished a compound betwixt the French, which was the exclusive dialect of the nobles, and the Saxon, which was spoken by the inferior orders. The golden period of our language he conceives to have been from the beginning of the reign of Elizabeth, until the breaking out of the civil war in 1642. Yet those who consider, on the one hand, the comparative poverty of the English of that period, and on the other the quaint affectations which have since become obsolete, will see no better reason for fixing upon the age of Elizabeth, than on any which has succeeded it, as the most improved period of the English tongue. The subsequent enlargement of science has rendered a proportional addition to our vocabulary altogether indispensable; and phrases at first introduced, as the language of philosophy, are aptly and properly employed in oblique and metaphorical senses, until they become a part of our ordinary speech. And this gradual progress of improvement, of enlargement at least, must continue to influence our language, until the pitch of national improvement shall be attained and passed, and until authors, as well as the public, to whom they address themselves, shall look back unanimously toward the compositions of some particular period, as what must ever be the objects of their imitation, but never of their successful rivalry. An era like this seems to have taken place, both in Spain and Italy, where the necessity of composing in the same language, and upon the same plan which was used by their ancestors, has indeed fixed the dialect, but has, at the same time, neutralized the genius of those writers by whom it is to be employed. The utility, therefore, of a society whose statutes should fix down the present generation to use the very language, which, under different circumstances, and when knowledge was less generally diffused, was used by their forefathers, may be greatly questioned. Of the practicability of the scheme, Dr Johnson has justly observed, that every man would have been willing, and many would have been proud, to disobey the decrees of the proposed academy, and that the institution being renewed by successive elections, would, in a short time, have differed from itself. There is but one mode in which the man of literature can contribute to the purity and stability of language, and in this the success of Swift himself has been at least equal to all that might have been expected from his projected institution. This can only be by such careful selection of words, and sedulous attention to style, as may attract at once the approbation of his contemporaries, and become the object of imitation to his successors. It is upon the permanent popularity of an author alone, that his influence upon the speech of succeeding ages can be founded; and when that popularity rests upon the sure basis of literary merit, his language will remain current and intelligible, not only from its own purity, but because it is used in writings with which it would be a disgrace not to be intimately acquainted.

Swift's letter to the lord-treasurer upon this subject was published in May, 1712, and the reception it met with might have convinced the author for what a refractory class of subjects he was proposing a legislation and constitution. Various answers were published to his proposal, all tending to impugn the authority of the institution, ere it was yet embodied, and several intimating, with the usual candour of disputants, that the chief purpose of the author was to create for himself an office of power and of profit;[1] for such is the alchemy of faction, whether literary or political, that it can extract scandal out of circumstances the most innocent or laudable. Meanwhile the lord-treasurer, according to his wonted custom, gave fair promises, but no-

[1] At the end of the 25th Medley, 26th May, 1712, appeared the following singular notice:—« In a few days will be published an Improvement of the Reverend Dr Jonathan Swift's late Proposal to the Most Honourable the Lord High Treasurer, for correcting, improving, and ascertaining the English tongue; wherein, beside abundance of other particulars, will be more clearly shewn, that, to erect an academy of such men, who (by being no Christians), have unhappily prevented their ecclesiastical preferment; or (by being buffoons and scandal-bearers), can never expect the employment of an envoy from those who prefer such services at home, to the doing them no service abroad; and that to give them good pensions, is the true and only method towards the end proposed, in a letter to a gentleman, who mistook the doctor's project.» And, in the succeeding Medley, was this advertisement. « Whereas, since my last, there has been published a very ingenious pamphlet, entitled, Reasons for not correcting, etc. which was advertised in my paper of Monday last, and was intended to be published the Monday following.»

thing more: and thus fell to the ground a proposal in which, as in many other cases, an inadequate remedy is proposed for an evil, which, if indeed it be a real one, is inherent in the progressive state of society. There is every reason to think that Swift was deeply interested in the success of his scheme; and it is probable that a small vocabulary, entitled, « An explanation of difficult English words, » may have been compiled by him on this occasion. The manuscript is imperfect, and of little value, unless in point of curiosity.[1]

[1] It was found among Dr Lyons' manuscripts, and is now before the editor. It seems to have occupied some time and attention, as it is alphabetically arranged, and additions occur from space to space upon the blank pages. It is, however, obvious, as in the notes upon Milton, either that the Dean had a mean opinion of those to whom the vocabulary was addressed, or else that words derived from the Latin had been in very rare use at that period. A few examples, taken at random, will make this evident.

A.

Abbreviation, a shortening.
Abbett, to stand by, to defend.
Abrogate, to disannul, make void, cancel.
Accession, a coming or arriving to.
Accumulate, to heap up, etc.

B.

Bacchanals, drunken feasts of Bacchus.
Baleful, dismal.
Ballot, the balls that votes are given by in Venice.
Battalia, order of battle, etc.

The Letter on the English Language is the only purely literary publication which Swift had leisure to produce during this bustling period; for the publication of the Miscellanies, which took place in 1711, contains nothing new. They were published for John Morphew, without Swift's name, and apparently without his knowledge, but in a respectable form, and with a preface, indicating the author, and apologizing for the liberty of giving these pieces to the world without his consent. We have seen that Swift himself designed such a publication, but he had probably given up his purpose when he found himself engaged in writing political tracts, which would arrange but indifferently with « The Contests in Athens and Rome.» He disowns Morphew's Miscellanies in his journal, yet expresses his doubts that Tooke, with whom he had corresponded on the subject of such a publication, was at the bottom of the undertaking. There may still be some room to believe, considering his habitual and myste-

C.

Cabal, a private club or company.
Cadence, the tone, or accent, or sound.
Cajole, to flatter, wheedle, etc. etc.

The vocabulary, so far as preserved, only reaches letter N, and may contain from a thousand to fifteen hundred words.

rious circumspection on these occasions, that the book was not absolutely a piracy.

We cannot account the history of the peace of Utrecht, which was undertaken by Swift about this time, a purely literary composition. The ministers, who had designed to lay the foundation of their power in that treaty, soon saw themselves assailed from the vantage-ground which it afforded to the opposition. Swift, whose popular arguments had reconciled the people to the prospect of a peace, was now required to conciliate their good opinion of its conditions. His work, afterwards enlarged into a history of the four last years of Queen Anne's reign, was accordingly commenced, and, from various passages in his journal, appears to have occupied much of his time about this period. But Oxford and Bolingbroke, who now quarrelled upon every occasion, could not agree upon the light in which particular incidents were to be represented, and the publication was postponed against the opinion of the author, who conceived it might have been of considerable service to the ministerial cause.[1]

If Swift was himself interrupted in the career of general literature, no part of his

[1] In his letter to Miss Vanhomrigh, 8th July, 1713, he says, « I verily think if the thing you know of had been published just upon the peace, the ministry might have avoided what has since happened. »

character is more admirable than his zeal in assisting and bringing forward all who seemed to cultivate its arts with success. He relieved the necessitous, he supported the dependent, and insisted that more distinguished genius should receive from his powerful friends that kindness and distinction to which it is so well entitled. Congreve, a Whig in politics, and who apprehended being deprived of his office under government, was treated by Harley, at Swift's request, with such marked regard and assurance of protection, as excited his astonishment, while it allayed his apprehensions.[1] « And thus, » says Swift, with the complacence of conscious virtue, « I have made a worthy man easy, and that's a good day's work. »[2] He obtained also for the ami-

[1] Journal to Stella, 22d June, 1711.

[2] Of this, among many others, take the following instances: Journal, Feb. 12, 1712. « I dined to-day with our society, the greatest dinner I have ever seen. It was at Jack Hill's, the Governor of Dunkirk. I gave an account of sixty guineas I had collected, and am to give them away to two authors to-morrow. And lord-treasurer has promised me one hundred pounds to reward some others. » — 13th. « I was to see a poor poet, one Mr Diaper, in a nasty garret, very sick. I gave him twenty guineas from Lord Bolingbroke, and disposed the other sixty to two other authors. »—In that of March 30th, « I was naming some time ago, to a certain person, another certain person, that was very deserving, and poor, and sickly; and the other, that first certain person, gave me one hundred pounds to give the other. The

able Parnell that prompt attention which is most flattering to the modesty of merit. At court, he contrived that the lord-treasurer should make the first advances to the man of letters, and thus, as he boasts to Stella, made the minister desire to be acquainted with Parnell, not Parnell with the minister. Pope, who was now labouring on his Homer, experienced that warm and effectual support which is acknowledged in the preface to the Iliad;[2] and the foundation was laid of the memorable friendship, which lasted until the conclusion of their lives. It was by Swift's interest that Gay was made known to Lord Bolingbroke, and obtained his patronage.

person who is to have it never saw the giver, nor expects one farthing, nor has the least knowledge or imagination of it; so I believe it will be a very agreeable surprise; for I think it a handsome present enough. I paid the 100*l.* this evening, and it was a great surprise to the receiver.»

[1] Journal to Stella, 31st January 1712-13. «I contrived it so that lord-treasurer came to me, and asked (I had Parnell by me,) whether that was Dr Parnell, and spoke to him with great kindness.» Dr Delany has given the anecdote too high a colouring, and certainly injured the grace of the compliment, by supposing that Swift made Lord Oxford, «in the height of his glory, walk with his treasurer's staff from room to room through his own levee, inquiring which was Dr Parnell.» *Observations on Orrery's Remarks*, p. 28. The attention was in the real case simple and delicate; in the other it would have been affected and ostentatious.

[2] See p. 140.

Arbuthnot, although he needed not our author's recommendation, having established himself by his prof essional merit, enjoyed in the most intimate degree the pleasure and advantage which were afforded by his society. Berkeley, afterwards the celebrated Bishop of Cloyne, owed to Swift those introductions which placed him in the way of promotion. « This, I think, » said Swift, upon that occasion, « I am bound to, in honour and conscience, to use all my little credit towards helping forward men of worth in the world. »[1] In like manner, he recommended Rowe to a post under government; and although Prior, with whom he lived in strict intimacy, had no occasion for his services during the reign in which he flourished as a political character of eminence, yet, in that which followed, he received, during his distresses, the most effectual support from Swift's experienced friendship. With such literary friends and associates, Swift might well despise the abuse of Dennis, Oldmixon, and Smedley, endure the enmity of Steele, and even the estrangement of Addison.[2] His attention was kindly and

[1] Journal, 12th April, 1713.

[2] The coldness between those great characters seems to have commenced on Steele's account. 22d October 1710, Swift expressed his wishes to Addison to mediate with the ministers in Steele's favour, but his offer was dryly received. On the 14th December, the breach seems to have grown wider, for Swift observes, « Mr Addison and I are different as black and white, and I

willingly extended, even where literary merit was less remarkable. Dr King, notwithstanding his having been Swift's personal antagonist,[1] was made Gazetteer through his influence. Diaper and others were relieved under the pressure of poverty; and Harrison was placed in a situation to have advanced his fortune, had life been spared to him. The early death of this young man, who had been recommended to Swift by Addison, was bewailed by his patron in terms which, from their plain and affecting simplicity, shew how deeply he was interested in those whom he honoured by his protection.[2]

believe our friendship will go off by this damned business of party. He cannot bear seeing me fall in so with the ministry; but I love him still as much as ever, though we seldom meet.» And again on the following day, he blames Addison as having been the means of preventing Steele's accommodation with the ministry. And shortly after the estrangement, for it cannot be termed a quarrel, reached its highest point, «I called at the coffee-house, where I had not been in a week, and talked coldly awhile with Mr Addison; all our friendship and dearness are off; we are civil acquaintance, talk words of course, of when we shall meet, and that's all. Is it not odd? but I think he has used me ill, and I have used him too well, at least, his friend Steele.» Addison and Swift, however, continued to meet occasionally, notwithstanding their difference, and a foundation was luckily left for the reconciliation which afterwards took place between them.

[1] See p. 134.

[2] «14th. I took Parnell this morning, and we walked

The benefit of Swift's protection was not limited to literary characters. All his friends, and even the friends of those friends, who had occasion for his good offices, Bernage, Beaumont, and many others, had the benefit of his intercession. He made the fortune of Barber the printer, who became afterwards lord mayor of London, and a man of great wealth. He recommended Dr Freind to be physician-general in the army in Spain. In short, he laid the basis of that list of upwards of forty persons, including many of the highest respectability, both in point of fortune and talents, whom he had a right afterwards to consider as his debtors, and, according to their conduct towards him, to distinguish into the classes of grateful, ungrateful, and dubious. In short, as he expresses it in his Journal to Stella, he found himself able to forward the interest of every one, excepting only his own.

While, indeed, Swift enjoyed so ample a power over the fortune of others, his own, to

to see poor Harrison. I had the hundred pounds in my pocket. *I told Parnell I was afraid to knock at the door; my mind misgave me.* I did knock, and his man in tears told me his master was dead an hour before. Think what grief this is to me! I could not dine with lord-treasurer, nor anywhere else, but got a bit of meat towards the evening. No loss ever grieved me so much; poor creature! Pray God Almighty bless you. Adieu. I send this away to-night, and I am sorry it must go while I am in so much grief."

the surprise of the public, and no doubt to his internal disappointment, remained entirely stationary. The ministers, who admitted him to their inmost confidence, and shared with him at once their hours of business and of relaxation, appeared to have forgotten, while disposing of numerous church preferments, that the chief pillar of their cause, so far as it depended upon influence over the public mind, was only an Irish vicar, with the aid of a very poor prebendary. Swift, who disdained to solicit the advancement which he considered as his due, seems to have imputed for a time the delay of its arrival to the habits of procrastination peculiar to Harley, and to the unwillingness of the ministry to raise him to such a dignified situation in the church, as might limit in its consequence his opportunities of affording them assistance in their politics. But when in their intimacy they called him Jonathan, and he retorted that he supposed they would leave him Jonathan as they found him, the expression indirectly implied expectation as well as reproach; nor did all the kindness and complacence of the lord-treasurer prevent Swift from expressing peevishness on the delay which occurred in making some honourable provision for his future life. But there was a lion in the path,

He expresses himself to Stella on his hopes of preferment at first with great caution. 16th January, and the ministers were deficient in the power necessary to do in Swift's favour what we must suppose they had sincerely at heart. The real obstacle was the prejudice entertained by Queen Anne against the warmest literary supporter of her administration. All princes are necessarily educated in ceremonials and formalities, and those of weaker minds seldom can stir beyond their magic circle. Queen Anne was of the latter description, and was hence led to consider a breach of decorum, or a departure from professional character and etiquette, as equivalent to a heinous offence

1710-11.—« It is the last sally I shall ever make, but hope it will turn to some account. I have done more for these, and I think they are more honest than the last: however, I will not be disappointed. I would make M. D. and me easy, and I never desired more.» 24th January.—« My new friends are very kind, and I have promises enough, but I do not count upon them.» May 23d, 1711.—« To return without some mark of distinction would look extremely little, and I would likewise gladly be somewhat richer than I am.» From a passage, July 1st, 1711, it would seem Stella had grown impatient, had expressed regret at his journey, and considered him as ill used by ministers, for he says in their vindication, « I had no offers of any living. Lord Keeper told me some months ago, he would give me one when I pleased, but I told him I would not take any from him, and the secretary told me the other day, he had refused a very good one for me; but it was in a place he did not like, and I know nothing of getting any thing here, and if they would give me leave, I would come over just now.»

against morals. Swift was now to experience the truth of Atterbury's prophecy, made while the author of the Tale of a Tub was yet unknown. « He hath reason to conceal himself because of the profane strokes in that piece, which would do his reputation and interest in the world more harm than his wit can do him good.»[1] While the author was generally accounted a Whig, Sharpe, Archbishop of York, who was in many respects Queen Anne's spiritual counsellor, conceived he was at once discharging his conscience and serving the high church party, by painting the Tale of a Tub as a ridicule upon religion in general, and the writer as little better than an infidel, who at once had disgraced his sacred order by profligate levity, and sapped the foundations of revealed religion: a scoffer, in short, and a deist, altogether undeserving of church preferment. This was a mode of reasoning, which, besides that the first part of the charge was not actually void of truth, was otherwise exactly adapted to the capacity and temper of a princess, who alleged as one reason for changing her prime minister, that he had appeared before her in a tie-wig instead of a full bottom. The prejudice which Sharpe's representation excited, appears to have been deeply imprinted upon the queen's mind from the beginning of Harley's administration. For

Letter to Bishop Trelawney.

although the lord-treasurer proposed, as a natural consequence of Swift's high favour with the ministers, that he should be presented to the queen, yet the introduction was delayed, and at length laid aside, without any reason being assigned,[1] a circumstance which plainly implied, that the queen declined so far to grace the author of the Tale of a Tub. But if the reasoning or importunity of the ministers could have overcome the scruples of the queen in this particular, Swift's imprudent zeal in their behalf had roused against him a more formidable enemy than the Archbishop of York, and passions much more irritable and vindictive than mere zeal for clerical decorum. Queen Anne, jealous of again being subjected to the domination of a single favourite, which had been so severely exercised by the Duchess of Marlborough,

The ministers expressed a resolution that Swift should preach before the queen, and Harley mentioned his intention of introducing him. But neither of these incidents took place. January 1710-11. « Mr Harley of late has said nothing of presenting me to the queen,—I was overseen when I mentioned it to you. He has such a weight of affairs on him, that he cannot mind all; but he talked of it three or four times to me, long before I dropt it to you. »

It has, however, been said, that the Dean received from the queen the beautiful seal with an Apollo and Pegasus. But this donation is extremely improbable, and the seal is mentioned in his will, as the gift of the Countess of Granville.

now divided her confidence betwixt Mrs Masham, the patroness of the Tories, and the Duchess of Somerset, who was inclined towards the opposite faction; and with the petty craft of a weak mind, amused herself by balancing the strength of the contending parties against each other, in order that both might be sensible of their dependence on her personal favour. Swift, although perfectly aware that such was the queen's line of policy, and that the rude shocks which the ministers received in the House of Lords arose entirely from the influence of the Duchess of Somerset, was rash enough to suppose that the evil could be remedied, by holding up the favourite, whose secret influence was so powerful, as an object of satirical contempt. With this view, and using the same medium of satire which had been successful in the case of the sapient Partridge, and of Merlin's prediction,[1] he wrote the « Windsor Prophecy. » In that satire the duchess is ridiculed for the redness of her hair, and upbraided as having been privy to the murder of her first husband. It may be doubted which imputation she accounted the

[1] Among the books in Swift's library, with notes in his own hand-writing, occurs a copy of Nostrodamus's true Prophecies, commented by Theoph. Garencieres, London, 1672. He probably consulted such works, to catch the mystical and emblematical style of the ancient soothsayers.

most cruel insult, especially since the first charge was undeniable, and the second only arose from the malice of the poet. The prophecy was printed and about to be published, but Mrs Masham, more alive than the ministers to the danger of offending the queen, prevented this consummation of Swift's imprudence. The impression was nevertheless brought to the club of Brothers; and as each of the sixteen members took twelve copies, it was, to use a legal phrase, so complete an utterance, as altogether to defeat the purpose of Mrs Masham's caution.[1] Having thus given

[1] Journal to Stella, 24th December, 1711.—« My prophecy is printed, and will be published after Christmas day. I like it mightily; I don't know how it will pass. I believe every body will guess it to be mine, because it is somewhat in the same manner with that of Merlin, in the Miscellanies.» 26th December.—« I called at noon at Mrs Masham's, who desired me not to let the prophecy be published, for fear of angering the queen about the Duchess of Somerset; so I wrote to the printer to stop them. They have been printed, and given about, but not sold.» And a little lower, he says, « I entertained our society at the Thatched House tavern to-day at dinner; but brother Bathurst sent for wine, the house affording none. The printer had not received my letter, and so he brought us a dozen a-piece of the prophecy; but I ordered him to part with no more. It is an admirable good one, and people are mad for it.» From a letter to Mr Tickell, written several years afterwards, Swift appears to have been fully aware of his imprudence, in suffering this piece to get abroad, and mentions it as a « thing which no friend would publish.»

mortal offence to a favourite, of whom he has himself recorded, that she had more personal credit than all the queen's servants put together, Swift was not long of feeling the effects of her resentment. He remained stationary, like a champion in a tale of knight-errantry, when, having surmounted all apparent difficulties, an invisible but irresistible force prevents him from the full accomplishment of the adventure. The promises of the ministers were in the mean while reiterated, and doubtless with the sincere purpose of their fulfilment. An opportunity occurred of making them good, by appointing Swift to the see of Hereford, which became vacant by the death of Dr Humphry Humphreys, on the 20th November, 1712. There seems little doubt that the lord-treasurer recommended his friend to the vacant mitre; and a letter from Lord Bolingbroke, dated during the vacancy of the bishopric, certainly relates to the same proposal. It is warm, cordial, and friendly in the highest degree.[1] But the prejudice excited by

[1] Thursday morning, two o'clock, January 5, 1712-13. « Though I have not seen, yet I did not fail to write to lord-treasurer. Non tua res agitur, dear Jonathan; it is the treasurer's cause; it is my cause; it is every man's cause who is embarked on our bottom. Depend upon it, that I never will neglect any opportunity of shewing that true esteem, that sincere affection, and honest friendship for you, which fill the heart of your faithful friend, BOLINGBROKE. »

the representations of the Archbishop of York, powerfully supported by the entreaties and

I conveive Hereford to have been the object in view for Swift, at this period, because the vacancy corresponds with the date of the above letter, and because it is twice mentioned by Swift, in his Journal, about the same period, 7th January, 1712-13. « The Bishop of Ossory will not be Bishop of Hereford, to the great grief of himself and wife. » 20th January. « Our English bishopric is not yet disposed of. » Upon the whole, I have no doubt that at this time occurred the incidents mentioned by Mr Sheridan.—« The ministers, he states, had recommended Swift to the queen, to fill a vacant bishopric. But the Duchess of Somerset, who entertained an implacable hatred against him, determined to move heaven and earth to prevent his promotion taking place. She first prevailed on the Archbishop of York to oppose it, whose remarkable expression to the queen was, « That her majesty should be sure that the man whom she was going to make a bishop was a Christian. » But as he could give no better colour for this surmise, than that Swift was supposed to be the author of the « Tale of a Tub, » the bishop was considered as acting officiously, out of too indiscreet a zeal, and his interposition was of no avail. The duchess then went in person to the queen, and, throwing herself on her knees, entreated, with tears in her eyes, that she would not give the bishopric to Swift: at the same time presenting to her that excessively bitter copy of verses, which Swift had written against her, called, « The Windsor Prophecy. » The queen, upon reading them, was stung with resentment at the very severe treatment which he had given to a lady, who was known to stand highly in her favour, and as a mark of her displeasure, passed Swift by, and bestowed the bishopric on another. » The See of Hereford was given to Philip Bisse, translated from that of St David's.

tears of the Duchess of Somerset, prevailed against the united influence of ministers, who seldom united in any thing, and the name of Swift was added to the list of clergymen recommended to Queen Anne for promotion in the church, against whom she stated her objection, that they were too violent in party.

At length he began to feel that his situation was awkward, and became desirous either of receiving some preferment suited to the figure which he had made in public life, or of taking permission to retire to Ireland, at the risk of sacrificing all future hope of preferment, and encountering what he equally dreaded, the condolence of those who might affect to pity him.[1] After sundry insinuations that the lord-treasurer shewed more personal kindness than attention to his interest, he at length expressed himself positively determined to relinquish labouring in the service of the ministers. « I will contract,» he says, « no more enemies, at least I will not embitter worse than I have already, till I have got under shelter, and the ministers know my resolution.»[2] At this time

[1] 4th March, 1712-13.—« Tisdal's a pretty fellow, as you say; and when I come back to Ireland he will condole with me with abundance of secret pleasure. I believe I told you what he wrote to me, that 'I have saved England, and he Ireland.' But I can bear that.»

[2] 26th Dec. 1712.—« I dined with lord-treasurer, who chid me for being absent three days. Mighty kind with a p—; less of civility, and more of interest.» 25th

three Irish deaneries, a canonry of Windsor and other church-livings in England, chanced to be vacant. On being informed that the warrant for the deaneries was filled up without mention of his name, Swift immediately announced his positive purpose of retiring, desiring Mr Lewis to inform the lord-treasurer that he took nothing ill of him, but his failure to inform him, as he had promised to do, if he found the queen would do nothing for him; a remarkable passage, which shews that Swift was now fully sensible of the fatal influence which obscured his prospects of promotion. Thus pressed, Oxford, with the concurrence of the Duke of Ormond, then lord-lieutenant, proposed that Dr Sterne should be removed to the Bishopric of Dromore, in order to vacate for Swift that Deanery of St Patrick's, the name of which has since become a classical sound, because connected with his memory. Sterne had no apparent interest of his own, and was rather obnoxious to the Duke of Ormond. The circumstance, therefore, of his being promoted to the higher dignity, while Swift, with all his influence, only gained that from which Sterne was re-

Feb. 1712-13.—« He chides me if I stay away but two days together. What will this come to? Nothing. My grandmother used to say,

> More of your lining,
> And less of your dining. »

moved, indicates a capitulation between the queen and her ministers, in which the latter, finding their influence too low to obtain a mitre for their candidate, were contented to compound by procuring his appointment to a wealthy deanery. A last effort was made by the joint interest of Oxford and Lady Masham, to exchange St Patrick's for a prebendary of Windsor. But the remonstrances of the prime minister, and the entreaties, even the tears of the favourite, were unavailing; and Swift, galled by the difficulty which attended his promotion, could only console his pride by the consideration, that a bishop had been created against great opposition, and without any interest of his own, in order to make way for his gaining the best deanery in Ireland. It is remarkable, that, neither during the agitating period when this business was in dependence, nor at any other time, did Swift suffer himself to glance a sarcasm at Queen Anne, or at her memory.[1] And this is the

[1] The following line can hardly be considered as an exception:

——— By an old [murderess?] pursued,
A crazy prelate, and a *royal prude*.

In the same piece he mentions in very different terms, the intrigues of Archbishop Sharpe and the Duchess of Somerset:—

York is from Lambeth sent to tell the queen,
A dangerous treatise writ against the spleen;

more striking, as he seems to have lost patience with his friend Oxford, even while he was sensible he laboured all he could to overcome the prejudices against his character in the royal breast. This respectful moderation is a strong contrast to the offence which he afterwards expressed against Queen Caroline for much slighter neglect. But in the former case, Queen Anne's favour for the church, and for the ministers with whom Swift lived in such intimacy, seems to have subdued his resentment for her personal dislike.[1]

Which by the style, the matter, and the drift,
'Tis thought could be the work of none but Swift.
Poor York! the harmless tool of others' hate;
He sues for pardon, and repents too late.
Now angry Somerset her vengeance vows
On Swift's reproaches for her murder'd spouse;
From her red locks her mouth with venom fills,
And thence into the royal ear distils.

It is remarkable, that in two passages of his Journal to Stella, Swift intimates that the Archbishop of York had expressed a strong wish to be reconciled to him; but it does not appear that they ever met. Delany, after expressing his surprise that Swift should ever have been represented as an infidel, mentions, as if it consisted with his own knowledge, « It will be some satisfaction to the reader, as I doubt not it was to Swift (though no reparation of the injury), to know that the archbishop lived to repent of this injury done to Swift, expressed great sorrow for it, and desired his forgiveness.»—*Observations upon Lord Orrery's Remarks, etc.* p. 271.

[1] Bolingbroke always affirmed, that the queen had no unfavourable impression of Swift, and that he had been

The warrant for the Deanery of St Patrick's was signed 23d February, and Swift set out for Ireland early in June, 1713, to take possession of a preferment, which he always professed to consider as at best an honourable exile. It must have been indeed unexpected, that his unexampled court favour should all terminate in his obtaining a deanery in a kingdom remote from those statesmen who equally needed his assistance, and delighted in his society. Nor can we doubt that he was disappointed, as well as surprised, since at one time he held his services too essential to the administration, to allow them even to create him a bishop in Ireland.[1]

assured by herself, that neither the Archbishop of York, nor any one else, had prejudiced her against him. He represented the whole as an invention of Lord Oxford, to keep Swift to his deanery in Ireland. Dr King shrewdly observes, « If Lord Bolingbroke had hated the Earl of Oxford less, I should have been readily inclined to believe him.»—*King's Anecdotes*, p. 61. Indeed no adequate reason can be assigned, why Oxford should have impeded the promotion of his most zealous friend and active partizan. Bolingbroke meant it to be inferred, perhaps, that Swift was likely to take his side and desert Oxford, when they came to an open rupture. But Swift's subsequent behaviour affords no room for such a belief.

[1] Journal, May 29, 1611. — « We hear your Bishop Hickman is dead; but nobody here will do any thing for me in Ireland, so they may die as fast or slow as they please.» Hickman, Bishop of Derry, was succeeded by Dr Hartstonge, translated from the see of Ossory.

To the very last, he confesses he thought the ministry would not have parted with him, and could only conclude, that they had not the option of making a suitable provision for him in England.[1]

[1] Journal, 18th April, 1713.—« Neither can I feel joy at passing my days in Ireland; and I confess I thought the ministry would not let me go; *but perhaps they cannot help it.*»

SECTION IV.

Swift takes possession of his Deanery—Is recalled to England to reconcile Harley and St John—Increases in favour with Oxford—Engages again in political controversy—Writes the Public Spirit of the Whigs—A reward offered for discovery of the Author—The dissensions of the ministers increase—Swift retires to the country—Writes Thoughts on the Present State of Affairs—Writes to Lord Oxford on his being displaced—And retires to Ireland on the Queen's Death—His reception—His Society—The interest he displayed in the misfortunes of his Friends.

THE biographers of Swift have differed in their account of Swift's reception as Dean of St Patrick's. According to Lord Orrery, it was unfavourable in the extreme. He was shunned by the better class, hissed, hooted, and even pelted by the rabble. This is contradicted by Delany and Sheridan, who argue on the improbability of his experiencing such affronts, when the high-church interest, which he had so ardently served, was still in its zenith. Indeed, there is no doubt, that Lord Orrery's account is greatly exaggerated, or rather that his lordship has confounded the circumstances which attended Swift's first reception with those of his final retirement to his deanery after the death of the queen. Yet, even on his first arrival, his reception was far from cordial. Many, even among his own order, beheld with envy the Vicar of Laracor elevated by mere force of talents to a degree of power and consequence seldom attained by the highest dignitaries of the church; and they scarce forgave him for his success, even in the very negotiation of which they reaped the benefit. « I remit them, » says Swift, with indignant contempt, « their first fruits of ingratitude, as freely as I got the others remitted to them. » He had also more legitimate enemies. The violent Whigs detested him as an apostate from their party; the dissenters regarded his high-church principles with dread and aversion; and both had at that time considerable influence in the city of Dublin.

The following copy of verses occurs in the works of Jonathan Smedley, and are said to have been fixed on the door of St Patrick's Cathedral on the day of Swift's instalment:

To-day this temple gets a Dean,
Of parts and fame uncommon;
Used both to pray, and to profane,
To serve both God and Mammon.

When Wharton reign'd, a Whig he was;
When Pembroke, that 's dispute, sir;
In Oxford's time, what Oxford pleased
Non-Con, or Jack, or Neuter.

The temper and manners of Swift were ill qualified to allay these prejudices, In assuming his new offices, with perhaps too much an air of authority, he soon provoked opposition from the Archbishop of Dublin, and from his own chapter; and he was thwarted and disappointed both in his arrangements with his predecessor, and in the personal promotions which he wished to carry through for his friends. Besides, he had returned to Ireland

This place he got by wit and rhyme,
   And many ways most odd;
And might a bishop be in time,
   Did he believe in God.

For High Church men and policy
   He swears he prays most hearty;
But would pray back again to be
   A Dean of any party.

Four lessons, Dean, all in one day!
   Faith! it is hard, that 's certain:
'T were better hear thy own Peter say,
   G—d d—n thee Jack and Martin.

Hard! to be plagued with bible, still,
   And prayer-book before thee;
Hadst thou not wit to think, at will,
   On some diverting story?

Look down, St Patrick, look, we pray,
   On thine own church and steeple;
Convert thy Dean on this great day,
   Or else, God help the people!

And now whene'er his Deanship dies,
   Upon his tomb be graven;
A man of God here buried lies,
   Who never thought of heaven.

a dissatisfied, if not a disappointed man, neither hoping to give nor receive pleasure, and such unhappy expectations are usually the means of realizing themselves. His intimate friendship with Vanessa already embittered the pleasure of rejoining Stella; and it was therefore no wonder, that, after hurrying from Dublin to his retirement at Laracor, he should write to the former in the following strain of despondency.

« I staid but a fortnight in Dublin, very sick, and returned not one visit of a hundred that were made me; but all to the Dean, and none to the Doctor. I am riding here for life; and I think I am something better. I hate the thoughts of Dublin, and prefer a field-bed, and an earthen-floor, before the great house there, which they say is mine.» — « At my first coming, I thought I should have died with discontent, and was horribly melancholy while they were installing me, but it begins to wear of, and change to dulness.»[1] He writes Archbishop King in the same strain of discontented melancholy,[2] and it is still more strongly expressed in his verses.

While Swift was in a state of seclusion, so different from the bustling scene in which he

[1] The letter is dated Laracor, 8th July, 1713.

[2] « I can tell your grace nothing from Dublin. I was there between business and physic, and paid no visits, nor received any, but one day.» Letter, 16th July, 1713.

had been for three years engaged, he received from the Tory administration the most anxious summons, pressing his instant return to England. Swift had early observed to Harley and St John, that the success and stability of their government depended upon their mutual confidence and regard for each other. But this was soon endangered by a variety of minute grounds of mistrust, as well as by the differing genius of these two statesmen. Oxford was slow, mysterious, and irresolute; St John vehement, active, and irregularly ambitious. The former was desirous of engrossing from his colleague, not only the essentials of ministerial power, but all its outward show and credit; the latter was ambitious of sharing the honours, as well as the fatigues, of public employment. These dissensions sometimes smouldered in secret, sometimes burst out into open flame; were frequently suppressed, but never extinguished. The disunion became visible to Swift, so early as within the first six months of their administration,[1] and in about four months after it, it was apparent both to friends and

[1] Journal, 27th April, 1711.—«I am heartily sorry to find my friend the secretary stand a little ticklish with the rest of the ministry; there have been one or two disobliging things that have happened. I will, if I meet Mr St. John alone on Sunday, tell him my opinion, and beg him to set himself right, else the consequences may be very bad, for I see not how they can well want him neither, and he would make a troublesome enemy.»

enemies.[1] While the increase of this unkindness became more and more apparent, Swift, at the risk of compromising his own influence with both, though his fortune appeared dependent on its subsistence, hesitated not to undertake the precarious and thankless office of mediating between them. In verse and in prose, by conversation and writing, by serious advice and jocular remonstrance, he endeavoured to alarm his powerful friends upon the hazards into which they were hurried by their dissensions. He reminded the minister, in the verses entitled «Atlas,» of the danger of attempting to conduct the whole government, without the confidential assistance of his colleagues; with St John he frankly expostulated upon the absolute necessity of his acting cordially with the lord-treasurer; and he was so far successful, upon more than one occasion, as to bring about a seeming and temporary reconciliation. But, ere he left England, the evil which he had twice patched up, as he expresses himself, with the hazard of all his credit, became more evident than ever; and

[1] «The Whigs whisper, that our new ministry differ among themselves, and they begin to talk out Mr Secretary; they have some reasons for their whispers, although I thought it was a greater secret. I do not much like the posture of things; I always apprehended, that any falling out would ruin them, and so I have told them several times.»

he was scarce settled in Ireland, before an hundred letters from different quarters recalled him to resume the hopeless task of ineffectual mediation. He obeyed the call so hastily, that he did not even take leave of the Archbishop of Dublin, at which that prelate was so much offended, that he threatened to take measures for obliging Swift to reside at his deanery; and it was probably his influence, aided by the envy of the inferior clergy, that prevented Swift from being in his absence chosen prolocutor of the House of Convocation; an honour with which he would obviously have been much pleased, though he declined to solicit it.

Upon Swift's arrival at London, he found that the disagreement between the ministers approached near to an explosion, and that he himself was the only mutual friend who would venture to mediate between them. There is reason to think his remonstranees produced some temporary effect. Meanwhile, he was once more engaged in the general contest of politics, and was not long without experiencing some of the perils of that envenomed warfare.

Swift's principal antagonists, on this occasion, had both been old friends. The first was Burnet, whom, in an ironical preface to the Bishop of Sarum's introduction to the third volume of the History of the Reformation, he treats as one whom he delighted to insult; upbraiding the venerable champion, who had produced a pamphlet as a precursor of his folio, with his mighty haste to take the field as a skirmisher, «armed only with a pocket pistol, before his great blunderbuss could be got ready, his old rusty breast-plate scoured, and his cracked head-piece mended.» It does not appear that Burnet ever noticed this harsh and disrespectful treatment, nor does Swift's name occur in that history of his own times, where he commemorates so many individuals of inferior note; and the Dean finally recorded the bishop's character as that of a man of generosity and good-nature, but who at last became party-mad, and saw popery under every bush.

Swift's controversy with Steele was longer, fiercer, and attended by more serious consequences for both parties. We gave an account of their rupture, p. 147; and it now was increased to a public controversy. In the Guardian, No. 128, Steele had attacked the ministers for negligence in enforcing that stipulation of the treaty of Utrecht, which respected the demolition of Dunkirk, and being then about to be elected Member of Parliament for Stockbridge, he pursued the subject in a pamphlet, entitled, «The Importance of Dunkirk Considered,» in a letter to the bailiff of that borough. Swift, with less feeling of their ancient intimacy than of their recent quarrel, appears readily and eagerly to have taken up the gauntlet. His first insulting and vindictive answer is entitled, «The Importance of the Guardian Considered,» in which the person, talents, history, and morals of his early friend, are the subject of the most acrimonious raillery; and where he attempts to expose the presumption of Steele's pretensions to interfere in the councils of princes, whether as a publisher of Tatlers and Spectators, and the occasional author of a Guardian; or from his being a soldier, alchemist, gazetteer, commissioner of stamped papers, or gentleman-usher. Besides this diatribe, there appeared two others, in which Swift seems to have had some concern;[1] and

[1] The «Character of Richard Steele, Esquire, with some remarks by Toby, Abel's Kinsman, 1713». Swift was the supposed author of this piece, which is, however, with more probability, ascribed to Dr Wagstaffe, under his directions. It is certain that Steele bestowed more attention upon it than on most of the satirical shafts by which he was assailed; and, from a particular expression, I conceive that he ascribed it, at least in a considerable degree, to Swift. «I think I know the author of this, and, to shew him I know no revenge, but in the method of heaping coals on his head by benefits, I forbear giving him what he deserves, for no other reason, but that I know his sensibility of reproach is such, as that he would be unable to bear life itself, under half the ill language he has given me.» *The Englishman, No. 57, being the close of the paper so called.* Swift himself alludes to the sensitiveness of disposition, here imputed to him, as having been an attribute of his earlier cha-

a ludicrous paraphrase on the first ode of the second book of Horace, in ridicule of Steele, which is entirely his composition. It is to Steele's honour, that although he appears to have rushed hastily, and without due provocation, into the quarrel with Swift, he did not condescend to retort these personalities. He was then engaged, with the assistance of Addison, Hoadley, Lechmere, and Marshall, in the composition of a pamphlet called the Crisis, intended to alarm the public upon the danger of the Protestant succession, and the predominating power of France. This treatise was brought forward with a degree of pomp and parade, which its contents hardly warrant, being chiefly a digest of the acts of parliament respecting the succession, mixed with a few comments, of which the diction is neither forcible, elegant, nor precise; while, by the extraordinary exertions made to obtain subscriptions, it was plain that the relief of the author's necessities was the principal object of the publication. The opportunity did not escape Swift,

racter. « I was originally as unwilling to be libelled as the nicest man can be, but, having been used to such treatment ever since I unhappily began to be known, I am now grown hardened.» See his letter to Dr Jinny, 8th June, 1732.

The other satire against Steele is « A Letter from the facetious Dr Andrew Tripe at Bath, to the venerable Nestor Ironside, 1714.» See this tract, in which Arbuthnot probably had some share.

who published his celebrated comment under the title of «The public spirit of the Whigs, set forth in their generous encouragement of the author of the Crisis; with some observations on the seasonableness, candour, erudition, and style of that treatise.» In this pamphlet, Steele was assailed by satire as personal and as violent as in the former. Still, however, he remained unmoved, and his only reply was moderate and dignified. In defence of himself and his writings, before the House of Commons, among several passages in former publications, from which he claimed the honours due to a friend of virtue, he quoted the favourable character given in the Tatler of the Project for the Advancement of Religion, and of its author, with the following simple and manly comment: «The gentleman I here intended was Dr Swift. This kind of man I thought him at that time: we have not met of late, but I hope he deserves this character still.» As it seldom happens that two intimate friends can descend to personal altercation without possessing means of mutual reproach, most readers will be of opinion, that Steele's forbearance, under gross provocation, deserved a better requital than the severe verses, entitled, «John Dennis the Sheltering Poet's invitation to Richard Steele, the secluded party-writer and member, to come and live with him in the Mint.» Dennis's share of the satire was undoubtedly and amply deserved, by his own scurrilities against Swift;[1] though the wit of the piece, as directed against Steele, is no apology for its cruelty. But, in political hostility, Swift had the attributes of Homer's champion,

> Impiger, iracundus, inexorabilis, acer,
> Jura negat sibi nata, nihil non arrogat armis.

Meanwhile, ere the controversy had ceased between those two eminent literary characters, the strong talons of power had well nigh

[1] Of which the following is perhaps too ample a specimen: « By thy wonderful charity, thou canst be nothing but a scandalous priest, hateful to God, and detestable to man, and agreeable to none but devils; who makest it thy business to foment divisions between communities and private persons, in spite of that charity, which is the fundamental doctrine of that religion which thou pretendest to teach. How amazing a reflection is it, that in spite of that divine doctrine, the Christian world should be the only part of the globe embroiled in endless divisions! From whence can this proceed, but from priests like thee, who are the pest of society and the bane of religion! But it is not enough to say thou art a priest; it is time to point out what priest thou art: thou art a priest who madest thy first appearance in the world like a dry joker in controversy, a spiritual buffoon, an ecclesiastical jack-pudding, by publishing a piece of waggish divinity, which was writ with a design to banter all Christianity.» What follows is too shocking for transcription, and only proves that all the mighty mad raved in the person of John Dennis. The whole piece, which is entitled a Letter to the Examiner, may be found in Dennis's Letters, 2 vols. 1721.

pounced upon both, like the kite upon the puny duellists in the old fable.

Of Steele it is only necessary to say, that, by the violence of a predominating majority, it was resolved that the papers called the Sequel of the Englishman and the Crisis were scandalous and seditious libels, and that Richard Steele, Esq for his offence in writing them, be expelled the House of Commons. By a singular coincidence, his antagonist, Swift, experienced the frown of authority at the same juncture. About this time the Scottish peers were greatly displeased with the court, and their discontent was fomented by the celebrated John, Duke of Argyle, who now openly opposed the ministers with whom he had once acted. Steele, therefore, both in the Englishman and in the Crisis, omitted no opportunity of panegyrizing the Scottish nation, and extolling the wisdom of the Union. Swift, who disliked the Scots, and had quarrelled with Argyle,[1] did not lose an opportunity of feeding full his grudge against both. In the Public Spirit of the Whigs the Scots are characterized as « a poor fierce northern people; » the Union treated rather as a measure of state-necessity,

[1] « How loved, how valued once, ava I'd him not! »

Swift's original respect for the duke is evident from many passages in the Journâl, as well as from an elegant letter, addressed to the duke while commanding in Spain, dated April 16, 1711.

flowing out of the Scottish act of security, than as that which was of itself desirable;[1] and the Duke of Argyle was glanced at as one of those Scottish nobles who appeared to be very zealous for dissolving the Union, although their whole revenues before that period would have ill maintained a Welsh justice of peace; and although they had since gathered more money than any Scotsman who had not travelled could form an idea of. It was besides stated, that the number of the Scottish nobility, joined to their poverty, was a great and necessary evil of the Union, and that to account it a benefit, as Steele had done in the Crisis, were as if, when a person of quality had married a portionless woman of inferior rank, it should be maintained as an advantage that she brought him as numerous a family of relations and servants as he had of his own. These expressions were higly resented in the upper House of Parliament. Lord Wharton, who certainly owed Swift little favour, made complaint to

[1] This was a favourite opinion with Swift, who enlarges upon it in the Examiner. See his Sarmatian Apologue in the 19th No. of the Examiner. Also his remarkable assertion concerning Lord Somers,—« Neither shall I ever forget, that he readily owned to me that the Union was of no other service to the nation, than by giving a remedy to that evil which my Lord Godolphin had brought upon us by persuading the queen to pass the Scotch act of security.»—*Memoirs relating to the Change of the Queen's Ministry.*

the House, and, being joined by a majority, the lord-treasurer was obliged to temporize and disown the pamphlet, and reprobate the expressions complained of. The offensive passage, which occupied about four pages, was hastily cancelled in the second edition; but this *amende honorable* had nearly come too late. Morphew the bookseller, and Barber the printer, were ordered into custody of the black rod. The former declared he knew nothing of the author, and Barber refused to answer any questions that might criminate himself. But Wharton, exclaiming that the House had nothing to do with the bookseller or printer, farther than they could be made the instruments of discovering «the villainous author of that false and scandalous libel,» proposed that Barber and his servants should be closely examined, and freed from those personal consequences, which they alleged as a reason for declining to give an answer. But the *finesse* of the ministers prevented a course of proceeding which must have led to the discovery of Swift. They directed a prosecution against Barber personally, which rendered it impossible to examine him in evidence against the author.[1] The resentment of the peers,

[1] This is the transaction to which Swift alludes in the lines upon himself, the concluding line of which former biographers have not explained particularly:—

« Now through the realm a proclamation spread
To fix a price on his devoted head,

and particularly of the Scottish nobles, was rather increased than allayed by this pretended sacrifice, which they considered in its true light of an evasion. The latter went in a body to the queen, headed by the Duke of Argyle, and required, that, in satisfaction for the affront which they had sustained, a proclamation should be issued, offering a reward for discovery of the author of the alleged libel. The same was moved by Wharton in the House of Lords; and a proclamation, proposing a reward of 300*l*., was issued accordingly. No one was in doubt as to the real author; but Swift, conscious of the protection of Oxford, exhibited no symptoms of alarm, though shunned by many of his former friends, who now conceived him to be singled out for prosecution. Meantime Lord Oxford indemnified Morphew and Barber by a sum of money (150.*l*), sent anonymously to Swift for the purpose of being conveyed to them; quashed, it would seem, the offer of a private informer to discover the author of the libel, provided he could be assured

While innocent he scorns ignoble flight,
His watchful friends preserve him by a *sleight*. »—

It appears, however, that Swift did meditate flight in case discovery had taken place. In the letter to his friend in Ireland about renewing his licence of absence, dated 29th July, 1714, he says, « I was very near wanting it some months ago with a witness,» which can only allude to the possibility of his being obliged to abscond.

of the reward; and finally, by discharge of the prosecution against Barber, when the clamour excited by the pamphlet was somewhat abated, consigned the whole matter to oblivion.

Swift's favour with the lord-treasurer, Oxford, had now ripened into the closest intimacy. How dearly Swift loved that statesman, in whom there were many qualities deserving of such attachment, appears from a thousand expressions in his letters and journal. The despair which he expresses at his being wounded by Guiscard is like that of a brother mourning for a brother. Swift retained to his dying day, as a sacred relic, the pen-knife with which the wound was inflicted; [1] and it would seem,

[1] Mr Deane Swift has thus described the weapon:—

« I have seen, » says Mr Swift, « the pen-knife, with a tortoise-shell handle, and when shut it was just about the length of a man's little finger. But, as the blade was broken within half an inch of the handle, by the violence of the blow, against one of the ribs of the earl, the doctor had a hole drilled through that part of the blade which was broken off, and another hole through that part of the piece which remained in the handle, and by that contrivance they were both held together by a little silver chain. »

Dr Delany, in a pamphlet published in 1755, containing some other remarks upon Mr Deane Swift's life of his great relative, gave, in very rude terms, an absolute contradiction to the above account, affirming that the knife, with the clothes which the lord-treasurer wore when he received the wound, were preserved as relics by the family of Oxford. In this last circumstance Delany's statement has since proved true, but it was not that, on one occasion, he secured his friend's life from a dangerous attempt of the same kind, at the hazard of his own.

This strange accident made much noise at the time, but has been unnoticed by Swift's numerous biographers. While the lord-trea-

so when made, and afforded no ground for the uncivil terms in which he controverted Mr Deane Swift's averment, since the knife was only given to the Oxford family after the Dean's death, and the publication of Delany's pamphlet. Dr Lyons gives a minute account of the circumstance in a letter now before the editor, dated 8th March, 1783, and addressed to Deane Swift, Esq.:—

« I have been honoured with the receipt of yours, dated 30th January, by the hands of my much esteemed friend and neighbour, Mrs Swanton, together with your animadversions on Dr Delany's erroneous account of that vile assassin Guiscard's penknife, with which he attempted to take away the life of Lord-Treasurer Harley.

« After the death of my ever to be honoured and admired friend and patron, Dr Swift, I took care of that knife, and also of the first plaster that was taken off the wound, both which the good Dean had preserved, and did afterwards wrap them together in a paper, with a short account of the villain's attempt. In 1760, when my private affairs occasioned my journey to London, I took this relic with me, in order to put it into the hands of Lord Oxford, or some branch of that noble family, to be delivered to him; and being one day invited by Alderman Harley, when Lord-Mayor, to dine at the Mayoralty House, I gave him the said knife, etc. to be given to the said Earl of Oxford, which knife he was much pleased to see, and did promise to put into his lordship's hand very shortly, as he expected to see him soon. I left London quickly after, and heard no more since.»

surer was dressing, a packet was delivered, the appearance of which excited the suspicion of Swift. He opened it with great precaution, and it was found to contain, according to the first account, three pistols cocked and charged, with a string attached so as to discharge them when the box should be opened. But afterwards the three pistols proved to be the barrels of large ink-horns filled with powder, connected with a pistol-lock for striking fire. This story was ridiculed by the Whigs, under the name of the band-box plot, and they did not hesitate to allege that Swift, the lucky discoverer, was also the ingenious deviser of the machine. But if the imputation had been just, there seems no reason why he should have disgraced his contrivance by the use of such ridiculous implements, since, though he had employed real pistols, he might easily have avoided danger in opening a box of which he knew the contents beforehand. Swift has himself assured Stella, that his life was actually in danger, and that he had saved that of the minister; and there appears no good reason for refusing our belief to both assertions. The attempt of Guiscard, and a much more melancholy and unfortunate example of our own time, may serve to convince us, that the life of a first minister may be endangered or destroyed by attempts as improbable as atrocious.

Swift was trusted by Oxford in his private as

well as public affairs. He was supposed to have assisted in the negotiations which preceded the alliance between the lord-treasurer's eldest son, and the only child of the Duke of Newcastle, and in the arrangements which followed for division of the duke's inheritance betwixt her and Lord Pelham, the male-heir. This was a point which Oxford had so greatly at heart, that Bolingbroke afterwards termed it the ultimate end of his administration.[1] Swift, upon this joyful occasion, wrote the poetical address to Lord Harley on his marriage.[2] But his sympathetic friendship is still more deeply manifested in his letter to the lord treasurer, on the death of his daughter,

[1] «In the management of this disagreeable business (Lord Harley's marriage, and the division of the inheritance of the Duke of Newcastle), the treasurer had the help of a priest's craft as well as his own, and it was said a good deanery was the reward of the Reverend Doctor's pains-taking in that pious negotiation.» Oldmixon's History, p. 559. This is invidiously recorded; nor is there any ground for the aspersion, supposing, which is highly probable, that the fact of Swift being consulted in the negotiation is in itself well-grounded.

[2] It is worthy of observation, that four lines in this poetical congratulation which were erased by the author, have been restored, and I think with taste and judgment, by his kinsman, Mr Deane Swift. The lines are those in Italics which conclude the following quotation:

Thus the bright Empress of the Morn
Chose for her spouse a mortal born,
The goddess made advances first,
Else what aspiring mortal durst.

the Marchioness of Caermarthen, than which there is nothing in the English language more beautifully and feelingly expressed. And the constancy of his attachment, at the most distressing period of Oxford's life, was such as well made good the manly expressions of regard with which, on retiring from London, he bade his lordship farewell. « When I was with you, I have said, more than once, that I would never allow quality or station made any real difference between men. Being now absent and forgotten, I have changed my mind: you have a thousand people who can pretend they love you, with as much appearance of sincerity as I; so that, according to common justice, I can have but a thousandth part in return of what I give. And this difference is wholly owing to your station. And the misfortune is still the greater, because I loved you so much the less for your station; for, in your public capacity, you have often angered me to the heart; but, as a private man, never once.»

The favour of Swift appears now to have been greater than ever, and most of the Irish affairs of consequence were determined by his advice and opinion[1]. It was the general

Though like a virgin of fifteen,
She blushes when by mortals seen,
Still blushes and with speed retires.
When Sol pursues her with his fires.

[1] See the Letters of Lord Primate Lindsay, Sir Con-

opinion, that he would soon be promoted to a bishop's see, and Lord Nottingham, on whom he had reflected severely in many of his satirical productions,[1] took an opportunity of retaliation when the celebrated schism bill was depending in the House of Lords. Adverting particularly to an enactment, that all teachers of youth should be licensed by the bishop or archbishop of the diocese, he proceeded thus: —« My lords, I have many children, and I know not whether God Almighty will vouchsafe to let me live to give them the education I could wish they had; therefore, my lords, I own I tremble when I think that a certain

stantine Phipps, etc., Earl of Anglesea, etc., in his correspondence at this period.

[1] See the « Excellent New Song, being the intended Speech of a famous Orator against Peace, of which Walpole complained in the House of Commons, and, pronouncing it to be written by Swift *and his Whimsical Club*, threatened to bring him to account for it. See also « Toland's Invitation to Dismal,» a name bestowed on Nottingham, from the gravity of his physiognomy. Nottingham was also assailed repeatedly in the Examiner and other satirical pieces, and in a ballad called the Hue and Cry after Dismal. To return these attentions, Nottingham seems, more than once, to have invoked the vengeance of the House of Lords against the author of this annoyance:

> Now Finch alarms the Lords: he hears for certain
> This dangerous priest has got behind the curtain,
> Finch, famed for tedious elocution, proves
> That Swift oils many a spring which Harley moves.
>
> *Verses by Swift on himself.*

divine, who is hardly suspected of being a Christian (meaning, as we read in the annals, Dr Swift), is in a fair way of being a bishop, and may one day give licence to those who shall be intrusted with the instruction of youth.»[1] And it appears from different passages in his correspondence, that the hopes of Swift's friends coincided with the fears of his enemies, respecting his expected promotion; and that there were expectations held out of a living in Yorkshire, to be obtained through the influence of Lord Keeper Harcourt. These hopes and fears, however, were so far disappointed, that Swift failed in obtaining a boon of much less consequence, though then essential to his comfortable settlement in life.

The debts which he was obliged to incur at entering upon his deanery were very considerable, amounting to at least a thousand pounds, an expense which he was unprepared to undergo. He therefore seems to have considered himself entitled, when accepting a promotion so much beneath the character in which he had acted, to be at least indemnified of the charges of induction;[2] and, in his own

[1] Oldmixon's History, p. 554.

[2] Journal, April 23, 1713. «I thought I was to pay but 600*l*. for the house, but the Bishop of Clogher says 800*l*.; first-fruits, 150*l*.; and so, with patent, 1000*l*. in all; so that I shall not be the better for the deanery these three years. I hope in some time they will be

peculiar manner, he stated that the queen should either pay up this debt for him, or hang him, since he had deserved the one or the other.[2]

The lord-treasurer, with his usual procrasti-

persuaded to give me some money here to clear off these debts. I will finish the book I am writing, before I can go over, and they expect I shall pass next winter here, and then I will drive them to give me a sum of money.»

Again, 16th May, 1713. «I shall be ruined, or at least sadly cramped, unless the queen will give me a thousand pounds. I am sure she owes me a great deal more. Lord-treasurer rallies me upon it, and I believe intends it, but *quando?*»—In a letter to Lord Keeper Harcourt, May, 1713, he hints at the same subject: «Lord-treasurer uses me barbarously, appoints to carry me to Kensington, and makes me walk four miles at midnight. He laughs when I mention a thousand pounds which he gives me, though a thousand pounds is a very serious thing.»

[1] This we learn from the following memorandum of Dr Birch: «The Reverend Mr Orr, Archdeacon of Ferns, gave me an account of a letter of Swift's, which has never been published, to Lord Bolingbroke. It was dated in July, 1713, from his living of Laracor, complaining of his being left by his friends in Ireland, and telling his lordship that he should remind him of David's prayer, which the lord-treasurer would direct him to the Psalm and verse for, 'Thou wilt not leave my soul in hell.' That when he returned to England, he would certainly petition the queen for the thousand pounds she had promised him; for that she ought to pay him that thousand pounds, or hang him, for he had deserved either the one or the other.»

nation, or from motives of public economy, jested on the subject, but did nothing, and Swift's situation must have been embarrassing to any one of less determined prudence. On his return to England, after his instalment, he addressed to Oxford that celebrated and beautiful imitation of Book I. epitsle vii. and sat. vi. Book II. of Horace, with which every reader must be familiar. The intention was to complain of the expenses attending his preferment,

——————— all vexations,
Patents, instalments, abjurations,
First-fruits, and tenths, and chapter-treats,
Dues, payments, fees, demands, and cheats,
The wicked laity's contriving,
To hinder clergymen from thriving.

It contains even a more plain intimation of his difficulties.

Poor Swift, with all his losses vext,
Not knowing where to turn him next,
Above a thousand pounds in debt,
Takes horse ———————

As well as

Lewis, the Dean will be of use;
Send for him up, take no excuse;
Or let it cost five hundred pound,
No matter where the money 's found,
It is but so much more in debt,
And that they ne'er consider'd yet.

All these hints of the loss he was actually

sustaining, seem to have been lost upon Oxford, and only attracted Bolingbroke's attention, at a time when his power was tottering, and his favour inefficient. Swift's solicitude on this subject, has been quoted as derogating from the high tone of independence assumed by him, on refusing the sum formerly offered by the treasurer; and it has been alleged that both cases were exactly parallel, unless in so far as the amount made a difference. But it must be considered, that three years public services had been remunerated with a professional situation of no common description of dignity indeed, and future emolument, but attended in the mean time with such an immediate expense, as must have embarrassed, for life perhaps, a man of less economy, and which reduced Swift to great temporary inconvenience. The grant of a sum of money, therefore, to render a preferment, which in every respect was beneath his pretensions, instantly productive and effectual, could no more be considered as an eleemosynary gratuity, than the acceptance of the deanery itself could be termed inconsistent with his having refused to be Lord Oxford's chaplain. Such grants have frequently been made in every department of the public service, and differ widely from the secret service-money doled out to party-writers from time to time, in proportion to the satisfaction which they afford to their patrons.

In another particular Swift was to undergo disappointment. He was still busy with his History of the Peace of Utrecht, and became disposed to extend it into a general account of Queen Anne's reign. With the view of obtaining access to materials, and perhaps of gratifying a wish long since entertained,[1] he was desirous to be named historiographer. The appointment is in the gift of the lord high chamberlain. But Swift, who seems to have had some reason for disliking the Duke of Shrewsbury,[2] whom he terms a person of no steadiness or sincerity, and by whom the office was held, endeavoured to supersede the necessity of applying to him, by presenting a direct memorial to Queen Anne.[3] His experience in courts might have taught him the jealousy entertained of official patronage; but he probably conceived, that his influence with ministers would surmount, in his particular case, all obstacles arising from it. He was mistaken. Oxford and Bolingbroke, each

[1] See his Letter to Addison, p. 116,

[2] This was erroneously applied to the Earl, afterwards Duke of Kent, in the first edition. But he was out of office at the time, and succeeded by the Duke of Shrewsbury.

[3] See his Memorial.

busied in preparing for an impending struggle, did not choose to excite the chamberlain's dislike, by encroaching on his rights of office; and Shrewsbury, to whom Swift made no personal application, filled up the situation with a dependent of his own.[1]

The dissensions among the ministers seem to have interrupted the meetings of the society of Brothers. But Swift had formed, in its stead, the celebrated Scriblerus Club, an association rather of a literary than a political character. Oxford and St John, Swift, Arbuthnot, Pope, and Gay, were the members. It was the well-known object of their united powers, to compose a satire upon the abuse of human learning. Part of their labours has been preserved in the Memoirs of Martinus Scriblerus, which gave name to the society, and part has been rendered immortal by the Travels of Lemuel Gulliver; but the violence of political faction, like a storm that spares the laurel no more than the cedar, dispersed this little band of literary brethren, and prevented the accomplishment of a task for which talents

[1] In a letter to Pope, mentioning the post of historiographer, as designed for him, he adds, « but as it was at the disposal of a person who had not the smallest share of steadiness or sincerity, I disdained to accept it.» This can only imply, he might have had it for asking it of the lord chamberlain, for it is certain he did apply to the queen by memorial, and was displeased with Bolingbroke for not obtaining it for him.

so various, so extended, and so brilliant, can never again be united.

Oxford and Bolingbroke, themselves accomplished scholars, patrons and friends both of the persons and of the genius thus associated, led the way, by their mutual animosity, to the dissolution of the confraternity. Their discord had now arisen to the highest pitch, and was scarce veiled under the thin forms of official intercourse. Swift again tried the force of humorous expostulation in his fable of the Fagot, where the ministers are called upon to contribute their various badges of office, to make the bundle strong and secure. With infinite delicacy the poet omitted all mention of Bolingbroke; the animosity between Oxford and him was too rankling a wound to endure being tickled. But all was in vain; and, at length, tired of this scene of murmuring and discontent, quarrel, misunderstanding, and hatred, the Dean, who was almost the only common friend who laboured to compose these differences, made a final effort, of which the result shall be given in his own words to Lord Oxford, son of the statesman: « When I returned to England, I found their quarrels and coldness increased. I laboured to reconcile them as much as I was able; I contrived to bring them to my Lord Masham's, at St. James's. My lord and Lady Masham left us together. I expostulated with them both, but could not find any good consequences. I was to go to Windsor next day with my lord-treasurer: I pretended business that prevented me; expecting they would come to some [reconciliation]. But I followed them to Windsor, where my Lord Bolingbroke told me, that my scheme had come to nothing. Things went on at the same rate: they grew more estranged every day. My lord-treasurer found his credit daily declining. In May, before the queen died, I had my last meeting with them at my Lord Masham's. He left us together; and therefore I spoke very freely to them both, and told them, 'I would retire, for I found all was gone,' Lord Bolingbroke whispered me, 'I was in the right.' Your father said, 'All would do well.' I told him, 'That I would go to Oxford on Monday, since I found it was impossible to be of any use.'

Nothing, indeed, was now left for Swift, but to execute the resolution he had repeatedly announced, of retreating from the scene of discord, without taking part with either of his contending friends. He set out for Oxford on the Monday succeeding his ineffectual interview, and from thence went to the house of the reverend Mr Gery at Upper Letcombe, Berkshire, where he resided for some weeks in the strictest seclusion. His feeling of this melancholy change, from all that was busy and gay, to the dulness and uniformity of a country vicarage, is expressed in a letter to Miss Vanhomrigh.[1] The secession of Swift from the political world excited the greatest surprise—the public wondered;[2]—the party writers exulted in a thousand ineffectual libels, discharged against the retreating champion of the high church,[3]—and his friends conjured him, in numerous letters, to return and reas-

[1] June 8, 1714.

[2] Pope's Letter, 18th June, 1714, and that of Thomas Harley, 19th June, 1714.

[3] One of these, which exhibits a good deal of humour, was called, A Hue and Cry after Dean Swift, containing a copy of his Diary, etc. It will surprise the reader, in perusing this, how closely the libeller has touched many of Swift's real habits; and the circumstance serves to shew, more plainly than a thousand general allegations, that even the most private particulars concerning him, had been for some years the object of public attention. His minute register of petty expenses, and the little shifts he adopted to diminish them, are mimicked very much in the style of his own Journal, and two or three circumstances in the Diary happened to coincide whimsically enough with the actual fact. *1mo*, He left Ford to settle for his handkerchiefs. *2dly*, If he did not borrow money of his bookseller, as in the Diary, he seems to have made such an arrangement with Barber, his printer, who tells him all his bills shall be answered. And though he did not then take exclusively to reading the civil wars of England, yet, after the decline of his faculties, it was the only work he perused, and he read it thrice over. In two particulars the Diary misrepresents his habits. Swift never appears to have smoked tobacco, and certainly never used wine, nor any liquor, to excess.

sume the task of a peace-maker. This he positively declined, but he seems to have meditated the extraordinary plan of an appeal to the public, at least to the Tory part at large, against those errors on which the administration seemed splitting asunder.

With this view, he composed the «Free thoughts on the State of Public Affairs,» in which it is remarkable that, although he loved Oxford far better than Bolingbroke, and indeed better than any other man who lived, yet almost the whole censure expressed in the piece falls to the share of that statesman. His affectation of mystery, his want of confidence in his colleagues, his temporizing with the opposite party, and maintaining many of the Whigs in office, are noticed at length, and with some severity. The infatuation of the internal dissension of the ministers, compared to a ship's crew quarrelling in a storm, or

The following notice of Swift occurs in a poem on the Late Examiner, which appeared about this time.

ON THE LATE EXAMINER.

O Jonathan! of merry fame,
As Swift in fancy as in name.
Here lie, as thou hast often done,
Thy holy mother 's pious son;
Deprived of paper, pen, and ink,
And, what is worse, deprived of drink;
For lo! thy idol Ox, thy Staff and Rod,
As thou would 'st say, are dropp'd by God, etc.

Political Merriment, 1714.

when within gun-shot of the enemy, is the only particular in which Bolingbroke shares the blame with Oxford. The measures recommended as a remedy for the imminent danger, are such as suited the headlong audacity of the former, rather than the slow and balancing policy of Harley. These are, *1st*, to achieve a complete predominance of the Tory party, by an absolute exclusion of the dissenters, termed the open enemies of the church of England, from every degree of power, civil or military; a disqualification to be extended likewise to all Whigs and low-church men, affirmed to be her secret adversaries, unless promotion be earned by a sincere reformation. This great work was to be accompanied by a new modelling of the army, especially of the royal guards, which are pronounced fitter, in their existing state, to guard a prince to the bar of a high-court of justice, than to secure him on the throne. *2dly*, After a thorough, and doubtless a sincere, disavowal of the exiled branch of the House of Stuart, it is strongly recommended that all secret intercourse between any party in England and the court of Hanover be broken off; that the visits of the presumptive heir, and his claims to be called to parliament, be no longer pressed upon the queen without her permission; and that the electoral prince should be required to declare his utter dislike of factious persons and principles, more especially of the party who affected to be peculiarly zealous for his rights, and to avow himself entirely satisfied with her majesty's proceedings at home and abroad. This was bold, daring, uncompromising counsel, better suited to the genius of him who gave it than to that of the British nation, and most likely, if followed, might have led to civil war. The treatise was, however, sent by Swift to his friend Charles Ford, and, with great precaution, through a circuitous channel, and, under a feigned name, transmitted by him to Barber the printer. Barber, being patronized by Bolingbroke, showed the manuscript, upon his own authority, to that statesman, who lost no time in making such additions and alterations, as were calculated to render it still more unfavourable to Oxford, and more suitable to his own political intrigues. On learning that such alterations were made, Swift, whose intention it had ever been to preserve the most perfect neutrality betwixt his great friends, and, if possible, to reunite them, but by no means to assist the one to the prejudice of the other, commissioned Ford to demand back the manuscript. It was recovered from the secretary of state and the typographer, after some hesitation, delay, and difficulty. And thus, the publication of this tract, which undoubtedly might have produced a great, though perhaps a dangerous effect, at that critical period, was laid entirely aside. He seems to have meditated another political pamphlet at the same time, apparently the memoirs relating to the change of ministry in 1710. But it must have been in somewhat a different form from that in which it was finally published.[1]

Meantime every post brought Swift, from various quarters, and with varying comments, accounts of the successful intrigues of Bolingbroke. It is curious to compare the differing lights in which the same facts are placed by his correspondents, as affected by their own feelings or interest. Lewis adheres to the falling fortunes of Oxford,—Ford seems half disposed to worship the apparently rising star of Bolingbroke,—Arbuthnot, like Swift, blames both, and laments the consequences of their division. Bolingbroke himself omitted no means of conciliating Swift to the revolution which he was about to accomplish in the cabinet. He wrote to the Dean in the kindest terms of friendship; and when Arbuthnot reminded him of the memorial for the post of historio-

[1] On 14th August, 1714, Ford writes, « I suppose Barber has given you an account of Lord Bolingbroke's pamphlet (*i. e.* the Free Thoughts, of which Bolingbroke had detained the manuscript). I long for the other;» and, 14th Sept. Swift writes to Bolingbroke, « The —— take this country; it has in three weeks spoiled two as good sixpenny pamphlets as ever a proclamation was issued out against.»

grapher, he exclaimed, that to have suffered Swift, who had deserved so well of them, to have the least uneasy thought about such matters, would be among the eternal scandals of their government.[1] His good intentions, however, were in that case frustrated, as the lord chamberlain had, three weeks before, bestowed the office upon another.[2] But, to manifest his own zeal for Swift's interest, Bolingbroke caused an order on the treasury to be signed by the queen for the thousand pounds which Swift had in vain solicited from Oxford, and this he did during his short ministry of three days. The warrant, indeed, was rendered nugatory by the queen's death, but the good will of St. John was equally manifested. At the same time Lady Masham, by whose secret influence Oxford had been displaced, wrote to conjure Swift, by his charity and compassion for the queen, not to desert her cause at this crisis, but to stay, and be assured his advice would not be thrown away on thankless and indifferent ears. Barber also was commissioned by Bolingbroke to inform Swift he would reconcile him with the Duchess of Somerset, place him on a right footing with the queen, and, what perhaps might have been an equal temptation, that it was intended to comply with his advice, by making a com-

[1] Letter from Arbuthnot.

[2] Mr Maddox.

plete sweep of those Whigs who had been left in office. These flattering proposals seemed to be attended with instant benefit, and to open a prospect full upon the path of honour, ambition, and preferment. But almost the same post brought an affecting letter from Lord Oxford, the disgraced minister, now going alone to his country seat in Herefordshire, and requesting Swift, if he had not tired him in their former *tête à tête* parties, to throw away so much time on one who loved him, as to attend him upon this melancholy journey. To Swift's immortal honour, he paused not a moment, but wrote to solicit a renewal of his licence for absence, then on the point of expiring, not that he might share the triumph and prospects to which he was invited by the royal favourite and the new prime-minister, but in order to accompany his beloved friend and patron to neglect and seclusion.[1] « I meddle not with his faults, as he was a minister of state,» are his manly expressions; « but you know his personal kindness to me was excessive; he distinguished and chose me above all men when he was great; and his

[1] A letter to a friend in Dublin, now published for the first time, shews that this proposal was not made in ceremony, but that Swift actually applied for licence of absence to attend his patron. The direction is lost, but it was probably addressed to Archdeacon Walls, as in another letter to him he mentions having corresponded with him on the subject.

letter to me the other day was the most moving imaginable.»[1] It lessens not the merit of this sacrifice that, within three days, fate closed the prospects of the Tory party by the death of Queen Anne, when the accession of George I. confounded the triumphant Bolingbroke and the disgraced Oxford in common peril and proscription.

Swift, under a shock sudden and overwhelming to his party in general, and deeply fraught with personal hatred to so active a partizan as himself, lost neither presence of mind, courage, nor perseverance. He gave the bold opinion, that it was yet possible to rally the Tories, providing common misfortune could unite those whom success had separated. He exhorted Bolingbroke to place himself at the head of the high-church party; and, like a veteran who assumes his arms to succour in peril the standard from which he had retired while it was victorious, he offered his own services in the field of political contest in the beginning of winter. It was on this occasion that Arbuthnot used the memorable expression,— « Dean Swift keeps up his noble spirit, and, though like a man knocked down, you may behold him still with a stern countenance, and aiming a blow at his adversaries.» But the spirit of the Tories was totally broken, as

[1] Letter to Miss Vanhomrigh.

is well described in a desponding letter of Lewis. And on the subject of reconciliation, Bolingbroke avowed such an inveteracy of hatred against Oxford, that he would rather have laid down his own life, than made common cause with him in defending that of both. His flight, and that of Ormond, with the imprisonment of Oxford, Wyndham, Prior, and others, completed the discomfiture and dispersion of Queen Anne's last ministry. These events took place when Swift himself, under the frown of power, had sought refuge in Ireland from the evils and dangers which impended over all the late ministers, and their adherents.

It was now he experienced that height of unpopularity which the narrative of Lord Orrery has somewhat anticipated. The Irish Protestants, remembering the civil wars of 1689 and 1690, looked with utter abhorrence on all who were suspected of being favourable to the interest of the house of Stuart. This was the charge brought against Queen Anne's last ministry by their successors; it was countenanced by a remarkable passage in the declaration of the Chevalier de St George, expressing the good intentions of his sister in his favour, when prevented by death; and, if limited to Bolingbroke's intrigues, that statesman's subsequent conduct, as well as Ormond's, give it great probability. But the spirit of party made no distinction. All who had favoured the high-church interest were involved in a sweeping charge of Jacobitism, of which calumny Swift had his share. Libels on libels were showered against him; the rabble insulted him as he walked the street; and even young men of rank forgot his station and their own so far as to set the same example of wanton brutality. Nor was this the worst evil of his situation.[1] His former friends, including

[1] Such disgraceful occurrences occasioned the following petition to the House of Lords, on the wanton aggression of one of their members:

"The humble PETITION of JONATHAN SWIFT, D. D. and Dean of the Cathedral of St Patrick's, Dublin.

Most humbly sheweth,

"THAT your petitioner is advised by his physicians, on account of his health, to go often on horseback; and there being no place, in winter, so convenient for riding as the strand toward Howth, your petitioner takes all opportunities that his business or the weather will permit, to take that road: That in the last Session of Parliament, in the midst of winter, as your petitioner was returning from Howth with his two servants, one before, and the other behind him, he was pursued by two gentlemen in a chaise, drawn by two high-mettled horses, in so violent a manner, that his servant, who rode behind him, was forced to give way, with the utmost peril of his life; whereupon your petitioner made what speed he could, riding to the right and left above fifty yards to the full extent of the said road; but the two gentlemen driving a light chaise, drawn by fleet horses, and intent upon mischief, turned faster than your petitioner, endeavouring to overthrow him: That by great accident your many who owed him civility and gratitude, paid court to the opposite party, by treating

petitioner got safe to the side of a ditch, where the chaise could not safely pursue; and the two gentlemen stopping their career, your petitioner mildly expostulated with them, whereupon one of the gentlemen said, Damn you, is not the road as free for us as for you? and calling to his servant who rode behind him, said, Tom (or some such name), is the pistol loaden with ball? To which the servant answered, Yes, my lord, and gave him the pistol. Your petitioner often said to the gentleman, Pray, sir, do not shoot, for my horse is apt to start, by which my life may be endangered. The chaise went forward, and your petitioner took the opportunity to stay behind. Your petitioner is informed, that the person, who spoke the words above-mentioned, is of your lordships' house, under the style and title of Lord Blaney; whom your petitioner remembers to have introduced to Mr Secretary Addison, in the Earl of Wharton's government, and to have done him other good offices at that time, because he was represented as a young man of some hopes and a broken fortune: That the said Lord Blaney, as your petitioner is informed, is now in Dublin, and sometimes attends your lordships' house. And your petitioner's health still requiring that he should ride, and being confined in winter to go on the same strand, he is forced to inquire from every one he meets, whether the said lord be on the same strand; and to order his servants to carry arms to defend him against the like, or a worse insult, from the said lord, for the consequences of which your petitioner cannot answer.

"Your petitioner is informed by his learned counsel, that there is no law now in being which can justify the said lord, under colour of his peerage, to assault any of his majesty's subjects on the king's highway, and put them in fear of their lives, without provocation, him with rudeness and insult.[1] He was obliged to secure his papers against the researches of government; and it would seem that a packet, addressed to him from the Duke of Ormond's chaplain, was seized by a messenger. The slight authority upon which it is affirmed, that Dean Swift actually absconded, lest he should be made answerable for the treasonable contents, may justly be neglected, since no steps were taken against a man so obnoxious to government, who would scarcely have been overlooked, had there occurred any grounds on

which he humbly conceives, that by only happening to ride before the said lord, he could not possibly give.

« Your petitioner therefore, doth humbly implore your lordships, in your great prudence and justice, to provide that he may be permitted to ride with safety on the said straud, or any other of the king's highways, for the recovery of his health, so long as he shall demean himself in a peaceable manner, without being put into continual fears of his life, by the force and arms of the said Lord Blaney. »

[1] Among these, Sir Thomas Southwell, one of the commissioners of the revenue, often mentioned as a friend in Swift's Letters and Journal, distinguished himself, by answering Swift, when he had addressed him on some ordinary occasion of business. « I'll hold you a groat, Mr Dean, I do not know you. » Afterwards, when created Lord Southwell, he expressed regret for his conduct during the heat of party, and attempted to regain Swift's acquaintance by saluting him with great politeness. But the Dean retorted his rudeness, prefaced by his own cant phrase, « I'll hold you a groat, my lord, I do not know you. »

which he could be made personally responsible.[1] That he was considered, however, as a person disaffected, and liable to accusation, is evident from an expression of his old correspondent, Archbishop King, who seems to have yielded to no one in the art of conveying a sarcasm under the mask of a friendly wish or amicable caution. « We have a strong report that my Lord Bolingbroke will return here and be pardoned: certainly it must not be for nothing. I hope he can tell no ill story of you.» This unfriendly hint the Dean repels with the most indignant spirit. « I should be sorry,» he commences, «to see my Lord Bolingbroke following the trade of an informer, because he is a person for whom I have always had, and still continue, a very great love and esteem. And as to myself, if I were of any importance, I should be very easy under such an accusation, much easier than I am to think your grace imagines me in any danger. I am surprised your grace could think, or act, or correspond with me for some years past, while you must needs believe me a most false and

[1] The authority for the whole story is but slender. Tindal in his Continuation of Rapin, copies, without quoting the words of Oldmixon, and Oldmixon refers to the Annals of Boyer. « Posterity,» says Oldmixon, « will be in amazement to find not one of these libellers made an example.» And, undoubtedly, posterity has been induced, from that very circumstance, greatly to doubt the grounds on which the historian has accused them.

vile man, declaring to you, on all occasions, my abhorrence of the Pretender, and yet privately engaged with a ministry to bring him in. I always professed to be against the Pretender, and am so still. And this it not to make my court, which I know is vain, for I own myself full of doubts, fears, and dissatisfactions, which I think on as seldom as I can : yet, if I were of any value, the public may safely rely on my loyalty, because I look upon the coming of the Pretender as a greater evil than any we are likely to suffer, under the worst Whig ministry that can be found.»

It would be in vain to waste more words on this accusation, excepting that no one had more reason to dread the accession of a Catholic prince than the determined champion of the Church of England; nor could a counter-revolution, which must have been achieved by foreign aid, and supported by arbitrary and military authority, have been so odious to any one as to the resolved and undaunted defender of the liberties of Ireland. His manuscript Notes upon Addison's Freeholder, a paper designed to support the government during the insurrection of 1715, indicate, indeed, compassion for the insurgents, and no great respect for the reigning family, but intimate no approbation of the Jacobite principles, nor any wish for a restoration of the Stuart line. It is true that, to be even the apologist of these unfortunate persons, might, in the rigorous judgment of more zealous partizans, misbecome one who professed himself a Whig, though without modern refinements. If this be judged an inconsistency, it must be considered as one of those which frequently occur from the accidental collision of human passions with political principle. But, excepting in these momentary flashes of satire, if we examine the whole tenor of Swift's life, writings, and opinions, there cannot be an action, or line, or sentiment derived from his history, writings, or letters, to countenance the charge of Jacobitism with which he was at this period of his life so generally slandered.

The imputation of disaffection has often the same effect with the reality, especially in a provincial capital, where the retainers of party endeavour to supply their deficiency in real importance, by zeal, clamour, and intolerance. Swift seems, therefore, for some time, to have been secluded from the society of the great, powerful, and distinguished; and the companion of Oxford and Bolingbroke, of Prior, Pope, Gay, had to select his society from the men of kindred taste in his own order, with a few of more elevated rank, who either had the sense and spirit to « forsake politics for wit, » or were not disinclined to high-church politics. Delany has enumerated several of these in a passage, where he repels, with equal success and indignation, the assertion of Orrery, that Swift delighted in company of low rank, and parasitical manners. He mentions, as Swift's principal companions, the Grattans, seven brethren of high honour, in their various walks of life,[1] as generally acquainted, and as much beloved as any family in England; their ally, the Rev. Mr Jackson, George Rochfort, and Peter Ludlow, both gentlemen of accomplishments, and, what Lord Orrery might think more material, of good birth and easy fortune. He also enumerates Dr Walsmley, Dr Helsham, Dr Sheridan, Mr Stopford, afterwards Bishop of Cloyne, and himself; and what he says of Rochfort and Ludlow may apply to most of Swift's society. « Greater companions he might have

[1] The eldest lived on his paternal fortune. One was a physician, one a merchant, and afterwards lord mayor of Dublin; one was head master of a free-school, with a large appointment, and the remaining three were clergymen. « Do you not know the Grattans?» said Swift to Lord Carteret, when he came over as lord-lieutenant; then pray obtain their acquaintance. The Grattans, my lord, can raise 10,000 men.» This was one of the first instances in which Swift shewed his desire of enhancing the importance of his friends. He alluded to the great popularity of the family, and Carteret seems to have found his report just, since Dr Grattan was named physician to the lord-lieutenant and his family. He wrote to the Duke of Dorset concerning the Grattans, making use of the same phrase.

conversed with, but better he neither did, nor could.»[1]

Amusing his leisure in this society, Swift had yet too much time remaining to reflect on his own disappointments, and the calamity of those who had lately been engaged with him on the public stage. Like a seaman wrecked upon a solitary island, we find him constantly lamenting the misfortunes and danger of the associates from whom he was divided,—longing for their society,—undervaluing, in his grief for their separation, the safety and the solitude which had fallen to his own lot. His thoughts were ever turning to « his friends in exile, or the Tower,» nor did he omit all that was in his power to manifest his sympathy with their distress, at every risk to his own person and fortune. He corresponded with Lord Bolingbroke, even while in banishment, through bad report and good report. He offered consolation to Lady Masham, and to the yet more unfortunate Duchess of Ormond. But to Oxford, his patron and his friend, then imprisoned in the Tower, and threatened with impeachment for high treason, Swift manifested that affection which only generous and noble minds can feel, and which glows highest when it most compromises the safety of him by whom it is displayed. He claimed it as his

[1] Delany's Observations.

right to offer his service and attendance during his friend's imprisonment—he entreated it as a boon: « It is the first time,» are his striking words, « I ever solicited you in my own behalf, and if I am refused, it will be the first request you ever refused me.» Oxford seems to have declined an offer, which, without being useful to him, could only have involved a noble and disinterested friend in suspicion and danger. But the generosity and self-devotion by which it was dictated, should be equally remembered in Swift's favour, and silence for ever the obscure and unproved calumnies, which are inconsistent with the very nature of such a mind. He writes to Pope in this melancholy strain, « You know how well I loved both Lord Oxford and Lord Bolingbroke, and how dear the Duke of Ormond is to me: do you imagine I can be easy while their enemies are endeavouring to take off their heads? *I nunc, et versus tecum meditare canoros.*»—And after an account of his living in the most secluded manner with a few servants, in the corner of a vast unfurnished house, he describes his amusements to be the task of defending his small dominions against the archbishop, and endeavouring to reduce his rebellious choir. *Perditur*, is the melancholy summing up, *perditur inter hæc misero lux.*

If it be possible that any one should peruse these pages, to whom the wayward history of

Swift's domestic misfortunes are altogether unknown, such a reader may be surprised, that, endowed with a competence which his economy was speedily increasing into opulence, he had not now at length relieved the tedium of celibacy, and diverted his painful reflections upon public affairs, and the fate of his friends, by seeking domestic comfort and society in an union with Stella, who had forsaken England on his account, and towards whom so much affection is expressed in the earlier part of his journal. But the fate of a third person was now entwined with theirs, and the misfortunes which followed must be the subject of an uninterrupted narrative.

SECTION V

Swift's first Acquaintance with Miss Vanhomrigh—She follows him to Ireland—Swift's Marriage with Stella—Death of Miss Vanhomrigh—Poem of Cadenus and Vanessa—Swift's Studies during his retirement from 1714 to 1720—His system of Life and Amusements—Engages in Irish Politics—His Proposal for Encouragement of Irish Manufactures—and other Tracts—Drapier's Letters—Swift's subsequent popularity.

AT the period of Swift's residence in England, he was possessed, in an eminent degree, of many of the qualities which are the surest passports to female favour. He was not only a man of the highest talents, but he enjoyed, in full extent, all the public notice and distinction which the reputation of such talents can confer. He moved in the highest circles, was concerned in the most important business of the time, and had all the advantage of a name blown wide abroad in the world. In private society, the varied richness of his conversation, the extent of his knowledge, his unequalled powers of wit and humour, even the somewhat cynical eccentricities of his temper, joined to form a character equally interesting from its merits and originality. His manners, in these his better days, were but slightly tinged with the peculiarities which afterwards marked them more unpleasantly, and his ease and address were such as became the companion of statesmen and courtiers:

> « He moved, and bow'd, and talk'd with too much grace,
> Nor shew'd the parson in his gait or face. »

Thus accomplished, Swift was readily admitted to the intimate society of many of the most beautiful and accomplished women of the age. His correspondence with the unfortunate Mrs Long, shews how well he knew to support the character of a favourite of the fair. The friendship of Lady Betty Germain, of Mrs Barton, of the Countess of Winchelsea, the Duchess of Ormond, Lady Masham, and many other ladies, eminent for beauty or accomplishments, rank or fashion, evinces how high he stood in the estimation of those by whom it is almost every man's ambition to be distinguished. But these enviable talents of pleasing became, through an unfortunate contingence, the means of embittering, if not of abridging, the life of the possessor.

Amongst the families in London where Swift was chiefly domesticated, was that of Mrs Vanhomrigh, a widow lady of fortune and respectability, who had two sons and two daughters.[1] The eldest daughter was Esther Vanhomrigh, better known by the poetical appellation of Vanessa. On her personal charms we are left in some uncertainty, since Cadenus[2] has said little upon that topic, and, by other authorities, they have been rather depreciated.[3] But, when Swift became intimate in the family, she was not yet twenty years old, lively and graceful, yet with a greater inclination for reading and mental cultivation than is usually combined with a gay temper. This last attribute had fatal attractions for Swift, who, in intercourse with his female friends, had a marked pleasure in directing their studies, and acting as their literary Mentor; a dangerous

[1] She was the daughter of Mr Stone, the commissioner, and widow of Bartholomew Vanhomrigh, a Dutch merchant, who had been commissary for stores for King William during the Irish civil wars, and afterwards muster-master-general, and commissioner of the revenue. Notwithstanding his having enjoyed a large income, and purchased forfeited estates to the value of 12,000l. in Ireland, he did not leave above 16,000l. to be divided among his children at his death. His widow and family settled in London about 1709, and had a house in Bury-street, St James's. Their vicinity to Swift's lodgings, and connexion with Ireland, probably first led to the intimacy which afterwards proved so fatal.

[2] The name of Cadenus is an anagram of Decanus.

[3] Lord Orrery says Vanessa was not handsome: but it is certain he only spoke of her by report. Mr Berwick has a picture of one of the Miss Vanhomrighs, but whether of Vanessa or her sister is, I believe, doubted.

character for him who assumes it, when genius, docility, and gratitude, are combined in a young and interesting pupil. From several passages in the Journal, Swift's constant and intimate familiarity in the Vanhomrigh family is manifest; and it is plain also, he soon felt that his acquaintance with Miss Esther was such as must necessarily give pain to Stella. While Vanessa was occupying much of his time, and much doubtless of his thoughts, she is never once mentioned in the Journal directly by name, and is only twice casually indicated by the title of Vanhomrigh s eldest daughter. There was, therefore, a consciousness on Swift's part, that his attachment to his younger pupil was of a nature which could not be gratifying to her predecessor, although he probably shut his own eyes to the consequences of an intimacy which he wished to conceal from those of Stella. Miss Vanhomrigh, in the mean while, sensible of the pleasure which Swift received from her society, and of the advantages of youth and fortune which she possessed, and ignorant of the peculiar circumstances in which he stood with respect to another, naturally, and surely without offence either to reason or virtue, gave way to the hope of forming a union with a man, whose talents had first attracted her admiration, and whose attentions, in the course of their mutual studies, had, by degrees, gained her affections, and seemed to warrant his own. It is easy for those who look back on this melancholy story, to blame the assiduity of Swift, or the imprudence of Vanessa. But the first deviation from the straight line of moral rectitude is, in such a case, so very gradual, and, on the female side, the shades of colour which part esteem from affection, and affection from passion, are so imperceptibly heightened, that they who fail to stop at the exact point where wisdom bids, have much indulgence to claim from all who share with them the frailties of mortality. The imprudent friends continued to use the language of friendship, but with the assiduity and earnestness of warmer passion, until Vanessa rent asunder the veil, by intimating to Swift the state of her affections; and in this, as she conceived, she was justified by his own favourite, though dangerous maxim, of doing that which seems in itself right, without respect to the common opinion of the world. We cannot doubt that he actually felt the « shame, disappointment, guilt, surprise, » expressed in his celebrated poem, though he had not courage to take the open and manly course, of avowing those engagements with Stella, or other impediments, which prevented him from accepting the hand and fortune of her rival. Perhaps he was conscious that such an explanation had been too long delayed, to be now stated, without affording grounds for the heavy charge of having flattered Miss Vanhomrigh into hopes, which, from the nature of his own situation, could never be gratified. This remorseful consciousness, too, he might feel, when looking back on his conduct, though until then he had blindly consulted his own gratification in seeking the pleasure of Vanessa's society, without being aware of the difficulties in which they were both becoming gradually entangled. Without, therefore, making this painful but just confession, he answered the avowal of Vanessa's passion, at first in raillery, and afterwards by an offer of devoted and everlasting friendship, founded on the basis of virtuous esteem. Vanessa seems neither to have been contented nor silenced by the result of her declaration, but to the very close of her life persisted in endeavouring, by entreaties and arguments, to extort a more lively return to her passion, than this cold proffer was calculated to afford. It is difficult to ascertain when this eclaircissement took place, but it seems to have preceded Swift's departure for Ireland to take possession of his deanery, though it must certainly have been made after obtaining that preferment. The effect of his increasing intimacy with the fascinating Vanessa may be plainly traced in the Journal to Stella, which, in the course of its progress, becomes more and more cold and indifferent, —breathes fewer of those aspirations after the quiet felicity of a life devoted to M. D. and the willows at Laracor, uses less frequently the affectionate jargon, called the « little language,» in which his fondness at first displays itself,—and, in short, exhibits all the symptoms of waning affection. Stella was neither blind to the altered style of his correspondence, nor deaf to the rumours which were wafted to Ireland. Her letters are preserved, but, from several passages of the Journal, it appears, that they intimated displeasure and jealousy, which Swift endeavours to appease. But there are two passages, in particular, worthy of notice, as illustrative of the history of Stella and Vanessa. The first occurs when Swift obtains the Deanery of St Patrick's. « If it be worth *L.* 400 a year,» he says, «overplus shall be divided . . . . besides usual . . .» an imperfect phrase, which however implies, that his relation with Stella was to continue on its former footing, and that she was only to share the advantage of his promotion by an increase of her separate income. This hint was probably designed to bar any expectations of a proposal of marriage. Another ominous sentence in the Journal is the following intimation : « His (Mr Vanhomrigh's) eldest daughter is come of age, and going to Ireland to look after her fortune, and get it into her own hands.» [1] This plan, which Miss Vanhomrigh afterwards ac-

[1] Journal, 15th August, 1711.

complished, boded no good to the unfortunate Stella.

Upon Swift's return to Ireland, we may guess at the disturbed state of his feelings, wounded at once by ungratified ambition, and harassed by his affection being divided between two objects, each worthy of his attachment, and each having great claims upon him, while neither was likely to remain contented with the limited return of friendship in exchange for love, and that friendship, too, divided with a rival. The claims of Stella were preferable in point of date, and, to a man of honour and good faith, in every respect irresistible. She had resigned her country, her friends, and even hazarded her character, in hopes of one day being united to Swift. But, if Stella had made the greater sacrifice, Vanessa was the more important victim. She had youth, fortune, fashion; all the acquired accomplishments and information in which Stella was deficient; possessed at least as much wit, and certainly higher powers of imagination. She had, besides, enjoyed the advantage of having in a manner compelled Swift to hear and reply to the language of passion. There was, in her case, no Mrs Dingley, no convenient third party, whose presence in society and community in correspondence, necessarily imposed upon both a restraint, convenient perhaps to Swift, but highly unfavourable to Stella. Vanessa could address Swift directly in her own name, and, as he was obliged to reply in the same manner, there is something in the eloquence of affection that must always extort a corresponding answer. There is little doubt, therefore, that Swift, at this time, gave Vanessa a preference in his affection, although, for a reason hereafter to be hinted, it is probable, that the death or removal of one of these far-famed rivals would not have accelerated his union with the other. At least we are certain, that, could the rivals have laid jealousy and desire to sleep, the lover's choice would have been to have bounded his connexion with both within the limits of Platonic affection. That he had no intention to marry Vanessa is evident from passages in his letters, which are inconsistent with such an arrangement, as, on the other hand, their whole tenor excludes that of a guilty intimacy. Before leaving England, he acquainted her with his determination to forget every thing there, and to write as seldom as he could; and in the same letter he expresses his doubts of ever visiting England again,—doubts which implied a gross insult, had he at any time held out a prospect of their union, but something still more villanous, if we suppose the parties to have passed the limits of innocence. On the other hand, his conduct, with respect to Stella, was equally dubious. So soon as he was settled in the deanery-house, his first care was to secure lodgings for Mrs Dingley and Stella, upon Ormond's Quay, on the other side of the Liffey; and to resume, with the same guarded caution, the intercourse which had formerly existed between them. But circumstances soon compelled him to give that connexion a more definite character.

Mrs Vanhomrigh was now dead. Her two sons survived her but a short time, and the circumstances of the young ladies were so far embarrassed by inconsiderate expenses, as gave them a handsome excuse for retiring to Ireland, where their father had left a small property near Celbridge. The arrival of Vanessa in Dublin excited the apprehensions of Swift, and the jealousy of Stella. However imprudently the Dean might have indulged himself and the unfortunate young lady, by frequenting her society too frequently during his residence in England, there is no doubt that he was alive to all the hazards that might accrue to the reputation and peace of both, by continuing the same intimacy in Dublin. But the means of avoiding it were no longer in his power, although his reiterated remonstrances assumed even the character of unkindness.[1]

[1] The effect which such severity produced upon a character of Miss Vanhomrigh's ardent cast, will be best illustrated from her own words, in a letter to Swift, dated 1714. "You bid me be easy, and you would see me as often as you could. You had better have said, as often

She importuned him with complaints of neglect and cruelty, and it was obvious, that any decisive measure to break their correspondence would be attended with some such tragic consequence, as, though late, at length concluded their story. Thus engaged in a labyrinth, where perseverance was wrong, and retreat seemed almost impossible, Swift resolved to temporize, in hopes, probably, that time, accident, or the mutability incident to violent affections, might extricate himself and Vanessa from the snare in which his own culpable imprudence had involved them. Meanwhile, he

as you get the better of your inclinations so much; or as often as you remember there was such a one in the world. If you continue to treat me as you do, you will not be made uneasy by me long. It is impossible to describe what I have suffered since I saw you last. I am sure I could have borne the rack much better than those killing, killing words of yours. Sometimes I have resolved to die without seeing you more; but those resolves, to your misfortune, did not last long. For there is something in human nature, that prompts one so to find relief in this world, I must give way to it: and beg you would see me, and speak kindly to me, for I am sure you'd not condemn any one to suffer what I have done, could you but know it. The reason I write to you is, because I cannot tell it to you should I see you. For when I begin to complain, then you are angry; and there is something in your looks so awful, that it strikes me dumb. O! that you may have but so much regard for me left, that this complaint may touch your soul with pity! I say as little as ever I can; did you but know what I thought, I am sure it would move you to forgive me, and believe, I cannot help telling you this and live » continued to bestow on her those marks of regard which it was impossible to refuse to her feelings towards him, even if they had not been reciprocal. But the conduct which he adopted as kindest to Miss Vanhomrigh was likely to prove fatal to Stella. His fears and affections were next awakened for that early favourite, whose suppressed grief and jealousy, acting upon a frame naturally delicate, menaced her health in an alarming manner. The feelings with which Swift beheld the wreck which his conduct had occasioned, will not bear description. Mrs Johnson had forsaken her country, and clouded even her reputation, to become the sharer of his fortunes, when at their lowest; and the implied ties by which he was bound to make her compensation, were as strong as the most solemn promise, if indeed even promises of future marriage had not been actually exchanged between them. He employed Dr St George Ashe, Bishop of Clogher, his tutor and early friend, to request the cause of her melancholy, and he received the answer which his conscience must have anticipated—it was her sensibility to his recent indifference, and to the discredit which her own character had sustained from the long subsistence of the dubious and mysterious connexion between them. To convince her of the constancy of his affection, and to remove her beyond the reach of calumny, there was but one remedy. To this communication Swift replied, that he had formed two resolutions concerning matrimony:—one, that he would not marry till possessed of a competent fortune; the other, that the event should take place at a time of life which gave him a reasonable prospect to see his children settled in the world. The independence proposed, he said, he had not yet achieved, being still embarrassed by debt; and, on the other hand, he was past that term of life after which he had determined never to marry. Yet he was ready to go through the ceremony for the ease of Mrs Johnson's mind, provided it should remain a strict secret from the public, and that they should continue to live separately, and in the same guarded manner as formerly. To these hard terms Stella subscribed; they relieved her own mind, at least, from all scruples on the impropriety of their connexion; and they soothed her jealousy, by rendering it impossible that Swift should ever give his hand to her rival. They were married in the garden of the deanery, by the Bishop of Clogher, in the year 1716.[1]

[1] The Bishop of Clogher, it is said, informed Bishop Berkeley of this secret, and by Berkeley's relict it was communicated to Mr Monck Berkeley. See the Inquiry into the Life of Swift, in his Literary Reliques, p. 36. But I must add, that if, as affirmed by Mr Monck Mason, Berkeley was in Italy from the period of the marriage to the death of the Bishop of Clogher, this communication could not have taken place. Dr Madden told the same

Immediately subsequent to the ceremony, Swift's state of mind appears to have been

story to Dr Johnson, upon the authority of Dr Sheridan, to whom Stella unfolded the secret shortly before her death. And neither Mrs Whiteway, nor any of Swift's intimate friends, excepting Dr Lyon, doubted the fact of this unhappy marriage. Mrs Sican's authority may also be added to the list of witnesses.

Since the first edition of this work appeared, some curious and elaborate notices concerning Swift's life have appeared in the History of the Cathedral of St Patrick's, Dublin, by William Monck Mason, Esq., who expresses his total disbelief of the prevailing report of a private marriage between Mrs Esther Johnson and the Dean, with many strictures on the credulity of those previous biographers of Swift, by whom it had been received as probable. It must be conceded to both parties, in such a controversy, that it respects a doubtful and dark transaction, entered into by two persons, whose exact situation and feelings, with respect to each other, could only be known with precise accuracy to themselves. It was also a transaction in which the Dean is said to have exacted the closest secrecy; and that all which is known with respect to it has rather transpired by the various channels intimated above, than become the subject of direct and positive evidence. It is therefore not wonderful, that the degree of testimony which establishes in the mind of one person a strong probability, may be of little weight in the opinion of another. Still, however, a report so distinctly traced to Sheridan, Delany, and Mrs Whiteway, Swift's nearest intimates and friends, will have great weight with persons who consider the question without prepossession. The opinion expressed by Dr Lyon is, however, certainly entitled to insertion, although the present editor is still of opinion, that it is almost entirely founded upon an argument *ex absurdo*, which might have been dreadful. Delany (as I have learned from a friend of his relict), being pressed to give his

very applicable to any other individual, but does not apply to so singular a person as Swift, and whom circumstances had placed in a very uncommon situation with respect to Stella on the one hand, and Vanessa on the other. An argument which sets out by obliging us to believe nothing with respect to Swift irreconcilable with the « common rules », from which he claimed emancipation for « nobler minds, » would either prove that Vanessa and Stella had never existed, or that Swift had never placed himself, with respect to these ladies, in the painful predicament which seems to have broken the heart of both, and to have gone far to breaking his own. Mr Monck Mason's opinion is thus stated.

« Notwithstanding Dr Delany's sentiments of Swift' marriage, and notwithstanding all that Lord Orrery and others have said about it, there is no authority for it but a hear-say story, and that very ill founded. It is certain that the Dean told one of his friends, whom he advised to marry, that he himself never wished to marry at the time he ought to have entered into that state; for he counted upon it as the happiest condition, especially towards the decline of life, when a faithful tender friend is most wanted. While he was talking to this effect, his friend expressed his wishes to have seen him married: the Dean asked why? 'Because,' replied the other, 'I should have had the pleasure of seeing your offspring; all the world would have been pleased to have seen the issue of such a genius.' The Dean smiled, and denied his being married, in the same manner as before, and said he never saw the woman he wished to be married to. The same gentleman, who was intimate with Mrs Dingley for ten years before she died, in 1743; took occasion to tell her that such a story was whispered of her friend Mrs Johnson's marriage with the Dean, but she only laughed opinion on this strange union, said, that about the time it took place, he observed Swift to be

at it as an idle tale, founded only on suspicion. Again, Mrs Brent, with whom the Dean's mother used to lodge in Dublin, in the queen's time, and who was his own housekeeper after he settled in Dublin in 1714, and who, for her many good qualities in that situation, was much confided in, never did believe there was a marriage between those persons, notwithstanding all that love and fondness that subsisted between them: she thought it was all platonic love, and she often told her daughter Ridgeway so, who succeeded her in the same office of housekeeper. She said that Mrs Johnson never came alone to the deanery, that Mrs Dingley and she came always together, and that she never slept in that house if the Dean was there, only in time of his sickness, to attend him, and see him well taken care of; and during this course of her generous attendance, Mrs Dingley and she slept together, and, as soon as he recovered, they returned to their lodgings on Ormond-quay. These ladies slept, two other times, at the deanery, at an **** pleasant house, and near his garden, called Naboth's vineyard, and that was for those months in 1726 and 1727 which he spent in England. It chanced that she was taken ill at the deanery, and it added much to his affliction that it happened at the deanery, for fear of defamation in case of her dying in his house, whether he was at home or abroad. Had he been married, he could not have lived in a state of separation from her, he loved her so passionately; for he admired her upon every account that can make a woman amiable or valuable as a companion for life. Is it possible to think that an affectionate husband could first have written, and then have used, those several prayers, by a dying wife with whom he never cohabited, and whose mouth must have been filled with reproaches for denying her all conjugal rites for a number of years, nay, from the very period (1716) that is pretended to be extremely gloomy and agitated, so much so, that he went to Archbishop King, to mention his apprehensions. On entering the library, Swift rushed out with a countenance of distraction, and passed him without speaking.

the time of the marriage? Would he have suffered his wife to make a will, signed Esther Johnson, and to demise 1500l. away from him, of which 1000l. is enjoyed by the chaplain of Stevens's hospital for the sick, and accept of a gold watch only as a testimony of her regard for him?—If he could direct, or rather command her, to leave her fortune as he pleased, it is probable he would have directed the application towards the future support of lunatics, which was the species of charity he thought most worthy the attention of the public. Is it not probable that two gentlemen of honour and fortune, still living, who knew them both intimately, and who were her executors, would have known of a marriage, if there was one? And yet they always did, and do positively declare, they never had cause to suspect they were married, although they were in company with both one thousand times; they saw proof of the warmest friendship, and any love but connubial love. If she made him a present of a book, you may read in the title-page these words—and so he distinguished every book she gave him:

Esther Johnson's gift to
Jonathan Swift—1719.

Would he deny his marriage with a woman of good fortune at that time, when he says 'she had a gracefulness somewhat more than human in every motion, word, and action?'"

The reader must judge of the force of this reasoning compared with the circumstances brought together in the text, and form the best opinion which he can upon an event which, take it either way, is enveloped in mystery and inconsistency.

He found the Archbishop in tears, and, upon asking the reason, he said, « You have just met the most unhappy man on earth; but, on the subject of his wretchedness, you must never ask a question. » Swift secluded himself from

[1] It is proper to state, that Delany's inference from this circumstance was a suspicion that Swift, after his union with Stella, had discovered that there was too near a consanguinity between them, to admit of their living together, and that he had then been stating the circumstance to the Archbishop. But it does not appear that the words used by the prelate necessarily indicated a connexion of this kind, and there are positive proofs that none such could possibly exist. The connexion was supposed to depend upon Sir William Temple, of whom the legend pronounced both Swift and Stella to be illegitimate children. It is needless to dwell upon the improbability that such a relationship should have been a secret to both parties, during their intimacy of so many years, and yet should all at once have become known to them upon their marriage in Ireland, when their parents were dead, and when they were at a distance from all persons who could be supposed the confidents of Sir William Temple's intrigues. It is enough to say, that Swift's parents resided in Ireland from before 1665, until his birth in 1667, and that Temple was residing, as ambassador in Holland, from April 1666, until January 1668. As for Stella, her mother being introduced into Sir William Temple's family, after her husband s death, by the compassionate friendship of Lady Gifford, there is every reason to suppose, that she was never even seen by Temple, until the future wife of Swift was two or three years old. We must, therefore, seek some other reasons for Swift's distress, and the expressions of King, than the construction assigned to them by Delany.

society for some days. When he reappeared, his intercourse with Stella and Mrs Dingley was reassumed, with the same guarded and cautious attention, to prevent the slightest suspicion of a more intimate union with the former, as if such intimacy had not now been legal and virtuous. Stella, therefore, continued the beloved and intimate friend of Swift; the regulator of his household and table on public days, although she only appeared there as an ordinary guest; the companion of his social hours, and his comforter in sickness;—but his wife only in name, and even that nominal union a secret from the world. Thus situated, Stella continued to experience, in some degree, the inconveniences attached to a situation so doubtful; for though she was known to several ladies, yet their intercourse was rather formal than friendly, and her intimacies lay entirely with Swift's male friends. The obliging friend of Mrs Delany,[1] whom I have already mentioned, says, that Stella « went with Mrs Dingley to Dr Delany's villa on Wednesdays, when his men-companions

[1] When I say that the lady from whom I have this information is equally distinguished for high rank, eminent talents, and the soundest judgment, I regret, as much as Mr Mason can do, that a dislike on her part to any thing approaching to appearance before the public, prevents me from adding her name. — See *History of Saint Patrick's*

dined, before he was married to my friend. She (Mrs Delany) once saw her by accident, and was struck with the beauty of her countenance, and particularly with her fine dark eyes. She was very pale, and looked pensive, but not melancholy, and had hair black as a raven.» This slight sketch of Stella, from the recollection of the venerable Mrs Delany, will probably interest the reader as much as the editor.[1]

If flattery and fame could have made up for domestic happiness, Stella might have been satisfied. Every year, on her birth-day, the Dean addressed her in a copy of verses, in which the most elegant compliments were bestowed with an affectation of bluntness, which seemed only to warrant for their sincerity. But they contain frequent insinuations of angry passions, and virtues which

————Suspended wait,
Till time has open'd reason's gate.

Hints which too plainly imply, that their unsa-

[1] The only portrait of Stella known to exist is in possession of my kind and respected friend, the Rev. Mr Berwick. Dr Tuke of St Stephen's Green has a lock of her hair, on the envelope of which is written, in Dean Swift's hand — « Only a woman's hair.»—If Stella was dead, as is most probable, when Swift laid apart this memorial, the motto is an additional instance of his striving to veil the most bitter feelings under the guise of cynical indifference.

tisfactory state of union neither lulled jealousy nor resentment to silence. These complaints of Stella's temper occur most frequently in the poems which precede the death of Vanessa, and the reason is sufficiently apparent. Under the impression of such feelings, she is said to have composed the following lines : [1]

ON JEALOUSY.

« O shield me from his rage, celestial Powers!
This tyrant that embitters all my hours.
Ah Love ! you 've poorly play'd the hero's part ;
You conquer'd, but you can't defend my heart.
When first I bent beneath your gentle reign,
I thought this monster banish'd from your train :
But you would raise him to support your throne,
And now he claims your empire as his own ;
Or tell me, tyrants, have you both agreed
That where one reigns the other shall succeed ?»

The mind pauses on this mysterious story, with an anxious wish to ascertain its secret causes : and, though time and death have destroyed the perfect clew to the labyrinth, a few speculations may be hazarded from the facts, so far as they are ascertained. The reasons alleged by Swift himself for the extraordinary conditions which he attached to his marriage seem merely ostensible; at least

[1] I say *said* to have composed, because there is room to suppose Stella received assistance (from Delany probably) both in these, and the much more beautiful verses addressed to Swift on his birth-day.

they are such as never influenced any reasonable being in the same situation; for they resolve into a desire to conceal from the world his having had the weakness to break two private resolutions concerning matrimony, of which resolutions the world could know nothing. Terror for the effects the news of his marriage might produce on the irritable feelings of Vanessa, and a consciousness that his long concealment of the circumstances which led to it placed his conduct towards her in a culpable point of view, must be allowed as one chief motive for the secrecy enjoined upon Stella. This dread would be increased to anguish, if we suppose that he married Mrs Johnson to satisfy his own honour, and her conscience, while his heart was secretly devoted to her rival. But had such been the only cause of his distress of mind, and of the injunctions of secrecy laid upon Stella, that secrecy would have ceased to be necessary after Vanessa was no more. A struggle there might have been between his pride and his affection; but it seems reasonable to suppose that the latter would have been victor, where the former had so little to support it. There remains a conjecture which can only be intimated, but which, if correct, will explain much of Swift's peculiar conduct in his intercourse with the female sex. During that period of life when the passions are most violent, Swift boasts of his « cold temper. » Since that time, the continual recurrence of a distressing vertigo was gradually undermining his health. It seems, in these circumstances, probable, that the continence which he observed may have been owing to physical, as well as moral causes. Were such the case, he might seek the society of Vanessa, without the apprehension of exciting passions, to which he was himself insensible; and his separation from Stella, after marriage, might be a matter equally of choice or of necessity. This much, at least, is certain, that if, according to a saying which Swift highly approved, desire produces love in man, we cannot find any one line in Swift's writings or correspondence, intimating his having felt such a source of passion;[1] nor indeed is there a single anecdote of his life recorded, which indicates his having submitted to what he irreverently terms « that ridiculous passion which has no being but in play-books or romances. » In his youth he sought female society merely as a relaxation from unpleasant thoughts, and from Stella and Vanessa he seems, at a later

[1] The sense of decency, which uniformly gave way before the slightest temptation to exercise his wit, would scarce have restrained him from expressing voluptuous, as well as disgusting ideas; and that he has nowhere done so, but uniformly expatiated on those of an opposite tendency, is perhaps the strongest confirmation of the conjecture expressed in the text.

period, to have required no other proof of affection than the pleasures of intimate friendship, enlivened by female wit, and softened by female sensibility. The qualities for which he extols both his celebrated favourites are uniformly mental, and not only so, but such as are rather of a masculine character, as courage, frankness, constancy, and sincerity; rather than delicacy, sensibility, and ardour of affection. In short, he praises in his female friends those attributes chiefly which are most frequently met with in the other sex, and appears embarrassed, rather than gratified, by the superior ardour of passion with which his temperate predilection was returned. He has himself characterized his affection for Vanessa as void of passion:

> His conduct might have made him styled
> A father, and the nymph his child.
> That innocent delight he took,
> To see the virgin mind her book,
> Was but the master's secret joy
> In school to hear the finest boy.»

And Stella he has thus addressed:

> « Thou, Stella, wert no longer young,
> When first for thee my harp I strung;
> Without one word of Cupid's darts,
> Of killing eyes, or bleeding hearts:
> With friendship and esteem possest,
> I ne'er admitted love a guest.»

[1] From the following lines a different inference might

If such was the goal of his expectations and hopes, he may have considered his regard for Vanessa as no breach of his faith to Stella, until taught by the unrestrained declaration of the former, as well as by their mutual rivalry, that the coldness of his own temper had prevented him from estimating tne force of passion in those who became his victims.[1]

After his marriage with Stella, Swift seems

be drawn. But although signed with the initials of the celebrated Drapier, I do not believe they came from his pen.

INSCRIBED IN STELLA'S PRAYER-BOOK.

When, dearest maid! with heavenly zeal possest,
In thy fair hand these pious leaves are prest;
While thy soft eyes devotion's glances wear,
And thy dear lips repeat the affecting prayer;
Would'st thou Heaven's pity to thy suit incline,
Oh! by its pity learn, and answer mine.

M. B.

From the Gentleman's Magazine, for March 1738.

[1] It must not be suppressed, that Mr Monck Berkeley mentions, with some hesitation, a report, which, if true, would totally destroy the hypothesis in the text, although supported by the opinion of Sheridan. Richard Brennan, the servant in whose arms Swift breathed his last, informed Mr Berkeley, that, when he was at school, there was a boy boarded there, who was commonly reported to be the Dean's son, by Mrs Johnson. He added, that the boy dined at the Deanery on Sundays, and was permitted to amuse himself in the Deanery yard, and that he died soon after Mrs Johnson. Admitting there may have been such a boy, and that he met with kindness from the Dean, the inference is only that drawn by a witness from

to have redoubled his anxiety to moderate the passion of Vanessa into friendship, or to give it, if possible, a new direction. The secret husband of another, he could not but be conscious how ill it became him to remain the object of such ardent affection. He introduced to her notice Dean Winter, a gentleman of character and fortune, as a candidate for her hand; but she rejected the proposal in the most peremptory manner. She was also unsuccessfully addressed by Dr Price, afterwards archbishop of Cashell. At length, about the year 1771, she retired from Dublin to her house and property near Celbridge, to nurse her hopeless passion in seclusion from the world. Swift seems to have foreseen and warned her against the consequences of this step. His letters uniformly exhort her to seek general

the lowest and most prejudiced of the common people, and is totally opposite to all which is recorded of Swift and Stella, by the numerous intelligent, and doubtless inquisitive persons by whom they were surrounded. In one of the letters to Mr Tickell, which are now for the first time published, Swift himself bears a curious testimony to the distance which was maintained between him and Stella. It is dated 7th July, 1726, ten years after their marriage: « I wonder how you could expect to see her in a morning, which I, her oldest acquaintance, have not done these dozen years, except once or twice in a journey. » To other improbabilities may be added, that so proud a man as Swift should provide no otherwise for his only child, than to board him in a school where so mean a person as Richard Brennan was a scholar.

society, to take exercise, and to divert, as much as possible, the current of her thoughts from the unfortunate subject which was preying upon her spirits. He even exhorts her to leave Ireland. But these admonitions are mingled with expressions of tenderness, greatly too warm not to come from the heart, and too strong to be designed merely to soothe the unfortnnate recluse. Until the year 1720, he never appears to have visited her at Celbridge: they only met when she was occasionally in Dublin. But in that year, and down to the time of her death, Swift came repeatedly to Celbridge; and, from the information of a most obliging correspondent, I am enabled to give an account of some minute particulars attending them.

Marley Abbey, near Celbridge, where Miss Vanhomrigh resided, is built much in the form of a real cloister, especially in its external appearance. An aged man (upwards of ninety by his own account) showed the grounds to my correspondent. He was the son of Mrs Vanhomrigh's gardener, and used to work with his father in the garden when a boy. He remembered the unfortunate Vanessa well, and his account of her corresponded with the usual description of her person, especially as to her *embonpoint*. He said she went seldom abroad, and saw little company: her constant amusement was reading, or walking in the garden. Yet, according to this authority, her society was courted by several families in the neighbbourhood. who visited her, notwithstanding her seldom returning that attention; and he added, that her manners interested every one who knew her. But she avoided company, and was always melancholy, save when Dean Swift was there, and then she seemed happy. The garden was to an uncommon degree crowded with laurels. The old man said that when Miss Vanhomrigh expected the Dean, she always planted, with her own hand, a laurel or two against his arrival. He showed her favourite seat, still called Vanessa's Bower. Three or four trees, and some laurels, indicate the spot. They had formerly, according to the old man's information, been trained into a close arbour. There were two seats and a rude table within the bower, the opening of which commanded a view of the Liffey, which had a romantic effect; and there was a small cascade that murmured at some distance. In this sequestered spot, according to the old gardener's account, the Dean and Vanessa used often to sit, with books and writing-materials on the table before them. And the verses composed among such objects, by that unfortunate lady, will perhaps help us to guess at the subject of their classical interviews.

AN ODE TO SPRING.

Hail, blushing goddess, beauteous Spring,
Who in thy jocund train dost bring
Loves and graces, smiling hours,
Balmy breezes, fragrant flowers,
Come, with tints of roseate hue,
Nature's faded charms renew.
Yet why should I thy presence hail?
To me no more the breathing gale
Comes fraught with sweets, no more the rose
With such transcendent beauty blows,
As when Cadenus bless'd the scene,
And shared with me those joys serene.
When, unperceived, the lambent fire
Of friendship kindled new desire;
Still listening to his tuneful tongue,
The truths which angels might have sung,
Divine impress'd their gentle sway,
And sweetly stole my soul away.
My guide, instructor, lover, friend,
(Dear names!) in one idea blend;
O! still conjoin'd, your incense rise,
And waft sweet odours to the skies.

AN ODE TO WISDOM.

O Pallas! I invoke thy aid!
Vouchsafe to hear a wretched maid,
By tender love deprest;
'T is just that thou should'st heal the smart
Inflicted by thy subtle art,
And calm my troubled breast.

No random shot from Cupid's bow,
But by thy guidance, soft and slow,
It sunk within my heart;

Thus, Love being arm'd with Wisdom's force,
In vain I try to stop its course,
In vain repel the dart.

O Goddess! break the fatal league,
Let Love, with Folly and Intrigue,
More fit associates find!
And thou alone, within my breast,
O! deign to soothe my griefs to rest,
And heal my tortured mind.

Vanessa, besides musing over her unhappy attachment, had, during her residence in this solitude, the care of nursing the declining health of her younger sister, who at length died about 1720. This event, as it left her alone in the world, seems to have increased the energy of her fatal passion for Swift, while he, on the contrary, saw room for still greater reserve, when her situation became that of a solitary female, without the society or countenance of a female relation. But Miss Vanhomrigh, irritated at the situation in which she found herself, determined on bringing to a crisis those expectations of an union with the object of her affections, to the hope of which she had clung amid every vicissitude of his conduct towards her. The most probable bar was his undefined connexion with Mrs Johnson, which, as it must have been perfectly known to her, had, doubtless, long excited her secret jealousy: although only a single hint to that purpose is to be found in their correspondence, and that so early as 1713, when she writes to him, then in Ireland, « If you are very happy, it is ill-natured of you not to tell me so, *except 'tis what is inconsistent with mine.* Her silence and patience under this state of uncertainty, for no less than eight years, must have been partly owing to her awe for Swift, and partly perhaps to the weak state of her rival's health, which, from year to year, seemed to announce speedy dissolution.. At length, however, Vanessa's impatience prevailed, and she ventured on the decisive step of writing to Mrs Johnson herself, requesting to know the nature of that connexion. Stella, in reply, informed her of her marriage with the Dean; and, full of the highest resentment against Swift for having given another female such a right in him as Miss Vanhomrigh's inquiries implied, she sent to him her rival's letter of interrogation, and, without seeing him, or awaiting his reply, retired to the house of Mr Ford, near Dublin. Every reader knows the consequence. Swift, in one of those paroxysms of fury to which he was liable, both from temper and disease, rode instantly to Marley Abbey. As he entered the apartment, the sternness of his countenance, which was peculiarly formed to express the fiercer passions, struck the unfortunate Vanessa with such terror, that she could scarce ask whether he would not sit down. He answered by flinging a letter on the table, and, instantly leaving the house, mounted his horse and returned to Dublin. When Vanessa opened the packet, she only found her own letter to Stella. It was her death-warrant. She sunk at once under the disappointment of the delayed, yet cherished hopes, which had so long sickened her heart, and beneath the unrestrained wrath of him for whose sake she had indulged them. How long she survived the last interview is uncertain, but the time does not seem to have exceeded a few weeks. In the mean while, she revoked a will made in favour of Swift, and settled her fortune, which was considerable, upon Mr Marshal, afterwards one of the judges of the Court of Common Pleas in Ireland, and Dr Berkeley, the celebrated philosopher, afterwards Bishop of Cloyne.[1] A remarkable condition is said to have accompanied her bequest: that her executors, namely, should make public all the letters which had passed between the testator and Swift, as well as the celebrated poem of Cadenus and Vanessa. It is said that Berkeley, from friendship to Swift, and Marshal,

[1] Dr Berkeley had been known to the Vanhomrigh family in London, by the introduction of Swift, but had not seen Miss Esther Vanhomrigh since she came to Ireland. Her succession amounted to about eight thousand pounds.

influenced by Berkeley's opinion, or perhaps dreading to bring on himself the displeasure of the satirist, resolved to disobey this injunction; and every biographer of Swift has hitherto recorded either the apology or censure of Vanessa's executors. But the truth is, that Miss Vanhomrigh's will contains no such injunction, so that, if it at all existed, it must have been delivered in a manner and at a time when Berkeley, honourable and virtuous as he was, felt himself entitled to dispense with obeying it. He probably thought, that giving publicity to the romantic expressions of Vanessa's passion, could only gratify idle or malignant curiosity, exasperate the sufferings of Swift, which were already beyond endurance, and perhaps expose to evil construction the reputation of his benefactress. Such might be the reasoning of Berkeley, supposing that Vanessa really enjoined this extraordinary posthumous revenge. But as the report, however uniform, is certainly inaccurate in ascribing a place to such a condition in Vanessa's will, it may be well doubted whether it is better founded in the general point of its existence.

Bishop Berkeley is said to have destroyed the original letters of this celebrated correspondence. But a full copy remained in possession of Judge Marshal, and, after his death, some mutilated extracts found their way to the public. By the friendship of Mr Berwick, the editor is enabled to fill up this curious desideratum in Swift's correspondence, which gives him the more pleasure, as any sinister interpretation of the former imperfect extracts, which, as was natural, were taken from those passages that expressed most warmth of passion, will be in a great measure confuted by the entire publication. The tone of feeling is lowered by the context, and those passages which, taken by themselves, might appear suspicious, especially while what was suppressed was left to imagination, are much modified, when restored to their place among grave maxims of advice, and trifling passages of humour. At any rate, all from which any inference, favourable or unfavourable, can be deduced, is now at length before the public. There are no fragments produced, from which suspicions may be excited, and no blanks remain to be filled up by the suggestions of detraction. If the correspondence proves less interesting than the reader might have expected, the admirers of Swift will be gratified with the confutation which the letters afford of the evil reports first propagated by Lord Orrery.

The sum of the evidence which they afford seems to amount to this,—that, while residing in England for years, and at a distance from Stella, Swift incautiously engaged in a correspondence with Miss Vanhomrigh, which probably at first meant little more than mere gallantry, since the mother, brother, and sister, seem all to have been confidants of their intimacy. After his journey to Ireland, his letters assume a graver cast, and consist rather of advice, caution, and rebuke, than expressions of tenderness. Yet neither his own heart, nor the nature of Vanessa's violent attachment, permit him to suppress strong, though occasional and rare indications of the high regard in which he held her, although honour, friendship, and esteem, had united his fate with that of another. It would perhaps have been better, had theiramours never become public; as that has, however, happened, it is the biographer's duty to throw such light upon them, as Mr Berwick's friendship has enabled him to do; in order that Swift's conduct, weak and blameable as it must be held in this instance, may at least not suffer hereafter, from being seen under false or imperfect lights.

Although the letters were suppressed, Cadenus and Vanessa was given to the world soon after Miss Vanhomrigh's death. In this extraordinary poem, it seems to have been the intention of the author to soothe the passion which the unfortunate Miss Vanhomrigh was unable to subdue. One passage in it has given rise to inferences yet more fatal to

Swift's character than can be deduced from the preceding narrative, or the perusal of the correspondence between the lovers. It begins with the well-known lines,—

> But what success Vanessa met,
> Is to the world a secret yet, etc.

To what purpose these lines were introduced, whether from Swift's usual vein of humour, which never could resist a jest, or whether they were meant jocularly to intimate the danger attending the intimacy between Cadenus and Vanessa, it were in vain to inquire. But to brand Swift as a seducer, and Miss Van homrigh as his victim, on account of a single passage, not only detached, but, if interpreted in so sinister a manner, at variance with all the rest of the poem, requires the cold-blooded ingenuity of Lord Orrery. Every other line of the poem ascribes to Vanessa a passion which had virtue for its foundation and object; and a similar picture is exhibited in the following lines, addressed by Swift to Vanessa, long after the date of his celebrated poem:—

> Nymph, would you learn the only art
> To keep a worthy lover's heart:
> First, to adorn your person well,
> In utmost cleanliness excel:
> And though you must the fashions take,
> Observe them but for fashion's sake;
> The strongest reason will submit
> To virtue, honour, sense, and wit:

To such a nymph, the wise and good
Cannot be faithless, if they would;
For vices all have different ends,
But virtue still to virtue tends:
And when your lover is not true,
'T is virtue fails in him or you.
And either he deserves disdain,
Or you without a cause complain.
But here Vanessa cannot err,
Nor are these rules applied to her,
For who could such a nymph forsake,
Except a blockhead or a rake?
Or how could she her heart bestow,
Except where wit and virtue grow?

The letters of Miss Vanhomrigh preserve the same tone, and plead, in extenuation of her uncontrollable affection, the high moral character of its object. The reproaches, too, which they occasionally contain, are uniformly of coldness, not of desertion; nor do her expostulations, like those of a forsaken paramour, upbraid her lover with the wreck of her fame and virtue, in the tone of Virgil's deserted heroine:—

——————— Te propter eundem,
Extinctus pudor et quâ solâ sidera adibam,
Fama prior———————

On the contrary, Swift, under Vanessa's pen, remains a matchless model of virtue, just and perfect in every thing, but in want of tenderness: the picture, in short, usually drawn by a male lover of his relentless mistress. It is the language of the most romantic attachment, but without the least tincture of criminal desire. Nay, in allusion, doubtless, to her rash declaration, she seems to take to herself, as the cause of their distress, those reproaches, which she was sensible she had no cause to impute to the perfidy of her lover. « Oh,» she exclaims, « how have you forgot me! You endeavour by severities to force me from you, nor can I blame you; for, with the utmost distress and confusion, I behold myself the cause of uneasy reflections to you. Yet I cannot comfort you, but here declare, that 'tis not in the power of time or accident to lessen the inexpressible passion which I have for.———» This remarkable and decisive passage proves, that it was the unrequited passion of Vanessa, not the perfidy of Cadenus, which was the origin of their mutual misery; for she states Swift's unhappiness as arising from her love, and declares herself at the same time incapable of abating her affection. Enough of blame will remain with Swift, if we allow that he cherished, with indecisive yet flattering hope, a passion which, in justice to himself and Vanessa, he ought, at whatever risk to her feelings and his own, to have repressed as soon as she declared it. The want of firmness which this conduct required made every hour of indecision an act of real cruelty, though under the mask of mercy, and while it trained his victim towards the untimely grave which it prepared, ruined at the same time his own peace of mind.

' It is singular that another female appears to have been inspired with a violent passion for Swift's person, in consequence of admiring his talents. The following « distracted scroll,» as the writer well terms it, is literally copied from the anonymous original among Dr Smith's papers.

FROM SACHARISA TO ——

Thursday Morning, Four o'clock.

If I was not thoroughly convinced that the author of this distracted scroll will for ever be sunk in oblivion, I would choose death in any shape, before I would reveal the continual anguish I have suffered, even before I saw your godlike form; for, believe me, my passion first got birth by perusing your inimitable writings.

If women were allowed to speak their thoughts, I would glory in my choice, and spread your fame (if possible) farther than these narrow limits of the earth.

'Tis my misfortune to be in the care of persons who generally keep youth under such restraint as won't permit them to publish their passion, though never so violent, and such I must confess mine for you to be. Could you conceive the many pangs, the many different pangs I feel, I flatter myself you would lighten the insupportable burthen of my love, by generously bearing a part. When I consider to whom I speak, that 'tis to the divine, immortal Swift, I am confounded at my vanity; but, alas! the malignity of my disorder is so great, that my love soon gets the better of the regard and homage I render even to his name; but certain it is, if you don't flatter this absurd but sincere passion of mine, I must expect death as the just reward of my presumption; and be assured if it were any but yourself,

Upon the death of Miss Vanhomrigh, Swift, in an agony of self-reproach and remorse, retreated into the south of Ireland, where he spent two months, without the place of his abode being known to any one. When he returned to Dublin, Stella was easily persuaded to forgive him, judging, probably, that the anguish he had sustained was a sufficient expiation for an offence which was now irremediable. We turn with pleasure from this painful but necessary detail, to trace Swift's occupation from the time of his settlement in Ireland, in 1714-15, till his first appearance as an Irish patriot, in 1723.

The business of the cathedral employed, doubtless, a considerable part of his leisure, embroiled as it was for some time by the resistance of his chapter, and the unfriendly interference of Archbishop King. But prejudices against the Dean wore off, as the rectitude of his intentions, and his disinterested zeal for the rights and welfare of the church, be-

I would cheerfully suffer that, before I would have my passion returned with disdain, and as I expect no other from you, beg you'll publish it in Faulkner's Journal, under what fictitious name you please; for, if I have the least understanding, I shall distinguish your writings (under ever so many disadvantages) from any other: (inscribe it to Sacharisa) you may easily imagine with what impatience I shall expect Friday; I can't add how much I am yours till the arrival of my doom.

SACHARISA.

came more and more evident. He soon obtained such authority in his chapter, that what he proposed was seldom disputed; after which, the business of leases and renewals, consulting old records, and compiling new ones, could not occupy any great portion of his time. There is every reason to believe that, during these five or six years, Swift dedicated many hours to study. Herodotus, Philostratus, and Aulus Gellius, seem particularly to have engaged his attention, as he has written his opinion concerning each of them in the blank leaves of the volume.[1] While such were his

[1] See his character of Herodotus, dated 6th July, 1720. From a Paris edit. of Philostratus, 1608, Mr Theophilus Swift copied the following note from the Dean's autograph. « In hoc libro, nugis, portentis, ac mendaciis undique scatente, non pauca sparsim inveniet lector, nec illepida nec inutilia : quæ autem mihi maxime arriserunt, ea punctulis quibusdam ad marginem appositis annotavi. Nov. 8, 1715. Jon. Swift. » The passages marked are but few.

The Dean's copy of Aulus Gellius, edited by Gronovius, An. 1706, was in the possession of the late Mr Theophilus Swift, and is now in that of E. L. Swift, Esquire. It bears the following inscription, in the hand-writing of Erasmus Lewis. « Beneficium dando accepit qui Digno dedit. E. L. » To which the Dean subjoins, « Donum Amici, de me optime meriti, Erasm. Lewis. April 10, 1712. » On a blank leaf occurs the following character of the work, given, as it appears, upon a second perusal.

« Post longum temporis intervallum, secundâ vice per-studies, we cannot suppose that the more pleasing paths of classical learning were neglected, even if we had not learned that the study of Lucretius was a favourite amusement during his residence at Gauls-town. But a list of books in his library, marked with his own manuscript remarks, affords the most authentic record of his taste in reading.[1]

legi hunc librum; et certè, mediante Fortuna, consultum optimè videtur autoris famæ, quod excerptis abundat e libris jamdiu deperditis, et quod lingua Latina apud annos M. manet in pretio. Supponamus enim hodiernum aliquem Scriptorem, Gallicum puta, Italicum vel Anglicanum, centones undique corrasos vernaculè scriptos in volumen congessisse, et critica quædam adjutasse in nonnulla vocabula cujusque linguæ; certè nil concipi possit futilius aut ineptius: opus igitur aliquanti æstimo, autorem nihili.»

«Quod ad commentatorem Gronovium attinet, magni nominis (ut dicitur) in hujusce generis eruditione: cave temerè speres ab eo lucem in difficultatibus enodandis; totum enim tempus insumit vel variantes lectiones confundendo, vel lectorem ad alios autores referendo; vel denique Oisellium quendam conviitiis insectando.

J. Swift.

«Nov. 1, 1719.»

[1] This list is extracted from

«A Catalogue of Books, the Library of the late Rev. Dr Swift, Dean of St Patrick's, Dublin. To be sold by auction. The time and place for the sale of them will be inserted in the Dublin Journal.—N. B. The books marked thus have remarks and observations on them in

These studies, however, were unequal to occupy the spare time which Dublin gave to

the hand of Dr Swift. Dublin, printed for George Faulkner, in Essex-street, 1745, 8vo.»

OCTAVO ET INFRA.

3 Mémoires de la Minorité de Louis XIV. Villefranche, 1690.

24 Virgilii Poëmata, cum Scholiis H. Stephani. Cura Pau. Steph. 1599.

25 Boetii Consolationes Philosophiæ, cum notis Vallini. Lugd. Bat. 1656.

26 Vidæ Poemata. Oxon. 1701.

18 Justini Historia, cum emendationibus Jan. Fabri. Salmur, 1671.

33 Valerii Maximi Dicta et Facta memorabilia, cum notis Lipsii. Amsterdam, 1647.

42 Rabelais, ses Œuvres. Lyon, 1558.

43 Eutropius et Paulus Diaconus de Gestis Romanis, cum annot. Eliæ Veneti. Paris, 1564.

46 Taciti Opera. Amsterdam, 1649.

65 Bernier, ses Voyages. Amsterdam, 1699, 2 tomes.

FOLIO.

78 Platonis Opera, Gr. Lat. cum comment. Jo. Serrani. Cura Hen. Stephani, 1578, 3 vol.

81 Xenophontis Opera, Gr. Lat. cum notis; Studio Leunclavii et Porti. Paris, 1625.

83 Philostrati Lemnii Opera, Gr. L. studio Fed. Morelli. Paris, 1608.

91 Strabonis Geographia, Gr. Lat. studio Casauboni et Xylandri. Paris, 1620.

92 Herodoti Historia, Gr. Lat. studio Vallæ et Sylburgii. Cura Pauli Stephani, 1618.

94 Suidas Lexicon. Gr. Lat. studio Æm. Porti. Col. All. 1619, 2 vol.

95 Dionis Cassii Romana Historia, Gr. L. studio Xylandri. Cura Hen. Steph.

Swift after his constant labour in the politics of London. It has been generally thought,

105 Historiæ Augustæ Scriptores sex, cum notis, studio Claud. Salmasii. Paris, 1620.

OCTAVO ET INFRA.

111 Satyre Menippée de la Vertu du Catholicon d'Espagne. 1621.

115 Jollyvet, ses Poésies Chrétiennes. Utrecht, 1700.

132 Boileau, ses Œuvres. Amsterdam, 1697, 2 vol.

QUARTO.

202 Hobbes Opera Philosophica. Amst. 1668, 2 vol.

216 Auli Gellii Noctes Atticæ, cum notis; studio Frederici et Gronovii. Lugd. Bat. 1706.

223 Antiquæ Musicæ Auctores, Gr. Lat. cum notis. Meibomi. Elzev. Amst. 1652, 1 et 2 vol.

228 Anthologia, Epigrammata Græcorum. Cura Hen. Stephan. 1566.

FOLIO.

238 Earl of Clarendon, his History of the Grand Rebellion. Oxford, 1707, 3 vol. large paper.

255 Hobbes, his Leviathan, or Matter and Form of a Commonwealth. London, 1651.

OCTAVO ET INFRA.

276 Child, his Discourse on Trade. London, 1693,

302 Marvel, the Rehearsal transposed. Lond. 1672.

309 La Bruyère, Les Caractères ou les Mœurs du Siècle, avec la Clef, Tome I. et II. et Ouvrage dans le goût de Théophraste et de Pascal. Amst. 1697.

QUARTO.

336 Horatii Opera, ad fidem optimorum exemplarium. Cantab. 1699.

337 Virgilii Opera, ad fidem optim. exemp. *Ib.* 1701.

338 Terentii Comœdiæ, ad fidem optim. exemp. *Ib.* 1701.

340 Doctor Gibbs's Translation of the Psalms, with Dr Swift's jests upon it. Lond. 1701.

and with great probability, that the outline of Gulliver's travels was drawn during this

FOLIO.

361 Procopii Arcana Historia, Gr. Lat. cum notis, studio Alemanni. Lugd. Bat. 1623.

363 Nieuhovii Legatio Batavica ad Magnum Tartariæ Chamum, Latine, per Geo. Hornium. Amstelod. 1668.

364 Nostradamus's true Prophecies, commented by Theoph. Garencieres. London, 1672.

365 Philip. de Comines, his History, translated by Tho. Danett. *Ib.* 1614.

366 Herbert, *Edw. Lord,* Life of King Henry VIII. *Ib.* 1649.

367 Polybii Opera, Gr. Lat. cum comment. studio Casauboni. Et Æneas de Obsidione toleranda, Gr. Lat. studio ejusdem. Paris, 1609.

369 Epiphani Episcopi Constant. Opus contra Hæreses. Basil. 1545.

374 Machiavel's Works. London, 1695.

375 Burnet, *Thomas,* his Theory of the Earth. *Ibid.* 1697.

377 Lawd's Relation of his Conference with Fisher. *Ib.* 1639.

378 Herbert, *Thomas,* his Travels *Ibid.* 1634.

381 Harrington's Commonwealth of Oceana. *Ibid.* 1656.

382 Meursii Historia Danica et Belgica. Amst. 1638.

383 Helvici Theatrum Histor. et Chronologicum. Oxon. 1651.

384 Livii Historia Romana, cum annot. variorum. Paris, 1625.

385 Isocratis Opera, Gr. Lat. cum annot. studio Hier. Wolfii. Basil. 1570.

OCTAVO ET INFRA.

419 Doloman's Conference about the next Succession. Lond. 1681.

period. There are many circumstances which favour this opinion. The germ of this cele-

420 Proceedings of the House of Commons, in impeaching the Earl of Clarendon. 1700.

431 Hale, *Sir Matthew*, History of the Common Law of England. Savoy, 1713.

447 Cotton's Virgil s Travestie. Dublin, 1728.

449 Tasso s Recovery of Jerusalem, by Fairfax. Dublin, 1726.

465 Garth's Dispensary. London, 1699.

482 Miscellanies in Prose and Verse, by Dr Swift and Mr Pope. Lond. 1727, 4 vol.

486 Dr Swift s Works. Dublin, 1734, etc. 6 vol.

492 Dr Swift's Gulliver's Travels. London, 1726, 2 vol. large paper.

QUARTO.

507 Speeches in the Parliament met 3d Nov. 1640. Lond. 1641.

513 Select Epistles of Horace, translated, imperfect.

514 L'Estrange's Dissenters' Sayings, and other Pamphlets. Lond. 1681, etc.

519 Pope's Works. Vol. II. containing his Epistles and the Dunciad. *Ib.* 1735.

FOLIO.

591 Bodin, ses six Livres de la République. Paris, 1579.

594 Davila's History of the Civil Wars of France. London, 1647.

599 Thuani Historia sui Temporis, cum continuatione. Aurel. 1628, 4 vol.

606 Baronii Annales Ecclesiastici. Antwerp. 1629, 12 vol.

627 Baconi, Fran. Opera omnia. Lond. 1630.

628 Stobæi Sententiæ. Gr. Lat. studio Gesneri. Basil. 1549.

632 Morery's Historical, Geographical, and Poetical Dictionary improved. London, 1694, 8vo.

brated work is to be found in the travels of Martinus Scriblerus, which was sketched probably before danger and proscription had dispersed the literary club. The exasperated spirit with which the Dean viewed public affairs in Great Britain, after the death of Queen Anne, coincides with many of the satirical touches of the Travels. Besides, a letter from Vanessa contains an allusion to the adventure of Gulliver with the Ape in Brobdignag, and from the same correspondence we learn, that Swift was, in 1722, engaged with the perusal of voyages and travels, studies congenial to the composition of the Travels. He told Mrs Whiteway, what he afterwards in substance told the world in person of the captain, that he had borrowed the sea-terms in Gulliver from the old voyages, which he had fully perused. All which circumstances favour the opinion, that the Voyages of Gulliver were sketched during the period of which we treat, though, in the state in which they were published, they bear reference to politics of a later date.

Swift's lighter literary amusements were such as arose from his habits of society. These habits appear to have been very regular. He

634 Letters of Sir William Temple, while he was ambassador abroad, from 1665 to 1671 inclusive, MS.

OCTAVO.

543 Ludlow's Memoirs, Vol. III. Switzerland, 1699.

boarded himself for the sake of economy with Mr Worral, whose wife preserved that neatness and good order which was particularly agreeable to him. But he kept two public days at the Deanery weekly. We can see that, according to the manner of the times, and the practice of his predecessor, Dean Sterne, Swift's entertainments were accounted rather economical, although his guests, so far as conviviality was consistent with decorum, were welcomed with excellent wine. Swift, who used to declare he was never intoxicated in his life, had nevertheless lived intimately with those at whose tables wine was liberally consumed, and he was not himself averse to the moderate use of it.[1] In some respects, however, his mode of life ill-suited the poorer clergy, who expected more frequent hospitality at the Deanery, and their disappointment exposed Swift to some obloquy. His best defence is, that he received his preferment on such terms as involved him considerably in debt, and that his parsimony never interfered with the calls of justice, or of benevolence. During all his life, there was a struggle between the rigour of his habitual economy, and his sense of justice, which led sometimes to instances of very ridiculous accuracy, in adjusting his conduct,

[1] Dr King says Swift drank about a pint (English measure) of claret after dinner, which the Doctor, him self very abstemious, considered as too much.

so as to compound matters between them The story of his giving Pope and Gay, after a narrow calculation of what a supper would have cost him, half-a-crown a-piece for the expense which they had spared him in coming after they had supped, is an excellent example.[1]

The anecdote is given by Spence, in the words of Pope. « Doctor Swift has an odd, blunt way, that is mistaken by strangers for ill nature—'Tis so odd that there is no describing it but by facts. I'll tell you one that first comes into my head One evening Gay and I went to see him: you know how intimately we were all acquainted. On our coming in, 'Heyday, gentlemen (says the Doctor), what 's the meaning of this visit! How came you to leave all the great lords that you are so fond of, to come hither to see a poor Dean?'—'Because we would rather see you than any of them.'—'Ay, any one that did not know so well as I do, might believe you. But, since you are come, I must get some supper for you, I suppose.'—'No, Doctor, we have supped already.'—'Supped already, that 's impossible! why, it is not eight o'clock yet —That 's very strange! but if you had not supped, I must have got something for you.—Let me see, what should I have had? a couple of lobsters; ay, that would have done very well; two shillings—tarts a shilling: but you will drink a glass of wine with me, though you supped so much before your usual time only to spare my pocket.'—'No, we had rather talk with you than drink with you.'—'But if you had supped with me, as in all reason you ought to have done, you must then have drank with me.—A bottle of wine, two shillings,—two and two is four, and one is five; just two and sixpence a-piece. There, Pope, there 's half-a-crown for you, and there s another for you, sir; for I won't save anything by you, I am determined.'—This was all said and done with his usual seriousness on such occasions; and,

Delany informs us, in like manner, that when Lady Eustace, or other women of rank, dined at the Deanery, Swift allowed them a shilling a-head to provide their own entertainment, and used to struggle hard that only sixpence should be allowed for the brat, as he called Miss Eustace, afterwards Mrs Tickell. And when he dined with his poorer friends, he insisted upon paying his club, as at a tavern, or house of public entertainment.[1] The social party who assembled round him at the Deanery were naturally led to exert themselves for his amusement, and the verses of Sheridan, Delany, and other literary friends, provoked his own replies, and lightened his more severe studies. In this contest of ingenuity, Sheridan seems to have been both witty himself, and the cause of wit in others. His simplicity and characteristic absence of mind were tempered with so much humour and readiness of repartee, that his company was invaluable to the Dean, and their friendship was never interrupted until the increasing irascibility and violence of Swift overcame the patience, and offended the honest pride of his respectful

in spite of every thing we could say to the contrary, he actually obliged us to take the money."

[1] There is a most excellent letter, in which the Dean introduces himself in the third person, as a stranger, to the hospitality of the Rev. Mr Blachford, and settles with great minuteness the allowance with which he proposes to compensate the expense of his reception.

friend. Delany was a character of a different description. He had risen from a low origin by the distinction due to his learning and genius. But prouder, more cautious, or more interested than Sheridan, he kept aloof from that horseplay of raillery which passed between the latter and the Dean, and which unavoidably lowers, in a certain degree, the man whose good humour is contented to submit to it. He made court to the Dean by verses less humourous, but more elegant than those of Sheridan, and he also had his answer in the style which he used. The distinction which the Dean made between them is obvious, from his exhorting Delany to impress on Sheridan the sense of propriety and self-respect in which he thought him deficient. Yet, though the guarded caution of Delany commanded more respect, the honest and precipitate good humour of Sheridan deserved better of Dean Swift, than that the former should have been exalted over him for an example. The high opinion expressed of Delany, in the piece to which we refer,[1] was afterwards in some respects qualified, as may be seen in the next section. Stella was active too in this poetical strife. It has been doubted whether she actually finished the verses to which her name is prefixed; but if she really wrote the

[1] Verses to Mr Delany.

last verse in the epitaph on Demar the usurer, she wrote by far the best lines in the poem.

Gaulstown House, the seat of Lord Chief Baron Rochfort, where Swift sometimes resided for months at a time, gave variety to these exercitations. The Chief Baron, it would seem, was not very friendly to the existing government, so that epilogues, songs, and other vehicles of political satire, abounded at his mansion. Besides these, Swift indulged himself in an humourous poetical record on the occupations of the family and visitors, which gross and stupid malice afterwards construed into a lampoon. The author's vindication we reserve till we find him charged with a similar offence. But Dean Percival, whom he had rallied severely in the poem, was so much affected as to attempt a poetical reply, which, besides being very scarce, contains such a curious account of Swift's housekeeping and hospitality, though obviously viewed with a malignant eye, that it deserves being preserved in a note.

[1] The following lampoon is mentioned by Swift in a letter to Mr Cope, 9th of October, 1722. The provocation given to Dean Percival was a reflection upon his pedantry and his wife's housewifery. Swift says, « Dean Percival has answered the other Dean's Journal in Grub-street, justly taxing him for avarice and want of hospitality Madam Percival absolutely denies all the facts; insists that she never made candles of dripping; that Charley never had the chincough, etc.» The first part of

The Dean's correspondence also occupied a good part of his leisure. It was chiefly con-

Percival's verses allude to the housekeeping at the Deanery, while Sterne held that preferment.—

A DESCRIPTION,

IN ANSWER TO THE JOURNAL. DUBLIN, 1722.

Near St Sepulchre, stands a building
Which, as report goes, ne'er had child in:
The house is large, and to adorn her,
From garret down to chimney corner,
The upper chambers were well lined
With antique books and books new coin'd;
Which plainly shew'd its founder's head
With learning of all sorts supplied.
The house on every part was stored
To entertain the greatest lord;
Nor did the poorest meet disdain,
But fill'd his belly with his brain.
The kitchen grate, like Vesta's altar,
Had fire in 't whene'er you call'd, sir.
There were appointed vestal dames
To stir up the devouring flames.
On these were laid fat pigs and geese,
All beasts and fowls for sacrifice.
The sea itself could not escape,
For fish of all sorts here would gape
And bleed, soals, salmon, lobsters, cods,
To gratify the hungry gods;
And, to drive off the mind's dejection,
Wit flew about, but no reflection;
To keep the spirits in vibration,
Wine join'd with wit for the libation.
The Dean was small, his soul was large;
He knew his duty to discharge;
He loved his chapter, treated all
His dignitaries, vicars choral,
From Tallboy down to little Worrall.

fined to Tory friends, as his acquaintance was dropped by those of differing sentiments in

In short, he lived, and that's what few can
Justly report of Swift our new Dean.
He sometimes to a chapter goes,
With saucy strut and turn'd-up nose;
Leans on his cushion, then he'll bid ye
Hearken to what all know already.
Perhaps he'll sneer or break a jest,
But de'il a bit to break your fast.
Go when you please, let the clock strike
What hour it will, 't is all alike.
Some country Preb. comes just at one
In hopes to dine, and so begone.
The Dean appears:—« I'm glad to see you,
Pray tell what service I can do you.
Be quick, for I am going out.»
The hungry Levite's vex'd no doubt,
To be thus baulk'd; tucks up his gown,
Makes a low scrape, and so to town:
Is welcome there, so makes a shift,
To drink a glass and rail at Swift.
But of this farce you'll know the reason,
You shall, I'm sure it can't be treason.
He dines abroad you think—mistaken,
He dines at home on sprouts and bacon.
Besides, his two chief slaves are missing,
To boil his drink and broil his grisking,
Pert Jack and Robin, I mean Grattan,
As suppliant slaves as e'er had hat on;
Such slaves as these you know delight him,
Who're sure to trudge when he invites 'em;
And that's as often as in his kitchen
A fire is made to broil a pigeon.
The seventeenth of March each year,
The chapter meets to make good cheer.
The Dean's allow'd five pounds or more,
To entertain about half a score.
You re sure to meet a handsome dish,
Of salmon, or some other fish;

party matters. With such conduct, it is pleasing to contrast the generosity of Addison, who

A dish of soup, a leg of mutton,
By servants are the table put on;
A plate with puddings then next comes,
One plain, one almond, t' other plums:
The second course adorns the table,
With loin of beef most formidable;
A sallad, with a dish of fowl,
Of this huge treat makes up the whole.
Now if some critic should accost him,
And ask how much this dinner cost him,
He could not say that he had lost
Any great matter by the roast;
The treat, just as the Dean bespoke it,
Put two pound ten into his pocket,
Besides, the fragments of the feast
Will feed his house a week at least.
As for himself, with draggled gown,
Poor-curate-like he 'll trudge the town,
To eat a meal with punster base,
Or buffoon call him, if you pleas e.
Sometimes to Gaulstown he will go,
To spend a month or two, or so,
Admires the baron, George and 's spouse,
Lives well, and then lampoons the house.
Thus far our bard in doggrel rhyme,
In the Dean's kitchen, spent his time;
He s dull, because there is no fire,
Or wine, his rustic muse t' inspire.
But let s proceed from these poor tricks
O' th' kitchen to his politics.
They stare, and think he knows as well
All depths of state as Machiavel.
It must be so, since from him flows
Whate'er the Earl of Oxford knows.
He swears the project of the peace
Was laid by him in Anna's days.
The South Sea ne'er could have miscarried
As he contrived, but others marr'd it:

took this period of adyersity to renew that intimacy, which had been broken off while the Tories were triumphant. He intimated to Swift, through the Bishop of Derry, that it was his generous intention and earnest wish, that party should give way to friendship; and the Dean's answer to this overture, now first made public, was at the same time an elegant congratulation upon Addison's being made Secretary of State: « Three or four more such choices,» he said, « would gain more hearts in three weeks, than the harsher measures of government in as many years.» But the death of Addison broke off their renewed correspondence, after some kind letters had been exchanged. Swift found a valuable successor in Tickell the poet, surviving friend and literary executor of Addison. He was secretary to the Lords Justices of Ireland, an office of high trust, and he often employed the interest which it gave him in compliance

Thus he goes on two hours and more,
And tells the same thing o'er and o'er.
The darkest plots he can unravel,
And split them ope from the head to th' navel,
What dire effects o'er bandbox hover'd,
Venice preserved, the plot 's discover'd.
Venice here stands for 's great Mæcenas,
The Earl of Oxford, not Æneas.
And yet when all is done and said,
A Tale of a Tub fills up his head.
Thus having given a description
Of this great wit and politician,
I now surrender my commission.

with Swift's recommendations. The Dean does not seem to have approved or shared the resentment of his friend Pope against Mr Tickell, but maintained an intimate and friendly intercourse with him till his death.

From these studies and amusements the Dean was roused in the year 1720, and again appeared on the stage as a political writer, no longer, indeed, the advocate and apologist of a ministry, but the undaunted and energetic defender of the rights of an oppressed people. No nation ever needed more a patriotic defender than Ireland at this period. The portion of prosperity which she had enjoyed under the princes of the House of Stuart had been interrupted by a civil war, the issue of which sent the flower of her native gentry, as well as her best and bravest soldiers into foreign exile. The Catholic part of the community laboured under disqualifications of various kinds, and, above all, under a suspicion of disaffection, the most insurmountable incapacity of all. They sought their safety in remaining quiescent, well aware that every complaint originating with them would be construed into the murmurs of rebellion. The Irish Protestants, or, as Swift himself loves to term them, the English settled in Ireland[1]

[1] Nothing is more remarkable in all Swift's writings than his anxiety to draw a line between the native Irish, and the English settled in Ireland. See the Drapier's

were divided among themselves into Whigs and Tories, Churchmen and Dissenters, and an hundred lesser factions, fomented by petty political leaders, who found their interest in dissensions, which raised them into notice and consequence. England, whose councils have been sometimes too easily swayed by a narrow-souled, and short-sighted mercantile interest, availed herself of the unhappy state of the sister kingdom, to degrade her into a subdued province, instead of strengthening the empire by elevating her into an integral part. The power of legislating for Ireland was assumed by the English Parliament, though contrary to principle and precedent; and it was so exercised, as to fetter, as far as possible, the commerce of the kingdom, and render it subordinate to, and dependent upon that of England. The statutes of 10th and 11th William III. prohibited the exportation of all Irish woollen goods, excepting into England and Wales, and thus, at once, ruined the woollen manufactories of Ireland, worth upwards of an annual million, and drove the staplers into a smuggling trade with France, by which the Irish wool was exported to that

Letters, and other passages of his works. Swift, patriot as he was, was prejudiced on this subject by birth, and by his situation as a dignitary of the Protestant church. But it was also prudent to make such a distinction, to avoid the clamour against Papists and Jacobites.

country, to the great benefit of the manufactures recently established in Picardy. Ireland did not want patriots to state these grievances. Molyneux, the friend of Locke, and of liberty, published, in 1698, « The Case of Ireland's being bound by Acts of Parliament in England, stated;» in which he showed, with great force, that the right of legislation, of which England made so oppressive an use, was never justified by the plea of conquest, purchase, or precedent, and was only submitted to from incapacity of effectual resistance. The temper of the English House of Commons did not brook this remonstrance. It was unanimously voted that these bold and pernicious assertions were calculated to shake the subordination and dependence of Ireland; as united and annexed for ever to the crown of England; and the vote of the House was followed by an address to the queen, complaining that, although the woollen trade was the staple manufacture of England, over which her legislature was accustomed to watch with the utmost care, yet Ireland, which was dependent upon, and protected by England, not contented with the linen manufacture, the liberty whereof was indulged to her, presumed also to apply her credit and capital to the weaving of her own wool into woollen cloths, to the great detriment of England, etc. etc. etc. Not a voice was raised in the British House of Commons, to contradict maxims equally impolitic and tyrannical, and which were much more worthy of the monopolizing corporation of some peddling borough, than of the enlightened senate of a free people. In acting upon these commercial restrictions, wrong was heaped upon wrong, and insult was added to injury, with this advantage on the side of the aggressors, that they could intimidate the injured people of Ireland into silence, by raising, to drown every complaint, the cry of rebel and of Jacobite.

These evils Swift beheld with all the natural ardour of a disposition which rose in opposition to tyranny. «Do not,» said he to Delany, «the corruptions and villanies of men eat your flesh and exhaust your spirits?»[1] The fire, in the words of the inspired writer burned within him, and in 1720, he gave vent to his indignation in a short treatise, entitled, «A Proposal for the universal Use of Irish Manufactures, etc. utterly rejecting and renouncing every thing wearable that comes from England.» In appreciating the courage of Swift in recommending a measure so obnoxious to the principles upon which Ireland had hitherto been governed, we must remember he was

[1] Delany having replied in the negative, «Why,» answered the Dean in a fury, «how can you help it?» «Because I am commanded to the contrary,» rejoined his friend,—«fret not thyself because of the ungodly.»

himself a marked and even a proscribed man, intimately connected with the measures of that minister, whose period of power was now usually termed *the worst of times.* The system of non-importation, which he recommends as a just retort upon the engrossing spirit of English commerce, was likely to excite hatred and alarm among the powerful bodies who, from self-interest or prepossession, took an interest in the monopoly; and there were unfortunately both judges and courts of justice with whom that alarm would have fearful influence. And all these risks Swift was contented to incur, for the sake of a country to which he came as to a land of banishment; which had received him with public expressions of insult and contumely; and to which, on every occasion, he expressed a rooted aversion. He incurred them also without the possibility of any other reward than attends the conscience of a patriot who has discharged his duty.

The storm which he had dared was not long of bursting. It was intimated to Lord Chief-Justice Whitshed by « a person in great office,» that Swift's pamphlet was written for the purpose of setting the two kingdoms at variance, and it was recommended that the printer should be prosecuted with the utmost rigour. Whitshed was not a person to neglect such a hint; and the arguments of government were so successful, that the grand juries of the county and city presented the Dean's tract as a seditious, factious, and virulent libel. Waters, the printer, was seized, and forced to give great bail. But upon his trial, the jury, though some pains had been bestowed in selecting them, brought him in not guilty; and it was not until they were worn out by the threats of the lord chief-justice, who detained them eleven hours, and sent them out nine times to reconsider their verdict, that they at length, reluctantly, left the matter in his hands, by a special verdict. But the measures of Whitshed were too violent to be of real service to the government. Men's minds revolted against his iniquitous conduct, and the trial of the verdict was deferred from term to term, until the arrival of the Duke of Grafton, the lord-lieutenant. A *noli prosequi* was then granted, which left the advantage, if not the honour of victory, with Swift and the patriots of Ireland. He failed not to improve it; for, as a victorious general sends off his light troops in pursuit of a routed enemy, he persecuted Lord Chief-Justice Whitshed, and Godfrey Boate, a judge of the King's Bench, who had also distinguished himself in the trial of the printer, by such an unrelenting train of lampoons and epigrams, as at once made his satirical powers dreaded, and excited, against the offenders and their memory, the odium which their conduct had deservedly excited.

The proposal of a National Bank next alarmed the vigilance of the Dean. This scheme, however useful when the principles of commercial credit are established and understood, was made at a time when chimerical schemes of every possible kind were circulated in such abundance, as if it had been the intention of the projectors to gage the utmost extent of human credulity. Not only were public trading companies proposed for the most ridiculous and extravagant purposes, as introducing the breed of asses (which seems to have been unnecessary at that period), sweeping the streets, maintaining bastard children, etc., but one ingenious projector actually obtained subscriptions to a large extent, and some advance in ready money upon each, for a project, the object of which he declined to explain farther, than by promising a return to the adventurers of cent. per cent. At such a crisis, and when the petition to Parliament for a bank was but supported by a few obscure stock-jobbers, Swift saw it could only produce national disappointment and distress, and wrote three or four satirical essays, burlesquing the proposal itself, and ridiculing those who had subscribed to it. The Irish parliament being of the Dean's opinion, the project was rejected in the ensuing session.

The execution of one Elliston, a noted street robber, gave Swift an opportunity of exercising that remarkable versatility of composition, by which he could assume any character which he chose to personate. The effect of this piece was to put an end, for many years, to the practice of street-robbery; for, being received as genuine by the companions of the sufferer, they really believed, as there asserted, that he had left a list of their names to be proceeded against, if they did not relinquish their evil courses. Some other trifles were published by the Dean about this time, and in general the eyes of the people of Ireland began to be turned towards him, as one who was not likely to be silent in asserting her rights. But his opposition to Wood's project raised him at once to the summit of popularity, and forms one of the most remarkable points in his history.

There being a deficiency of copper coinage in Ireland, the king, in 1723, granted to William Wood, upon certain conditions, the patent right of coining halfpence and farthings to the extent of 108,000 *l.*, to be current in that kingdom. Abstractedly, there could be no objection to this mode of supplying the want of copper, providing the coinage was of proper weight and quality. But the patent had been obtained in what may be termed a surreptitious manner, through the influence of the Duchess of Kendal, the mistress of George I. to whom Wood had promised a share of the profits. It was passed without consulting either the lord-lieutenant or privy-council of Ireland; and, in devolving upon an obscure individual the right of exercising one of the highest privileges of the crown, the dignity of the kingdom was disgracefully compromised. The Irish parliament felt the insult, and caught the alarm; and the family of Broderick, then almost the chief of the Whig interest, from conviction, or from dislike to the lord-lieutenant, or from a mixture of these motives, threw their weight into the scale of opposition, and, by their countenance secured those who made it from the charge of disaffection. While the struggle was impending, the voice of Swift was heard in the celebrated Drapier's Letters,—strong in argument, and brilliant in humour, but unequalled in the address with which those arguments are selected, and that humour applied. It cannot be supposed that he really considered Wood's project, simply and abstractedly, as of a ruinous or even dangerous tendency. There was, doubtless, a risk of abuse; but, setting that apart, the supply of copper money which it provided was advantageous, and even necessary to Ireland. Nor was the hazard of Wood's misusing the patent so great, but what might easily be guarded against. The half-pence of William Wood were remarkably handsome, and well executed, and they were proved by the experiments at the Mint, under the direction of Sir Isaac Newton, to equal, or exceed, in weight, purity, and value, coins of the same denomination in England. That the coinage was exposed to be counterfeited, is an evil incidental to current money of every description; but precautions were taken that the patentee himself should not lower its value, by the nomination of a comptroller on the part of the crown, to inspect and assay from time to time the copper, whether coined or uncoined. It may be doubtful whether, in the abstract, a more economical and unexceptionable mode of supplying the acknowledged want of copper money in Ireland could have been devised by government.

But, as already hinted, the danger and dishonour of the measure lay in its application to Ireland in its existing state. Within the last thirty years, repeated and oppressive steps had been taken to reduce this ancient kingdom, though still retaining the outward insignia of national legislation and sovereignty, into the condition of a conquered province, bound by the acts of the British Parliament, where she had neither friend, patron, nor representative.[1] The aphorism that Ireland was, and ought to be, dependent on Britain in this servile sense, had not only been loudly pronounced, with a denunciation of vengeance against those who should dare to deny it, but it had been already acted upon. Ireland was subject to a commercial slavery, which left neither her credit, her commodities, nor her havens, at her own disposal; and how long the civil and domestic freedom of her people might be spared, was a question which seemed to depend on the moderation of those who usurped the right of being her legislators. Such was the condition of the kingdom when Wood's scheme was brought forward; a measure, therefore, of far less importance in its real merit, than as it necessarily involved the grand question of the servitude or independence of Ireland. That the king should, without the consent either of the Irish parliament or privy-council, delegate a branch of his prerogative to a private projector, give, as it were in a farm, to an ordinary contractor or mechanic, the exercise of a privilege, which has, in every country, been deemed a peculiar and unalienable attri-

[1] And all this in despite not only of national law and reason, but of the express maxim adopted so early as the reign of Richard III. *Hibernia habet parliamentum et faciunt leges: et nostra statuta non ligant eos quia non mittunt milites ad parliamentum.*

bute of regal power, indicated such a contempt for the very form of independence, that, where decency was so little consulted, the patriots of Ireland were justified in apprehending consequences still more fatal, and more arbitrary. The language of Wood himself, who imprudently boasted of his favour with Walpole, and threatened that his coin should be imposed upon the Irish by force, if rejected upon fair terms, was at once irritating and alarming. The formality of a vice-regal court, the supposed representative of majesty, and depositary of the executive power in Ireland, would only in future be necessary to hold levees, and give birth-day balls, while the essential exercise of the royal prerogative might be exercised in England, or leased out by wholesale to adventurers and projectors, with power to them, like the farmers-general of France, to call in military assistance where opposition required it. Thus, deprived alike of the power of making and of executing her own laws, the kingdom must have remained mocked with the semblance of a court, a parliament, and a free government; forms serving only to irritate the people with the recollection of the rights which were no longer protected or enforced. Such was the state of Ireland; and the inference which might fairly be drawn from the disrespectful and unceremonious manner in which the sovereign's right of coinage was exercised in the case of William Wood. But to have proclaimed this truth, would have been construed into a misdemeanour, little short of high treason; and Swift had in recollection the example of Molyneux, as well as his own narrow escape on the publication of his Proposal for encouraging Irish manufactures. He took his ground, therefore, with infinite address and caution, and confined himself, in opening the controversy, to the objections which applied to Wood's project in detail, cautiously veiling the grand question of national right, which was necessarily involved in the discussion.

The first three letters of M. B., Drapier in Dublin, dwell, therefore, upon arguments against Wood's halfpence, derived from their alleged inferiority in weight and value, and the indifferent or suspicious character of the projector himself. These arguments, also, had the advantage of being directly applicable to the grosser apprehensions of the «tradesmen, shopkeepers, farmers and country people,» to whom they are professedly addressed. Such persons, though incapable of understanding, or being moved by the discussion of a theoretical national right, could well comprehend, that the pouring into Ireland a quantity of copper coinage, alleged to be so base in denomination, that twelve pence were not intrinsically worth more than a penny, must necessarily drain the country of gold and silver, and occasion great individual loss, as well as national distress. The bitter and satirical passages against Wood himself were also well adapted to the taste of the vulgar, whose callous palate is peculiarly excited by the pungency of personal satire. Whether Swift himself believed the exaggerated reports which his tracts circulated concerning the baseness of the coin, and the villainy of the projector, we have no means of discovering. Once satisfied of the general justice of his cause, he may have deemed himself at liberty to plead it by such arguments as were most likely to afford it support, without rigid examination of their individual validity, or (which is most likely), like most warm disputants, he may himself have received, with eager faith, averments so necessary to the success of his plan. But it is certain that, in these first three letters, the king, the minister, the mistress, and the British privy-council, are not mentioned, or treated with studied respect; while the whole guilt and evil of the scheme are imputed to the knavery of William Wood, who, from an obscure ironmonger, had become an avaricious and unprincipled projector, ready and eager to ruin the whole kingdom of Ireland, in order to secure an exorbitant profit to himself.

The ferment produced by a statement so

open to the comprehension, and so irritating to the feelings, of the nation at large, became unspeakably formidable. Both the Irish Houses of Parliament joined in addressing the Crown against Wood's scheme. Parties of all denominations, whether religious or political, for once united in expressing their abhorrence of the detested halfpence. The tradesman to whom the coin was consigned refused to receive them, and endeavoured, by public advertisement, to remove the scandal of being concerned in the accursed traffic. Even Wood's near relatives were compelled to avert public indignation by disavowing all concern with his contract.[1] Associations were

[1] See the advertisement of John and Daniel Molyneux, ironmongers, one of whom I take to have been Wood's brother-in-law. The following is a similar disclamation now before me:

« ADVERTISEMENT.

« Whereas I, Thomas Handy, of Meath Street, Dublin, did receive by the last packet, from a person in London, to whom I am an entire stranger, bills of lading for eleven casks of Wood's halfpence, shipped at Bristol, and consigned to me by the said person on his own proper account, of which I had not the least notice until I received the said bills of lading.

« Now I, the said Thomas Handy, being highly sensible of the duty and regard which every honest man owes to his country and to his fellow-subjects, do hereby declare, that I will not be concerned, directly or indirectly, in entering, landing, importing, receiving, or uttering any of the said Wood's halfpence, for that I am fully formed for refusing their currency; and these extended from the wealthy corporation of Dublin down to the hawkers and errand-boys, who announced to their employers, that they would not receive, nor offer in change, Wood's drossy halfpence, since they could « neither get news, ale, tobacco, nor brandy, for such cursed stuff.» The matter being thus adopted by the mob, they proceeded according to their usual custom; made riotous processions, and burned the unfortunate projector in effigy. In short, such was the state of the public mind, that it was unsafe for any one to be supposed favourable to Wood's project.

Swift, finding the people in a disposition so favourable for the maintaining their rights, did not suffer their zeal to cool for lack of fuel. Not satisfied with writing, he preached against Wood's halfpence. One of his sermons is preserved, and bears the title « On doing good.» It verifies his own account, that he preached not sermons, but political pamphlets. At his instigation, also, the grand-

convinced, as well from the addresses of both houses of Parliament, as otherwise, that the importing and uttering the said halfpence will be destructive to this nation, and prejudicial to his Majesty's revenue.

« And of this my resolution I gave notice by letter to the person who sent me the bills of lading, the very day I received them, and have sent back the said bills to him.

« THO. HANDY.

« Dublin, 29th August, 1724.»

jury, and principal inhabitants of the liberty of St Patrick's, joined in an association for refusing this odious coin.[1] Besides the celebrated Drapier's Letters, he supplied the hawkers with a variety of ballads and prose satires seasoned with all the bitterness and pungency of his wit, directing the popular indignation against the contractor, without sparing some very intelligible innuendoes against his patrons and abettors in England. By such means the timid were encouraged, the doubt-

[1] "Dublin, August 20, 1724.

"This day, the grand-jury, and the rest of the inhabitants of the liberty of the Dean and Chapter of St Patrick's, attended the Dean of St Patrick's, with the following declaration, which they read to him, and desired that he would give orders to have it published.

"The Declaration of the Grand-Jury, and the rest of the inhabitants of the Liberty of the Dean and Chapter of St Patrick's, Dublin.

"We, the grand jury, and other inhabitants of the liberty of the Dean and Chapter of St Patrick's, Dublin, whose names are underwritten, do unanimously declare and determine, that we never will receive or pay any of the halfpence or farthings already coined, or that shall hereafter be coined, by one William Wood, being not obliged by law to receive the same; because we are thoroughly convinced by the addresses of both houses of Parliament, as well as by that of his Majesty's most honourable privy-council, and by the universal opinion of the whole kingdom, that the currency of the said halfpence and farthings would soon deprive us of all our gold and silver, and therefore be of the most destructive consequence to the trade and welfare of the nation.

ful confirmed, the audacious inflamed, and the attention of the public so rivetted to the discussion, that it was no longer shocked at the discussion on the more delicate questions which it involved; and the viceroy and his advisers complained, that any proposition, however libellous and treasonable, was now published without hesitation, and perused without horror, providing that Wood and his halfpence could be introduced into the tract. The Duke of Grafton (then lord-lieutenant) found himself unable to stem the popular torrent; and it became evident, that the scheme, if enforced, would occasion a civil war.

In this emergency Walpole was not wanting to himself. His first object was, if possible, to appease the general ferment, by such a composition as to the extent of the proposed issue of coin, as would leave unquestioned the assumed right to utter it. He therefore endeavoured to let the scheme drop gradually, by a proclamation which limited the issue of halfpence to 40,000*l.* instead of 108,000*l.* And when this failed, he contrived, by a bold turn of political intrigue, to impose the task of enforcing Wood's project, and subduing the discontent of the Irish, upon a rival statesman, who was supposed to have had no small share in obstructing the one, and fomenting the other. This was the celebrated Lord Carteret, then secretary of state, learned, accomplished, eloquent, ambitious, and a personal favourite of his sovereign. He had maintained a war of intrigue in the interior of the cabinet, against Walpole, and his brother-in-law, Townsend; and, by caballing with the Brodericks, and furnishing, it was said, the private history of the mode in which Wood's patent was obtained, he had greatly encouraged the discontents of Ireland, trusting that all the odium would be imputed to Walpole. But his interest in the cabinet gradually sunk before that of his rival, who unable, perhaps, to remove Carteret entirely from office, enjoyed the refined revenge of sending him to Ireland as lord-lieutenant, in the room of the Duke of Grafton, with the injunction of carrying on Wood's project if it were possible; but otherwise with permission to drop it, by the suspension or surrender of the patent. But ere Carteret arrived on the scene, to extinguish the fire which he himself had fanned, the discussion had begun to assume its real character.

It was now obvious, from the temper of Ireland, that the true point of difference between the countries might safely be brought before the public. In the Drapier's fourth letter, accordingly, Swift boldly treats of the royal prerogative, of the almost exclusive employment of natives of England in places of trust and emolument in Ireland; of the dependency of that kingdom upon England, and the power assumed, contrary to truth, reason, and justice, of binding her by the laws of a parliament in which she had no representation. It is boldly affirmed (though in terms the most guarded), that the revolutions of England no farther affected Ireland, than as they were consonant to freedom and liberty; and that, should an insurrection fix a new prince on the throne of the sister kingdom, the Irish might still lawfully resist his possessing himself of theirs. The threats of the English ministers to enforce the currency of Wood's halfpence by violent measures are next alluded to; and the Drapier concludes this part of his reasoning in the following very marked passage: « The remedy is wholly in your own hands, and, therefore, I have digressed a little, in order to refresh and continue that spirit so seasonably raised among you, and to let you see, that, by the laws of GOD, of NATURE, of NATIONS, and of your COUNTRY, you ARE, and OUGHT to be, as FREE a people as your brethren in England.»

This tract pressed at once upon the real merits of the question at issue, and the alarm was instantly taken by the English government. The necessity of supporting their domination devolved upon Carteret, who was just landed; and, accordingly, a proclamation was issued, offering 300*l.* reward for the discovery of the author of the Drapier's fourth letter, described as a wicked and malicious pamphlet, containing several seditious and scandalous passages, highly reflecting upon his majesty and his ministers, and tending to alienate the affections of his good subjects in England and Ireland from each other. Harding, the printer of the Drapier's Letters, was thrown into prison, and a prosecution directed against him, at the instance of the Crown. Swift, bold in the merit of his cause, and in the support of the people, was not to be appalled by this menacing procedure. He went to the levee of the lord-lieutenant, burst through the circle with which he was surrounded, and, in a firm and stern voice, demanded of Lord Carteret the meaning of these severities against a poor industrious tradesman, who had published two or three papers, designed for the good of his country. Carteret, to whom Swift was personally well known, and who could have no doubt of his being the author of the Drapier's Letters, evaded the expostulation, by an apt and elegant quotation from Virgil:—

> Res dura, et regni novitas, me talia cogunt
> Moliri.———

The courtly circle, astounded at the daring conduct of Swift, were delighted and reassured by the lord-lieutenant's presence of mind and urbanity.

Two other anecdotes occurred, which served to show the bold, stern, and uncompromising temper of the Dean. The first is well known: A servant, named Robert Blakeley, whom he intrusted to copy out, and convey to the press the Drapier's Letters, chanced one evening to absent himself without leave. His master charged him with treachery, and, upon his exculpation, insisted that at least he neglected his duties as a servant, because he conceived his master was in his power. « Strip your livery, » he commanded, « begone from the Deanery instantly, and do the worst to revenge yourself that you dare do. » The man retired, more grieved that his master doubted his fidelity, than moved by this harsh treatment. He was replaced at the intercession of Stella; and Swift afterwards rewarded his fidelity, by the office of verger in the cathedral of St Patrick's. The other anecdote bears, that while Harding was in jail, Swift actually visited him in the disguise of an Irish country clown, or *spalpeen*. Some of the printer's family or friends, who chanced to visit him at the same time, were urging him to earn his own release, by informing against the author of the Drapier's Letters. Harding replied steadily, that he would rather perish in jail before he would be guilty of such treachery and baseness. All this passed in Swift's presence, who sat beside them in silence, and heard, with apparent indifference, a discussion which might be said to involve his ruin. He came and departed without being known to any one but Harding.

When the bill against the printer of the Drapier's Letters was about to be presented to the grand jury, Swift addressed to that body a paper, entitled « Seasonable Advice, » exhorting them to remember the story of the league made by the wolves with the sheep, on condition of their parting with their shepherds and mastiffs, after which they ravaged the flock at pleasure. A few spirited verses addressed to the citizens at large, and enforcing similar topics, are subscribed by the Drapier's initials, and are doubtless Swift's own composition. Alluding to the charge that he had gone too far in leaving the discussion of Wood's project to treat of the alleged dependence of Ireland, he concludes in these lines:—

If, then, oppression has not quite subdued,
At once, your prudence and your gratitude;
If you yourselves conspire not your undoing,
And don't deserve, and won't draw down your ruin;
If yet to virtue you have some pretence;
If yet you are not lost to common sense,
Assist your patriot in your own defence.
That stupid cant, He went too far, despise,
And know, that to be brave, is to be wise:
Think how he struggled for your liberty,
And give him freedom, whilst yourselves are free.

At the same time was circulated the memorable and apt quotation from scripture, by a Quaker: —« And the people said unto Saul, shall JONATHAN die, who has wrought this great salvation in Israel? God forbid: as the Lord liveth, there shall not one hair of his head fall to the ground; for he hath wrought with God this day. So the people rescued Jonathan that he died not.» Thus admonished by verse, law, and scripture, the grand-jury assembled. It was in vain that the same Lord Chief-Justice Whitshed, who had caused the Dean's former tract to be denounced as seditious, and procured a verdict against the printer, exerted himself strenuously upon this similar occasion. The hour of intimidation was past, and the grand-jury, conscious of what the country expected from them, brought in a verdict of *ignoramus* upon the bill. Whitshed, after demanding, unconstitutionally, and with indecorous violence, the reasons of their verdict, could only gratify his impotent resentment, like his prototype Scroggs, on a similar occasion, by dissolving the grand-jury. They returned into the mass of general society, honoured and thanked for the part which they had acted, and the chief-justice, on the contrary, was execrated for his arbitrary conduct.[1]

[1] See two spirited letters addressed to him, probably by the Dean's friend and legal adviser, Robert Lindsay,

Such means would injure a good cause, and, unless supported by tyrannical force, can never prop a bad one. The next grand-jury of the county and city of Dublin presented Wood's scheme as a fraud and imposition on the public, and omitted not to express their gratitude to those patriots by whom it had been exposed. Three other Drapier's letters were published by Swift, not only in order to follow up his victory, but for explaining more decidedly the cause in which it had been won. The fifth letter is addressed to Lord Molesworth, and has for its principal object a justification of the former letters, and a charge of oppression and illegality, founded upon the proceedings against the author and printer. The sixth letter is addressed to Lord Chancellor Middleton, who strenuously opposed Wood's project, and resigned his office in consequence of the displeasure of the court being expressed on account of such resistance. It is written in

whose counsel he had used during the whole controversy. And he received another broad hint of his unconstitutional proceeding, by publication of the Resolutions of the House of Commons in 1680, declaring the discharging of a grand-jury before the end of the term, or assizes, arbitrary, illegal, and destructive to public justice. There is room to believe, that his death, which speedily followed, was hastened by the various affronts which were heaped upon him. See Boulter's Letters. But Swift was determined to gibbet his very memory, and vindicates himself for doing so.

the Dean's person, who pleads the cause of the Drapier, and, from several passages, does not appear anxious to conceal this identity. This also relates chiefly to the conduct of Whitshed, and the merits of the prosecution against Harding. The seventh letter, though last published, appears to have been composed shortly after the fourth. It enters widely into the national complaints of Ireland, and illustrates what has been already mentioned, that the project of Wood was only chosen as an ostensible and favourable point on which to make a stand against principles of aggression, which involved many questions of much more vital importance. This letter was not published until the Drapier's papers were collected into a volume. Meantime Carteret yielded to the storm,—Wood's patent was surrendered,—and the patentee indemnified by a grant of 3000*l.* yearly, for twelve years. Thus victoriously terminated the first grand struggle for the independence of Ireland.

The eyes of the kingdom were now turned with one consent on the man, by whose unbending fortitude and pre-eminent talents this triumph was accomplished. The Drapier's head became a sign, his portrait was engraved, woven upon handkerchiefs struck upon medals, and displayed in every possible manner, as the liberator of Ireland. A club was formed in honour of the patriot, who held regular meetings to commemorate his excellencies, study his doctrines, and carouse to his health.[1] In all this, Swift's popularity did not probably exceed that of other patriots, who, at some decisive and critical period, have had the fortune to render a striking service to their country. Nor is it singular that the Dean's memory should, after death, be

[1] To the Drapier's Club we owe the first collection of the Drapier's letters, published by Faulkner at their desire, under the following title :—" Fraud Detected ; or, the Hibernian Patriot, containing all the Drapier's letters to the people of Ireland on Wood's coinage, etc. interspersed with the following particulars, viz.—1. The address of the Lords and Commons of Ireland against Wood's coin.—2. His Majesty's answer to the said addresses.—3. The report of his Majesty's most honourable Privy-Council.—4. Seasonable advice to the Grand-Jury.—5. Extract of the votes of the House of Commons of England, upon breaking a grand-jury.—6. Considerations on the attempts made to pass Wood's coin.—7. Reasons showing the necessity the people of Ireland are under to refuse Wood's coinage. To which are added, Prometheus, a poem. Also, a new poem to the Drapier; and the songs sung at the Drapier's Club in Truck-street, Dublin, never before printed. With a preface explaining the usefulness of the whole."—Dublin. Reprinted and sold by George Faulkner, in Pembroke Court, Castle-Street, 1725, 12mo.

This publication contains five songs to the honour of the Draprer, to which some others might be added from the broadsides before the Editor But they would only show the zeal and attachment of the worthy members of the Drapier's Club at Taplin's, Truck-Street, without doing any credit to their literary talents.

honourably and tenderly cherished by the nation which he did so much to rescue from subjection. But the period between the deeds on which a patriot rests his fame, and the time when they are recorded on his tombstone, is but rarely distinguished by the unclouded and steady glow of uniform popularity. History affords, in all countries, too many instances of the mutability of public favour, and exhibits a long list of those benefactors of nations who have heard the songs composed in their praise turned into libellous parodies, and the acclamations of their countrymen exchanged for as loud and general shouts of reprobation or derision. To the honour of the warm-hearted and generous people for whom he exposed his safety, the sun of Swift's popularity shone unclouded even after he was incapable of distinguishing its radiance. While he was able to go abroad, a thousand popular benedictions attended his steps, and if he visited a town where he was not usually resident, his reception resembled that of a sovereign prince. The slightest idea of personal danger to THE DEAN, for by that title he was generally distinguished, aroused a whole district in his defence; and when, on one occasion, Walpole meditated his arrest, his proposal was checked by a prudent friend, who inquired if he could spare ten thousand soldiers to guard the messenger who should execute so perilous a commission. His foibles, though of a kind which seem peculiarly obnoxious to the observation and censure of the vulgar, were overlooked with the pious respect paid by filial affection to the imperfections of a parent. The governors of Ireland, from the courtly Carteret to the haughty Dorset, even while disliking his politics, if not his person, saw themselves under the necessity of respecting his influence, and temporizing with his zeal. And as he was mourned in his last stage of imbecility, and followed to the grave by the lamentations of his people, so there have been few Irish authors who have not since that period paid to the memory of Swift that tribute of gratitude, which is so peculiarly his due. One of the latest, as well as the most eloquent panegyrics which have decorated his monument, occurs in « A Sketch of the State of Ireland, past and present,» published in 1810. With the just and concise character of the Dean of St Patrick's, viewed as an Irish patriot, we close the present section.

« On this gloom one luminary rose, and Ireland worshipped it with Persian idolatry; her true patriot—her first, almost her last. Sagacious and intrepid—he saw, he dared; above suspicion, he was trusted; above envy, he was beloved; above rivalry, he was obeyed. His wisdom was practical and prophetic—

remedial for the present, warning for the future; he first taught Ireland that she might cease to be a despot. But he was a churchman. His gown impeded his course, and entangled his efforts,—guiding a senate, or heading an army, he had been more than Cromwell, and Ireland not less than England. As it was, he saved her by his courage—improved her by his authority—adorned her by his talents—and exa ted her by his fame. His mission was but of ten years; and for ten years only did his personal power mitigate the government; but though no longer feared by the great, he was not forgotten by the wise; his influence, like his writings, has survived a century; and the foundations of whatever prosperity we have since erected are laid in the disinterested and magnanimous patriotism of Swift.»

END OF VOL. I.

Lightning Source UK Ltd.
Milton Keynes UK
UKOW052148260911
179343UK00001B/76/P

9 781108 034180